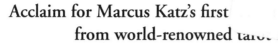

# Acclaim for Marcus Katz's first
## from world-renowned tar...

"In precise detail, with clarity but also with wit and a playful and explorative mind, Marcus Katz maps out a course for the serious tarot reader. Ranging across culture, myth, and history as well as the tarot tradition itself, [*Tarosophy*] is a major contribution."

—Rachel Pollack, author of *78 Degrees of Wisdom*
and *Rachel Pollack's Tarot Wisdom*

"*Tarosophy* is a work of intelligence and depth, featuring tons of tarot tips and exercises that will help you explore the wisdom of the cards in a manner that is accessible, playful, and practical. Highly recommended!"

—Mary K. Greer, author of *21 Ways to Read a Tarot Card*

"A bright star in the firmament of tarot."

—Lon Milo DuQuette,
author of *Understanding Aleister
Crowley's Thoth Tarot* and *Low Magick*

"Marcus Katz has recovered the spiritual dignity of tarot."

—Naomi Ozaniec, author of *The Watkins Tarot Handbook*

# Around the

# TAROT

## in 78 Days

# —About the Authors—

## Marcus Katz

Marcus Katz is a professional tarot teacher at the Far Away Centre, a contemporary training centre in the Lake District of England. As the co-Director of Tarot Professionals, the world's largest professional tarot organization, he has studied and taught tarot for thirty years and has delivered more than 10,000 face-to-face readings. His first book, *Tarosophy*, has been termed a "major contribution" to tarot by leading teachers. Marcus is also the co-creator of *Tarot-Town*, the social network for tarot, with over 10,000 people worldwide sharing innovative tarot development.

## Tali Goodwin

Tali Goodwin is the Marketing Director and co-founder of Tarot Professionals Ltd., the largest professional tarot organization in the world. She has co-authored innovative teaching books such as *Tarot Flip*, which is regularly in the top ten best-selling tarot books on Kindle. Tali is a skilled researcher and is credited with bringing the long-hidden Waite-Trinick Tarot to publication in *Abiding in the Sanctuary: The Waite-Trinick Tarot*. She also co-edited the leading tarot magazine, *Tarosophist International*, from 2010–11.

# To Write to the Authors

If you wish to contact the author or would like more information about this book, please write to the author in care of Llewellyn Worldwide, and we will forward your request. Both the author and the publisher appreciate hearing from you and learning of your enjoyment of this book and how it helped you. Llewellyn Worldwide cannot guarantee every letter written to the author can be answered, but all will be forwarded. Please write to:

Marcus Katz & Tali Goodwin
℅ Llewellyn Worldwide
2143 Wooddale Drive
Woodbury, MN 55125-2989

Please enclose a self-addressed stamped envelope for reply, or $1.00 to cover costs.
If outside the USA, enclose an international postal reply coupon.

# Around the TAROT in 78 Days

## A Personal Journey Through the Cards

## MARCUS KATZ & TALI GOODWIN

Llewellyn Publications
Woodbury, Minnesota

FIRST EDITION
First Printing, 2012

Book design by Bob Gaul
Cover art: Illustration © Autumns Goddess Design/Jena DellaGrottaglia
  Tarot cards © Universal Tarot © Roberto De Angelis—LoScarabeo
Cover design by Ellen Lawson
Editing by Laura Graves
Interior tarot card art (reprinted by permission):
  Legacy of the Divine Tarot © Ciro Marchetti—Llewellyn
  Shadowscapes Tarot © Stephanie Pui-Mun Law and Barbara Moore—Llewellyn
  Universal Tarot © Roberto De Angelis—LoScarabeo
  Ithell Colquhoun Tarot—Adam McLean
Other interior illustrations © Llewellyn Art Department

Llewellyn is a registered trademark of Llewellyn Worldwide Ltd.

Library of Congress Cataloging-in-Publication Data
Katz, Marcus, 1965–
  Around the tarot in 78 days: a personal journey through the cards/Marcus Katz & Tali Goodwin.—1st ed.
    p. cm.
  ISBN 978-0-7387-3044-8
1. Tarot.  I. Goodwin, Tali, 1969–  II. Title.
  BF1879.T2K38 2012
  133.3'2424—dc23
                              2012003257

Llewellyn Publications
A Division of Llewellyn Worldwide Ltd.
2143 Wooddale Drive
Woodbury, MN 55125-2989
www.llewellyn.com

Printed in the United States of America

# Dedications

This book is dedicated to all those townsfolk, citizens, and honoured patrons of Tarot -Town.com who engage tarot with life and share their experience and insight. You can discover an active and passionate study group for the 78 Days workbook in Tarot-Town.

We would particularly like to dedicate this work to the main road-testers of 78 Days, the gifted and talented tarot readers Shannon Gorton, Sarah Perks, Nadine Roberts, Claire Greener, Jennifer Dickensheets, Jera Babylon Rootweaver, Ann (Pearl) Coghlan, Annick Van Damme, Carole McCleery, Linette Voller, Sharon Woolf, and Donna. To the other 240+ readers and students who read through the entire course and offered suggestions, this work is also dedicated to you.

*Around the Tarot in 78 Days* is most deeply dedicated to our partners, leading astrologer Lyn Birkbeck (who also kindly provided the Sabian Symbols nameplates from his work *The Astrological Oracle*) and author Brina Katz, whose patience and inspiration supported the writing of every word of this book.

Dedicated to my father for his continual support and for buying me the *Encyclopaedia of Tarot* for a Christmas present in 1985, when I was seven years into my tarot studies.

—Marcus Katz

Dedicated to my mother, Margaret Goodwin (1929–1990), in memory of her loving grace and my father, Geoffrey Goodwin (1924–1996). To my sister Avril Garside for being there from the beginning.

—Tali Goodwin

As ever, and above all, this book is spiritually dedicated to *Anistita Argenteum Astrum,* The Priestess of the Silver Star.

She whose light leads the way to the Arcanum Arcanorum, the Secret of Secrets.

Vos Vos Vos Vos.

V. V. V .V.

## Acknowledgments

We would like to acknowledge Barbara Moore for providing the opportunity to create this workbook from our courses and teachings, and the members of Tarot Professionals whose encouragement and support over the years continue to raise the level of tarot worldwide.

A number of the techniques in this workbook have been created from our work in NLP, Neuro-Linguistic Programming. Marcus is a licensed trainer of NLP with the Society of NLP with over twenty years experience and would like to acknowledge the creative work of Richard Bandler, John Grinder, Robert Dilts, Doug O' Brien, and Stephen Gilligan, amongst many of those whose training continues to inspire him, assist clients, and provide new ways of teaching tarot.

# —Contents—

---

---

## Gate Nine: The Temple of the King

---

## Gate Ten: The Throne Room

# Introduction

$\mathcal{I}$n this book, you are going to discover that the tarot is not just a deck of seventy-eight cards; it is a real place—a place where your mind meets the mysteries and your imagination floats over the landscape of time itself, gaining insight into your past, present, and future. It is into this magical place that we are going to travel together, on a tour around the tarot in seventy-eight days.

This book contains a progressive and comprehensive tarot course that can be completed a day at a time, or ad-hoc, and then used as an invaluable reference guide as you continue to deepen your studies and practices in the future. It is written for absolute beginners to enjoy and seasoned readers to gain new ways of looking at their work.

On this journey, you will be introduced to each and every card as an exciting adventure of discovery, building up a conversation with the whole deck by learning new methods and insights along the way. These include tarot spreads for reading for yourself and others, and new methods to fully deepen your experience of the cards.

We will ensure that you are fully prepared by packing your map, phrasebook and guidebook, your compass—and even an emergency kit!

Over the years we have been teaching tarot, we know from thousands of students that the best way to learn tarot is to have fun, to engage in-depth with the deck as a living landscape and a voyage of self-discovery. You will soon visit such mystical places as the Clockwork Museum and the Mountain of the Sun, where you will find tarot gates opening up whole new areas in your life.

In fact, in no time at all, you will be working with the tarot to divine your future, change your present, and understand your past—and these seventy-eight days will open your magical and personal journey through the cards.

We are delighted to have you along for this trip of a lifetime.

# Let's Get Started

## Section One: Packing for the Journey

As with any journey, we need to first pack whatever we might need on the way. You won't need any other equipment for this workbook other than the book itself and a pack of tarot cards. The workbook is structured around the standard deck of seventy-eight cards (twenty-two majors, forty minors, and sixteen court cards) so you will need to ensure you have this type of deck rather than an "Oracle" or variant deck. It doesn't matter if the deck is illustrated or a "pips-only" deck, although you will probably find it easier with a deck such as the Waite-Smith Tarot or other "clone" deck based on that model.

You may like to use any of the following decks which illustrate this book:

• Shadowscapes Tarot (Stephanie Pui-Mun Law & Barbara Moore, Llewellyn)

• The Legacy of the Divine Tarot (Ciro Marchetti, Llewellyn)

• The Universal Tarot (Roberto de Angelis, Lo Scarabeo)

We also refer to the Thoth Tarot deck by Aleister Crowley and Frieda Harris during our journey ahead. There are many online sites that provide images and reviews of decks for you.[1] We also love the limited edition majors-only and other decks of our friends at:

• Adam McLean Artwork Tarot
  (www.alchemywebsite.com/tarot/tarot_decks.html)
• Beth Seilonen Tarot (www.catseyeart.com)

We refer to the Waite-Smith Tarot or its various versions as WST throughout this workbook.

You may wish to keep a journal of your tarot travels as you explore this workbook. We would highly recommend this recording of your experiences, particularly if you take the route of the ten gated spreads we have provided in the journey. A journal can be a simple notebook or a treasured handmade item; each traveller must decide what suits his or her style.

Having packed the bare essentials, let's take a look now at the landscape we are about to explore, and then we can decide what else we might require before setting off.

# Section Two: Your Tarot Mapbook
## The Tarot Landscape

The incredible country in which you are about to travel is a place with which you already have familiarity. In fact, you already spend all of your time there; it's just that you don't notice. Tarot is a place of dreams, symbols, and the unconscious. When you see a red light and stop, when you see two doors with a male and female figure on them, when you say "life is like a box of chocolates" you are already living in the symbolic landscape of tarot.

You have practiced tarot your whole life—in dreams and in waking.

The tarot landscape of the unconscious mind is one that has been explored in many films, most recently *The Matrix* and *Inception*. Tarot, however, is a particular place. Whilst it follows dream rules, we can soon learn to find our way around using signposts and learning the language of the place.

## The Landmark Cards (Major Arcana)

There are twenty-two significant landmarks in the landscape—these are the twenty-two major arcana. In our life these are always present at every moment; they are so big we can see them from anywhere and get our bearings. We are never lost when we use these landmarks to discover where we are. In fact in Kabbalah these twenty-two landmarks correspond to the twenty-two Hebrew letters which create the entire language. Each of them has its own path on the Tree of Life so we can discover our way along the spiritual journey.

At any time in your life journey you may be closer to some of these landmarks than others. You can guide yourself, as you will discover in this book, in any situation.

In this book we begin from the landscape of the last major arcana card, the World. We then move upwards through the cards, to the first card of the Magician. This symbolises our journey in the world to acquire the skill of tarot. Of course we will be accompanied by the Fool throughout our journey although he will only make an actual appearance when we are ready.

As an example, suppose you are in an experience or situation to which the Wheel (card X) is closest. This describes the ups and downs of life. We can see from the Wheel that the landmark cards closest one way and the other are the Hermit (IX) and Justice (XI). This tells us we can either move towards removing ourselves from the situation (Hermit) or balancing it to achieve some outcome (Justice).

Using the landmark cards to guide you is a first step to being confident as a navigator in the world of tarot. Over the years you may come to use this book and the cards as an invaluable guide to life, as they are the very map and GPS of our soul.

## The Signpost Cards (Minor Arcana)

The minor arcana provide useful signposts in the realm of tarot. When we are working in any situation the minor arcana provide illustrations of all human activity. As they construct a matrix in four elements and in ten stages within each element, they also provide a logical progression, teaching us how to move from one state to another.

We call this the "next step" method.

As you travel over the next seventy-eight days and beyond, you can take any moment to identify the card in the minors that most sums up your present state and then consult the page in the workbook for that card. Your "next step" direction is to the following card, which indicates how you can look to move forwards—simply read the next page for the way ahead.

## The Direction Cards (Court Cards)

The court cards provide us directions in our journey, as they represent the forces at play in the universe, either through people or through events themselves. We can turn to the court cards for assistance when we need to kickstart something in our lives or when we feel out of balance.

Again, as you make our way through a life lived with tarot, if you shuffle your sixteen court cards whilst considering your present imbalance, then lay them out in a circle, you can identify which card feels closest to your present state (or use your significator card, which you will choose here in this workbook) and look across the circle to find your "Kickstart" court card which is the one now placed opposite to your current state.

Consult the relevant court card page in this workbook, and this will give you the voice of advice from the card itself in the "[Card] Says" section.

Don't be afraid to ask for directions if you find yourself a little lost in the world of tarot. The court cards are always around to assist you.

## Pitstop Points

The major arcana can provide our journey and our readings with pitstop points, important moments when we can take heed and review the fundamental forces that shape our lives. They are like the deep current on which we sail, often unaware of the tides yet sometimes swept up in them. When we know the nature of these points we can quickly adjust our course to make the most of the flow.

### Change Cards

There are several Change cards in the tarot. When these appear in the landscape, change is foretold, in one of a number of different manners. Whether this change is beneficial or malign is determined by the other cards in the vicinity.

- High Priestess—The change is happening subtly and without your knowledge
- Death—The change is happening by transforming the current situation
- Blasted Tower—The change is sudden and brings new elements into play
- Moon—The change is a slow cycle requiring a long journey

## Teaching Cards

When any of the following cards appear in your view, there is a lesson to be learnt, as they are the main teaching cards of the tarot realm. Actually, all the major cards are lessons and teachers in some way or another (being images of "archetypes"), but these are most powerful:

- Magician—Direct teaching by experiment and example
- Hierophant—Traditional teaching, learning by rote, following a structure and code
- Wheel—Teaching by life experience

## Challenge Cards

There are a few cards which present you a challenge to overcome on the way through tarot. Their appearance in your area brings a call to action and requires response and energy.

- Last Judgement—A calling which awakens a new state, if you answer quickly

## Opportunity Cards

Whilst all cards present both a challenge and an opportunity, teachings and lessons alike, some cards open wide opportunities when they appear:

- Sun—The opportunity to be open
- Lovers—The opportunity to choose
- Fool—The opportunity to be free

## Initiation Cards

The Initiation cards of the majors are:

- Strength—Engaging with the path of right relationship and appropriate response
- Chariot—Being on the path with all energies harnessed
- Hermit—Becoming the path itself as a living example of the way

*Stop Cards*

The Stop card of the majors is:

- Hanged Man—When this card appears, you should take notice and realise that your values are being called into question. Make no progress and stop until you are truly manifesting what is most important to you at this time.

The position of the Hanged Man can show where you are suspended; for example, if in the past position of a spread, it shows you are still in need of reviewing an experience in memory. If in the outcome position, it indicates that your current route will take you to a full stop and review.

We will now take a look at a number of other ways of exploring this tarot landscape.

## Going Beyond Spreads

Another manner in which you can use this journey is to provide an innovative way of working with tarot beyond your own spreads when you read for yourself. A three-card spread can be converted here to a series of activities or meditations, affirmations, or oracular advice from the card itself by selecting the "Days" for the cards you have dealt in answer to your question. This provides a real-life magical ritual to activate the forces of the cards in daily life.

## Gated Spreads

You'll also be given opportunity in this book to explore the concept of "Gated Spreads," which is an intrinsic part of Tarosophy®—tarot to engage life, not escape it. A Gated Spread is a series of spreads which are linked together by the activities you undertake in response to each spread. They are designed by "reverse engineering" to ensure you are taken into a powerful experience if you follow the sequence of spreads and activities they request.

You can only perform a Gated Spread in the sequence it is given; without the activity between the linked spreads, there is no way in which the next gate will open properly.

Gated Spreads are also used here to teach specific aspects of tarot, Kabbalah, and magick.

# The Titles of the Cards

As an intermediate method, once you have begun to learn the basics of each card, we have given each card two oracular titles that capture the essence of each stage of the journey as both an **invitation** and an **engagement**. Every card along the way presents you an invitation to learn from it—and a lesson which is experienced if you choose to engage with the card at that time.

These titles have been drawn from the experience of many hundreds of readers by asking them unusual questions about the cards which required them to unconsciously process their deep-seated meanings for the cards in practice rather than from books. In effect, we processed the cards through thousands of readings to see what they really mean in practice. Sometimes these were much the same as most accepted meanings in books, sometimes they were very different and yet insightful and relevant to the card.[2]

When we resolved the keywords from these unconscious responses, we then turned them into provocative card titles, such as turning "Resources" for the pentacles into "Finding Yourself…" or "Ambition" for the wands into "Working Towards…" These provide the **invitation** title.

Furthermore, we have simplified the concepts of Kabbalah in the four worlds of tarot so we can use the differences of the four suits to generate our **engagement** titles.

The wands become "expressions," the cups "creation," the swords "examination," and the pentacles "a place." These are lowering vibrations in four worlds, from the first emanation of the wands to the final manifestation of the pentacles. Again, you don't need to understand Kabbalah to use the titles as a guide to interpreting the cards; we have simplified this whilst remaining true to the source. It also means if you plan to study Kabbalah further in tarot, you will have already picked up a useful background.[3]

The court card titles are also taken from this research, which shows the pages to be *channelers,* the knights to be *responders,* the queens to be *connectors,* and the kings to be *demonstrators.* Thus, the titles for the invitation/engagement aspects of these cards are:

- Pages—Setting & Readiness
- Knights—Proving & Responding

- Queens—Caring & Being
- Kings—Doing & Declaring

You will also see that the titles create your own story through the deck, from the "finding yourself returning" of the Ten of Pentacles to the "finding the beginning at the end" of the Fool. The titles for the major arcana are also modified from our earlier work asking hundreds of readers for unconscious keywords, such as "success" for the Magician and "revelation" for the High Priestess.

## The Order of the Cards

Whilst it may be the usual format to learn the cards one at a time in numerical sequence, the strangest thing is that you will never get a reading—or only rarely—that follows a number sequence in order. It is like learning the alphabet and then expecting words to be created like "abc," "defg," "hi," "jklm," and so on. We have never found it very important to teach in number sequence. There are still discussions about the precise order of the majors, such as swapping the positions of Strength and Justice, and their original order was variable too because there were sometimes different cards in the early decks.

Similarly, occultists such as A. E. Waite listed the cards naturally from TEN to ACE in that order because of their background in esotericism and Kabbalah.

We have used a structure here in this workbook based on the soul's journey on the Tree of Life. Although we do not cover this in detail, you will experience a trip from the lowest plane of matter, where we encounter the pages of the court cards and the tens of the minors, all the way up to the rarefied and abstract heights of the aces and the mysterious High Priestess, the Magician, and finally the Fool—who is often seen as unnumbered and outside of any sequence.

The major cards are introduced in order from the World, the highest numbered card, to the Magician, the lowest numbered card, throughout our journey according to their positions on the Tree of Life. This provides a good opportunity to learn some of the esoteric patterns in the tarot without getting too obscure.

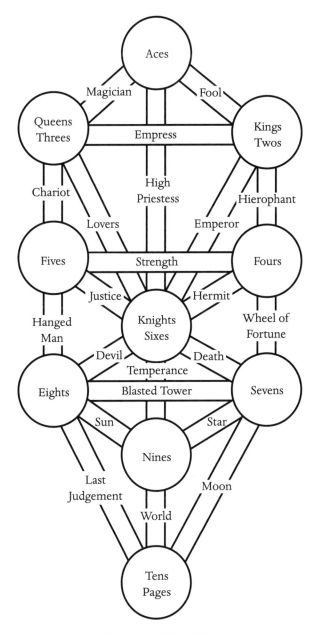

*The Tarot Card Tree of Life*

# Connecting with the Cards

As you traverse the tarot, as a quick handbook, you can find for every card a brief connection sequence, with two levels:

- Affirmation
- Meditation

These are two progressive stages of connecting with the deeper meanings of each card, and can provide another "fast-track" route through learning tarot. By using an affirmation (you'll learn how to create your own later) you can jolt the card into your life.

Once you have experienced a little of the flavour of the card, you can meditate regularly on a particular aspect of the symbolism or interpretation of the images. This allows the card to "sink into" your awareness.

As with most of the techniques in this workbook, it is intended that these practices benefit you in all areas of your life—spiritual and mundane—outside of your tarot practice. We aim to bring tarot into your life as an intrinsic spiritual system.

# Resonances

The tarot has resonances with other Western esoteric systems, such as astrology, numerology, the Sabian Symbols, and Kabbalah. In this section for every card you will locate the resonances or correspondences which apply to that card. These magical correspondences can be used to make magic—and you'll be learning a few techniques throughout the workbook!

# Tarot as a Teacher

The occultist Eliphas Levi observed that a man in prison could learn everything he needed to know about the world through a tarot deck alone. In this workbook you will be presented a lesson from every card, as if you were meeting each one as your own personal tutor. These lessons will vary depending on the teacher! Some will be conceptual, some will be practical.

# Tarot in Your Life

Whether you are applying the card and your interpretation in a reading to a general question, or a career, health, or relationship issue, we will discover how the card can apply to any aspect of life. It is often a limitation that books of interpretation will be too specific so that it becomes impossible to apply the meanings given to the particular question you are asking—this is a skill tarot readers have to learn over many years of experience.

We will find in this section for each card how to apply the card to a range of questions and learn that the cards are "multivalent"—they hold an infinite number of meanings, sometimes beyond the apparent simplicity of the card itself. You'll soon unlock the secret of how to apply any card to any question in any position of any spread.

Better yet, you'll come to see how the tarot teachers are present in your everyday life, until you become a living oracle able to interpret signs, symbols, portents, and secrets to guide your life.

## Tarot Connect

Whilst everyone has a "full deck of possibilities" in life, we often find ourselves askew or blocking our natural flow into creativity, whether we are trying to create a life, career, relationship, family, or other project. We can use tarot to inform us as to how we are blocking the energies that make up life itself—depicted in the deck—and take corrective action. In this section for each card, you'll discover how to use tarot as a GPS for your very soul.

One powerful method you may choose to adopt is to perform a three-card reading for any situation in which you are presently stuck. Take out the three cards and place them somewhere noticeable and then make a note of the "Connect to Your Card" activities appropriate to each card. Then perform those three activities on the same day, whilst you have the cards out, thus aligning the actions and energies of your life to the divination. You may be surprised how this breaks you out of old outworn patterns and behaviours, or even magically changes your situation.

## The Cards Speak

Sometimes experienced tarot readers simply explain themselves by saying that the "cards just speak to me." Here we will allow the cards to find their voice and speak to you! This section for each card can be used as an oracle for parties, brief readings, making snap decisions, or advising a friend. You'll often find yourself listening to a card after doing a few of these readings—another new skill.

## Getting to Know the Court Cards

We have provided two extra pages for page cards called "Where You Might Meet" and "What People Say About." These give you contemporary places and statements about the character and energy embodied by these sixteen cards so you can get to know them in person. They will likely remind you immediately of people in your life.

WAYSIDE LESSON: COURT CARDS

At certain points in our seventy-eight-day journey into the world of tarot, we will provide Wayside Lessons. These are optional lessons for intermediate travellers in the realm.

# Section Three: Your Tarot Phrasebook
## Learning the Tarot Language

When we are thinking about travelling to a new place, particularly one quite far away, we usually try and learn a few things about the place, the culture, the people, and the language. Our seventy-eight-day tarot journey involves exactly the same considerations. We will first look at the peculiar language of tarot and discover a good way of learning the basics so we can at least ask for directions during our journey.

If we were to describe tarot as a language, it is a language by which we communicate the connections of life, seen and unseen. The big difference with tarot language is that it is not bound by the usual considerations of time, it is *a-temporal*. If you have given or received a tarot reading, you'll have heard the reader talking about the past, present, and future all together.

Our first lesson in tarot language is to learn how to turn the present of the card into the future of the querent. This is something most students struggle to learn, as it is often something that only comes with practice. We will try and shortcut to this skill by teaching it first. We should also remember "it is not necessary to learn all the speech one is going to need: speech can be improvised, once the systems governing it have been mastered. A child learns its first language this way."[4]

# The Language of Tarot

The tarot is full of objects such as cups, swords, hats, windows, wheels, horses, and much more. Whilst each of these can be considered a symbol pointing to a meaning, such as "cup = emotion," they are simply nouns, things. Nouns are objects and they are the first thing we learn as children, for example, "C" is for "cat."

We have twenty-two main nouns in tarot language; these are the major cards such as the Devil, the Wheel, the Tower, and the Lovers. They require a little bit of rote-learning to study, and you can start by learning a single keyword/concept for each one, such as Devil=Attachment, Wheel = Cycles, Tower = Shock, etc. We have given keywords and a kaleidoscope so you can have fun generating your own personal words for each card, not only the majors!

So those of the main objects of tarot and our major landmarks are in our tarot journey too. We then tend to learn our verbs in tarot language. A verb is an action or a state of being; for example, running or sitting. It is a "doing" word that describes something happening or in process. We will imagine that in the language of tarot, the forty minor cards are the "verbs" of the language. They represent activities and events, situations, which can be summed up as a keyword, for the Three of Cups is the act of "celebration" and the Six of Swords is the act of "resting." Again, every card in our language and journey is given a range of Keywords throughout this workbook.

So if we took the Blasted Tower (keyword = shock) and the Three of Cups (keyword = "celebration") together, what sentence would those two words make? Perhaps "a shock and a celebration," "a celebrating shock," or "a shocking celebration"? As we make sense of this, what arises in our mind is maybe "a surprise party" or a "sudden announcement leading to celebration," both great ways of interpreting these two cards together.

Take a couple of major and minor cards out of your deck (if it is a court card, return it to the deck and choose another) and try reading them in your new language—which like any language will soon become second nature with practice. Now see if you are learning the language. If I asked for a two-card reading on my question, "What is the outcome of my date tonight," shuffled the deck, and picked these two cards, what would tarot's answer be in the Two of Cups and the Sun?

Finally, for our basic primer in tarot language, we have our adjectives. These are the descriptive words, which modify (by describing, identifying, or quantifying) a noun, such as "big" or "small." In tarot these are the court cards. They represent influences and forces applying in the reading which change the speed, level, or magnitude of the situation. Whilst this is not always the case, it is enough for us to get to grips with the basics of the language of tarot for now.

In English, we put these three components together in a sentence, such as putting the noun "cat," the verb "sitting," and the adjective "small" together as: "The small cat is sitting."

For more detail in our language you can also add an adverb, to further describe the verb, telling us "how" the "doing" is done; for example, "he sang loudly," or "the door opened slowly." If we added the adverb "quietly" (how the sitting is being done) to the sentence above, we get: "The small cat is sitting quietly."

We can see these forms of language in tarot too, and start to make our first sentences using the Keywords for the cards selected in a spread. We'll use a simple three-card spread for learning our language before we take to the air on our journey. This spread is simply the selection of three cards to answer a question, such as "What is the future of my new rock band?"

To recap, the major cards are the *nouns*, the minor cards are the *verbs*, and the court cards are the *adjectives*. We can add a word ourselves to describe how we interpret the sentence which becomes the *adverb*—a verb we have added ourselves.

To make it even easier, you can spend some time learning the basics of tarot language by splitting your deck into three piles; the majors, the minors (numbered), and the court cards (pages, knights, queens, and kings). Then shuffle each of the three decks, and select out one card from each, laying them face-up.

So if we shuffled our decks and got these three cards from each deck in order:

• Blasted Tower (from the majors)
• Three of Cups (from the minors)
• King of Pentacles (from the court cards)

Referring to our Keywords and concepts in this workbook, we would read this sentence in the language of tarot as: The friendly group (Three of Cups) broke up (Tower) steadily (King of Pentacles).

You can see we have slightly rearranged the cards in our sentence to form a clear communication. This is fine when you are reading several cards together in a non-positional spread, and it is also a good way to practice powerful readings with just a few cards.

Now we must turn this into a "future" predictive or advisory sentence, by simply casting it into the future tense—no need to learn more language to do this, just do it in English. According to these cards, the friendly group will steadily break apart. That doesn't sound too good for the rock band question, although usually one might not need a tarot card reading to predict that for most bands!

Suppose we had instead these three cards for the same question:

· The Wheel

· The Hermit

· Six of Swords

*The Wheel, the Hermit, and the Six of Swords*

Here we have two nouns—the major cards the Wheel and the Hermit—and a verb, the Six of Swords. If we look into our Keywords we could select: Luck (Wheel), Solitude (Hermit), and Recovery (Six of Swords).

Turning that into a tarot sentence we would say, "You will recover your luck by going solo." Have another look at the actual images of the cards (a method which we will look at later) and see if that reading makes any more sense to you with those words, or if you can now see images in the cards that support or add to that interpretation. However we read it, it doesn't bode very well for the forthcoming rock band.

We look forward to practising this new language of tarot in the best way possible—as we encounter the real situations and landscapes of the world in which the language is spoken. This is the world of the tarot, so our final preparation must be to grab a guidebook.

## Section Four: Your Tarot Guidebook

In our preparation for our voyage into the world of tarot, a seventy-eight-day journey, we will need a good guidebook. Whilst the tarot is itself a map of the world, there are three triangulation points we can always use to get our bearings. These are time/space, values/beliefs/actions, and self-image.

### Time/Space

Tarot arises out of the same universe as the stars, the planets, you and I, and even time and space itself. We hold that it is indivisibly connected to all events and that all events are connected likewise. As such, tarot can tell potential futures and define the mysteries of the past as well as providing a clear picture of the present, both known and unknown.

When we lay out the cards in a spread, it is a unique moment in space and time and should be treated as a small ritual separate from daily activity. Whilst it is possible to perform a reading at any time under any circumstances, take a moment to ensure that it is honoured and recognised as a divine moment.

### Values, Beliefs, and Actions

No matter what beliefs people have about tarot, it is widely acknowledged as a means of connecting to the unseen, and some people fear that it may have an undue influence on their life. You should assure your client or anyone for whom you read that their life is in their hands and the advice the tarot offers should be considered as the advice of a close and personal friend. Whilst it usually insightful, it is still up to the person to take action.

## Self-Image

Over time it is important to use the tarot to create a more comprehensive and consistent viewpoint of the universe and yourself as well as the relationship between these two. Tarot provides a bridge and mirror for that relationship. Our role as a living oracle becomes a central facet of our life the more we use tarot. Always ensure you maintain a good balance and approach to your tarot and treat it as a constant companion rather than an all-powerful dictator.

## The Tarot Culture

The place of tarot is steeped primarily in the wonders of the image. It is a culture derived from pictures and symbols, metaphors, myths, and meaning. Nothing is ever as it seems in tarot. As a result, the culture is open, flexible, and constantly shifting. The only steadfast rule seems to be "go deeper." As a traveller in tarot, you will get to know the place and people far better by respecting the story and the imagination—if you can tell a tale or two, you will win instant respect.

The standard greeting in tarot is "may a full deck of possibilities be yours," to which the response is, "and yours, a full deck (…indeed, this day, today, this evening, in our passing, etc.)," which also indicates the cultural importance of possibility and wholeness in tarot.

The motto of the state of tarot is "Tarot to Engage Life, Not Escape It" and over the Tarot University doors you will see the Latin for "Developing the Diversity of Divination."

You may get a flavour of tarot as a culture by visiting such sites as Tarot-Town.com where the spirit of tarot flows in every street and alleyway. We also recommend reading the book *Invisible Cities* by Italo Calvino, particularly where he describes the city of Tamara, which could be taken as a statement of tarot culture made real.

## The Tarot History

Tarot's history is slightly unclear, although we do know that it derived from Italy in the fifteenth century and the name itself appeared some one hundred years later. There is no evidence at all to suggest that tarot came from anywhere else or was used or created any earlier in history for anything other than a card game.

It is therefore quite a contemporary tool, historically speaking, and we are at the earliest days of its origins and development, so who knows what may become of the art? Perhaps this might be a question you would like to ask your tarot deck at some point during the next seventy-eight days—not "where are you from?" but "where are you going?" and even more importantly, "where are you taking me?"

Now that we have good grounding in the landscape, language, and culture of tarot, and have packed what we need, we'll just ensure we have an emergency kit to deal with all the possible events and then we can set off in our journey!

## Section Five: Your Emergency Kit

In this Fool's Bag, or emergency kit, we will provide you a compass, a kaleidoscope, and a number of other essential tools that we have seen are in the possession of all those experienced travellers in the realm of tarot.

### The Keyword Kaleidoscope

If you've ever wondered how to reconcile the different meanings you find in every book for a particular card, this Keyword Kaleidoscope method will soon install a whole new way of looking at the interpretation of any tarot card. Against every card you'll find a comprehensive survey of keywords—boiled down—and concepts which arise from the card.

You can then feed these into the Kaleidoscope and generate an interpretation for any question whilst remaining true to the card. This is a method modelled by NLP of the greatest and most experienced tarot readers alive today—here presented for the first time.[5]

One of the first problems encountered as a beginner to tarot is the bewildering difference of interpretations and keywords offered in the multitude of books available on the shelves.

At first, the student finds it difficult because the "little white book" that comes with the deck is often very brief, and only gives a few keywords, such as for the Ten of Cups: "happiness." If that card then comes up in the recent past position of a spread, where the querent has said they have certainly **not** been happy in their recent past—what do you do? Or if the question was "How will I progress in my new job?" and the card came up for the future—is it simply that they will have "happiness" or is there something more we can say from the card? The querent will certainly want to know more than a single word!

Usually the student then buys a couple more books. When looking at the various interpretations and keywords, the variations seem immense and conflicting. So often the student despairs and gives up, or stalls in their learning.

However, when looking at experienced teachers and readers of tarot, they seem to have no difficulty applying any card to any reading—in fact this may be one of the true skills of an experienced reader, whether they have natural talent, learning, experience, or all three.

We offer here an NLP method to train your brain in producing lateral but relevant interpretations based on keywords, no matter how different they may be! We call it the "Keyword Kaleidoscope," and it is a conscious model or template of an unconscious competence possessed by great tarot readers. With just a little practice use of the template, you'll find yourself being able to use it naturally whilst reading—as if by magic.

Simply take the template and make a few copies, choose a card—we've chosen the Ten of Cups as mentioned above—then fill in the template with some of the keywords you've discovered which relate to that card. We've gone for four extremely different sources for our example keywords—the notorious occultist Aleister Crowley in his *Book of Thoth*, the *Feminist Tarot* book, the classic A. E. Waite's *Pictorial Key to the Tarot*, and the contemporary Kim Huggens's *Tarot 101*.

So we write onto the template "Friendship (Perfected)," "Childhood memories," "Safety" (from Crowley), and "Home."

We then pair the keywords and using the same technique as we will see in the "Difference Engine," we come up with an "arising meaning" or feeling from the two keywords, concepts, or phrases. So we put together and play with "Childhood Memories" and "Homecoming"; the general feeling is "Security." We write this down on the template between the two original keywords. We repeat this for "Friendship" and "Childhood Memories" and get "Nostalgia" and do the same for the other two pairs of words.

We then fractal or kaleidoscope outwards, and do the same with the pair "Security" and "Nostalgia." When we think about these two words we come to a feeling, a concept of "safe and secure past," and it's a warm glow of a feeling. This is exactly what experienced tarot readers do with their knowledge, wealth of disparate keywords, and experience—they **see** them fractal out, making a kaleidoscope of words and meanings branching out from the original meanings until they get a **feeling** that arises—then they apply that actual feeling to **spoken** words which apply to the question.[6]

"Before you know it, you'll feel comfortable
and welcome there, although it is important not
to be too clingy...give it time, take a relaxed stance,
everything new becomes familiar eventually..."

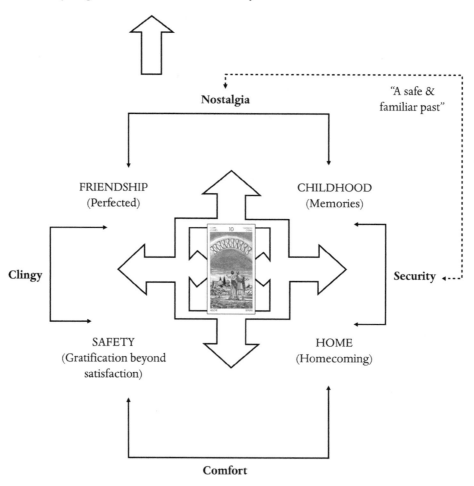

Nostalgia

"A safe &
familiar past"

FRIENDSHIP
(Perfected)

CHILDHOOD
(Memories)

Clingy

Security

SAFETY
(Gratification beyond
satisfaction)

HOME
(Homecoming)

Comfort

"How will I progress in my new job?"
(Future position of spread)

*The Keyword Kaleidoscope Spread*

So we would then take that feeling of a "safe and secure past," apply it to the question and the position in the spread which is in the future, and what would come out is "after a while it will seem as if you have been working there for a long time—you'll find a lot of security in this job … "

You can then repeat this as often as you like with each of the pairs, the pairs that arise, and so on. In Kabbalah this technique is known as "exploring the orchard" as each Tree (of Life) contains another tree and so on forever!

The idea here though is just to practice until you find yourself doing it automatically. And the best thing is that the more diverse and conflicting the Keywords you discover, the better and more interesting your readings will become!

## The Difference Engine

In this teaching tool we take two cards together and generate what tarot mentor Janine Worthington calls an "in-between" card. That's to say, it's the bridging or "5" card between an imaginary sequence of two cards. The best way to picture this is as if every card were a still frame in a movie. Take two cards, starting with two "in sequence" (i.e., the Five of Swords and the Six of Swords), and place them apart as follows:

*The Five of Swords, blank card, and the Six of Swords*

In the middle of the two cards, imagine what scene you would put there to connect the story told by the cards. What is the relationship between the figures in the cards? What happens between the two scenes you are viewing? It could involve one of the characters, both of them, or something entirely different still connected to the unfolding scenario.

By making this connecting card, we unconsciously train our mind to recognise sequential patterns in individual cards, extracting meaning out of them to make connections. This is another invaluable skill of experienced readers, and by practising this technique, you will shorten the amount of time it takes to learn this unconscious competence. Once you have practised with several pairs of cards in sequence, you can try picking any two cards out of the whole deck.

*The Three of Wands, blank card, and the Six of Cups*

You will also find after this practice you will begin to read your spreads very differently. It is hard to explain exactly how this works, but notice for yourself as you start to weave more meaningful connections between the cards in front of you during a reading.

## Tarot Life Story

In this tool, we use the workbook to generate a life story for our whole life, a year, or even a particular point of a relationship, career, or project. We accept that the cards have settled themselves in a sequence which reflects the nature of the Universe—or at least our perception of it—and work as if this is a comprehensive and sequential map of the general flow of creation.

So at any point we can take a snapshot of where we are in life, a sort of GPS positioning of our soul in its evolution. This is the deepest part of any tarot reading, whether it is for a simple or apparently frivolous question, it is always asking and answering "where am I in life?" and "where do I go from here?"

We would recommend spending a whole day preparing to use this tool. Sort through old photographs and diaries and/or journals, review the objects you own in your house, take a trip to somewhere from your childhood—generally recount your life.

When you are ready to use this tool, simply take out the twenty-two major arcana cards of your deck and shuffle them. When you feel ready, take out one card and lay it face-up. This is your current position in your life story.

You can now consult this workbook and discover where you are in life, and your past and future currents. These indicate the lessons you need to learn from your past to release your present self and the opportunities and challenges you must face to move into the future.

For example, if we were presented the Hermit card, this would teach us that our present is summed up by the phrase "What burns within you illuminates your truth, enabling you to inspire and encourage others." How this manifests in our health, career, and relationships can also be discovered on the relevant page.

It also shows that we need to learn the lessons of the Strength card—come to a better relationship with our own instincts, and take the opportunities presented by the Wheel card—look out to take a chance and not plan so much ahead (amongst other messages indicated by that page).

You can take a Life Story card for any relationship, project, or creative task and read the current state, previous lessons to be learnt, and next stage of the process in the relevant pages.

## The Compass Spread

Whenever you need to get your bearings in the world of tarot, you can lay out a compass spread with the deck. This uses one, five, nine, or thirteen cards, depending on your growing confidence in reading as you progress through your journey.

It uses what we call a Split Spread, where we split the deck into separate mini-decks depending on our requirements. In this case, we split the deck into three piles—the twenty-two major arcana, the forty numbered minor arcana (aces to tens), and the sixteen court cards.

The simplest version of the compass spread just to get your bearings in the overall landscape is to use the major cards pile only, and select just one card. Shuffle the mini-deck of twenty-two cards and consider your question, for example, **"What do I need to do to resolve my situation?"** Then select a card when you feel it is right.

When you have looked over the card and got your first reaction to the image, you can look up the "Card Says" section in this workbook for your answer.

If you require more bearings, you can try the next level of the compass spread, by laying out four cards from the court card pile in a cross surrounding the central major card.

These four cards represent the four quarters of your life in response to your question:

1. How to be/What to do
2. How not to be/What not to do
3. Who to be for the safest route
4. What you will be if you do nothing

You can then extend this spread as you gain more confidence with the minor arcana by adding another cross outside the court cards to explore your environment. Select the pile of minor arcana cards and shuffle and select as before:

5. What to aim for
6. What to move away from
7. What resources you can call upon
8. How to make progress

Finally, you can perform the full compass spread, which takes the past and future into its scope. Add four more cards from the minor arcana pile to your outer circle:

9. The past
10. The future
11. The future if you do nothing
12. The future if you follow the compass

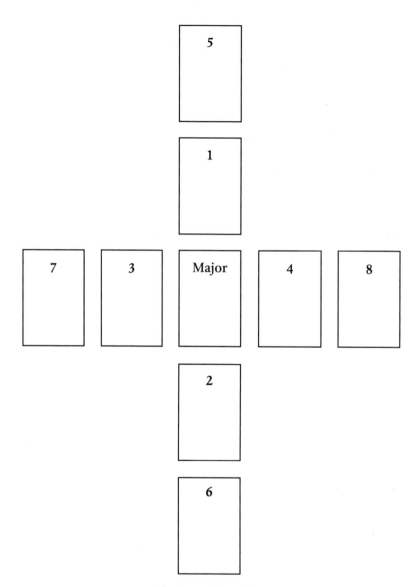

*The Compass Spread: One*

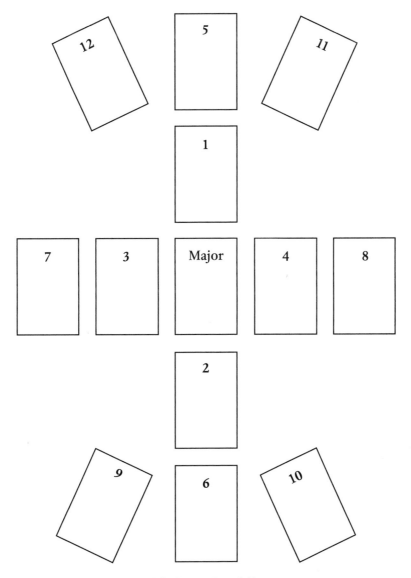

*The Compass Spread: Two*

## How to Turn Any Question into a Spread

Many of the spreads and methods here have been designed in real time with particular querents asking questions which have turned into a spread. A case in point is the "Strange Attractors" or "Whirlpool" method, which arose because a querent presented a particular case.

He asked a question which was framed as "I have two options, both of which are possible, one probably more desirable than the other, but I could sort of do both, and they're both a little bit out of my hands." However, whilst he was asking the question, he was motioning with both hands in circular motions on the table. This was to express his own unconscious model of how the two situations were moving and placed relative to each other.

So it was suggested we use the "classic whirlpool method," where we first lay two cards down, in two positions on the table, to show the source of the two situations, their essential nature. We then placed a ring of three cards around each of those two source cards to show how that particular situation would ripple out. We then placed a ring of six cards around each ring to show the final results of how the two situations would develop.

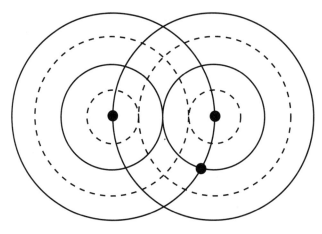

*The Whirlpool Method*

However, by then, the two rings had expanded on the table to overlap each other, with two cards in particular touching each other from both situations. The querent pointed these out and said, "I suppose this is what happens if I try to do both, they'll interfere with each other."

I nodded and said, "So let's look at what happens in that case," and we laid out three cards around those two cards to show the interference pattern, like ripples on water. I now use this "classic" method whenever anyone presents a similar situation.

There is a simple method for learning this skill, which I have modified from the NLP-derived method of Clean Language, based on the work of the late David Grove, a therapist in New Zealand.

When someone expresses a question, it usually has an emotional content which can be turned into a metaphor by a specialized but straightforward series of clean questions. It only takes a minute, and then you'll have a precise metaphor of the question against which to design your spread in real time.

The sequence of questions is as follows, with the essential sequence highlighted in bold:

*Querent:* My question is X [including some emotional content, such as "and I'm concerned that I may not make the right choice"].

*Reader:* … and your concern. **Where is** your concern?

*Querent:* In my head [or querent will gesture unconsciously even if they say "I don't really know"].

*Reader:* … in your head. **Is it outside or inside?**

*Querent:* Inside, in my head.

*Reader:* … inside, in your head. I'm wondering how you'd best **describe the shape or size** of that?

*Querent:* Well, it's just everywhere and it's rushing about.

*Reader:* … rushing about? **And that's like what?**

*Querent:* It's like a bull in a china shop, really.

So now you have a metaphor, the bull in a china shop. You can frame the questions in any particular way, following the querent's own language. The faster you do it and the more you pay attention to their whole communication (including nonverbal gestures), the more noticeable it will be that the question suggests its own spread in response.

You can then apply the "bull in the china shop" as a reading method.

The querent has asked whether to take an early retirement. They have described their question and given a metaphor which represents how their worries are rushing about like a bull in a china shop.

We take the symbols of **bull** and **china shop** to quickly lay out a reading.

1. The Bull cards: What is it that drives the client? [Three cards]
2. The China Shop card: What is it they will gain or lose from taking early retirement? [Three cards around the Bull cards]
3. The China card: What will be broken by taking this step? [One card]

Or any other variant that may strike you at the time of the reading, or as the querent explains his or her question, or as the cards are laid down. In this approach, we are using our intermediate experience to be more responsive to the question in our divination rather than forcing it into a predetermined spread. It also allows us to be more flexible and promotes an active dialogue with the deck and an engaging unique experience for the querent.[7]

## Turning a Word into a Spread

If you are performing email readings, you can use a keyword in the querent's question to design an elegant and relevant spread. If a querent has sent you this question, for example:

*Hello, I am asking about my relationship. I have been married for one year and we are discussing children. I wondered if I could have a reading because my parents used to say I was too **irresponsible** for such things and I am asking what my future might be with children.*

Then we might take the word "irresponsible" (highlighted above) as the main concern in the question. We then look up the etymology or derivation of the word in a dictionary or online source.

The word "irresponsible" comes from "to not be responsible." In turn, "responsible" comes from a similar root idea to "obligation." The word "obligation" comes from a Latin source, "to bind," and of course leads to its later use as meaning "to make someone indebted by conferring a benefit or kindness."

We take that concept of debt and kindness and turn it into the questions for a straightforward linear spread as follows.

## The Parents Response Spread

1. What debt does the querent owe her parents?
2. What kindness did the querent learn from her parents?
3. What binds the querent in their attitude to children?
4. What of benefit will the querent be able to give to children?
5. What responsibility will the querent take on?
6. What kindness will their child(ren) bring to them?

You can of course then go from those questions as the cards are placed and engage in conversation with the spread itself. This can be a very powerful method because it takes much of the expectation of the reading out of your hands and places it from the querent's question directly in dialogue with the cards themselves. Your job is simply to interpret the reading.

## How to Make Any Card Meaning Fit the Question

No matter what card arrives in which position of a spread, or in answer to a general question, an experienced reader is able to interpret its meaning. However, when we start from basic keywords and concepts, this can often be difficult for those new to tarot. How does one apply a card whose word is "trespass" to a question about a college exam?

In NLP, we use a method called "chunking" which describes levels of detail applied to thinking. A model of lateral thinking shows how people chunk in a particular "strategy" (which is unconscious) to solve problems in a creative way. We have applied this model to produce a kickstart version of "making a card fit" as follows.

**Example:** Three of Wands in the "past" position of a spread where the question was about a relationship. This card has the keyword of **building** and the title "Expression of Ambition." To make this fit, we map the context (or metaphor) in which building makes sense to the context of the question—the relationship. So "building" takes place in a context of "building a house." We then compare building a house to a relationship. Obviously, the building comes early on in the process (as it would do in the relationship)—the house is also about security. So we then apply this to a relationship, perhaps seeing that the relationship was "cemented" in the past, based on the person's high ideals for the union. Those "foundations" are now in the past denoting the relationship—like the building—has moved on.

**Example:** Four of Cups in the Advice position of a particular spread. This card has the keyword of **Weariness.** This is part of the context of "entertainment," so we would fit it into the reading by saying the querent is advised not to treat the situation as a game, otherwise they will tire of it.

We believe that by using the "flip" method to derive these keywords, they will prove fairly universal. However, insight always comes by working with the cards themselves in a range of questions—go practice!

You can then look at any court cards in the reading to see how close the energies are to manifesting the result (i.e., lots of kings means "really close" and lots of pages means "far away" because the energy hasn't started out properly).

The major cards then signify the archetypal forces at work in the whole situation. Again, if these are more immediate (Blasted Tower or the Fool, for example), then that adds weight to the time being closer rather than far away. Cards such as the Wheel, Moon, Sun, etc., signify more longer-reaching archetypal forces at play.[8]

So if you are now ready to begin, having packed your tool kit, learnt the language basics, and grabbed your map, we can commence our seventy-eight-day journey into the world of tarot!

Around the

# TAROT

in 78 Days

# —Day 1: Page of Pentacles—
### *Humble Beginnings • Delivery of Good Fortune*

## Resonances

*Numerology:* 68/5

*Astrology:*
Capricorn/Taurus

*Kabbalah:*
Malkuth (Kingdom)

*Elemental:*
Earth of Earth

*Perfume:* Storax

FANTE DI DENARI · KNAVE OF PENTACLES
VALET DE DENIERS · SOTA DE OROS

BUBE DER MÜNZEN · MUNTEN SCHILDKNAAP

## Quick Connections

*Affirmation:* With every breath I am growing more into the self I am to be.

*Meditation:* "How does the oak know the seasons ahead in order to grow so strong?"

## The Lesson of the Page of Pentacles
### *An Introduction to the Court Cards*

Our first lesson on the journey into tarot is from the Page of Pentacles. This card is one of the sixteen court cards in the deck, which represent the pages, knights, queens, and kings of a royal court. These four ranks or social stations are part of the four tarot families or suits: pentacles, cups, swords, and wands.

If we are going to travel into tarot, we need to know a lot about these families whom we encounter on our journey and throughout tarot history.

As with any collection of families, such as at a wedding or funeral, there's always lively action when they get together. In fact, the court cards can be seen as just that—levels of energy and action in interaction. Sometimes these energies come through people or events, and sometimes they are a part of ourselves that requires attention. We'll learn how to read at these levels later in our journey. For now, we'll get to know the personalities.

They are very much elemental and fixed to their family, these court cards. They represent four levels of each element, and you can bet that the children (pages) also take after their fathers and don't always play well together. The children too are neither male nor female; they can be either gender. This makes a page card sometimes difficult to read in a spread, but we will provide some rules later to ensure we don't make any social gaffes!

On our first-day lesson, we have a page from the court or family of Earth, the Page of Pentacles. We will soon meet the other three pages and see how these children differ so much in each family. Here we see a young energy, in the earthy pentacle family, the world of matter, material, and money. He (we will use "he" for today) is looking to manifest! This is a card of good intent and meaning when gained in response to a question with regard to finances.

Take a look at the keywords and description of our Colin of the Coins to get real insight into this character and his concerns. We'll first learn to appreciate the card as a person before moving on to the more abstract energy behind the personality.

In terms of the general reading of this card, when the Page turns up on our path, it may also be viewed as a card calling us to appraise our environment, be it financial or otherwise. When it turns up in a relationship reading, it is likely to signify that the relationship needs to be considered in terms of its health and security aspects. We have provided for every card and character a range of suggested meanings for the card in response to the main types of questions asked of tarot readers.

When you have considered the information and introduction today for the Page of Pentacles, Colin of the Coins, what would you say would trip him up in life? If you have chosen this card as your "starting page" (significator), this will be very important for you to think about before we set off on our journey together.

### Colin of the Coins

Colin, the Page of Pentacles, is the guileless realist of the tarot court cards. You know the youngster who just says it as it is? When it comes to tarot, Colin says, "keep it simple." They're only seventy-eight pictures on cardboard, after all. What's the big deal? We can all read pictures, we all have responses to art, even if we don't understand it—and there are comic books with more complexity than some tarot decks.

So Colin looks at the deck and teaches us to read what we literally see. Say it out loud. In this picture, I see a man on a horse. In this image, I see a woman who appears to be crying. In this card I see five young men fighting—or appearing to fight. Then go on to describe more—they appear to be fighting, but I see one of them is trying to find some direction. You'll be surprised what happens when you literally read the cards. Nothing more, nothing less. This is Colin's lesson.

*Where you might meet Colin:* Building site, accountant, football or baseball league.

*What people say about Colin:* He's very down-to-earth and calls a spade a spade.

## The Card in Your Life/Reading

*Careerwise & Financially* this card indicates the start of a financially rewarding prospect. It can signify a lot of work to be done and that employment is forthcoming. It generally shows positive opportunities are there to be grasped and advises going for them.

"There is definitely a good job ahead if you are willing to take it."

*Healthwise* this card indicates the start of recuperation and slow recovery. It indicates that patience is necessary in order to maintain an effective health regime. The card shows that one must manage the details of health in every way.

"With this card we see that there is a steady recovery and potential for healing."

In *Relationships* this card indicates that there is a firm basis for a growing relationship, although it may be based on practicalities and convenience rather than any deep emotional bond. It could also signify a very physical relationship.

"There is a marriage of convenience that works well on the level on which you have found it."

In *Travel & Lifestyle* this card indicates the potential to save for travel, and not the travel itself. It can signify that there will be slow progress, even delays in travel. Whilst it is a card of security, it can also mean that you should withhold your current plans until a later date.

"Make plans for travel and a change, but the time is not yet. Secure your current position first."

In *Education* this card indicates a realistic attitude toward the resources you have available for your course and studies. You should take time to evaluate your circumstances and ensure that you have the necessary environment for sustained study. On a positive note, it indicates the steady grasping of new material of practical benefit.

In *Spiritual Awareness & Self-Development* this card shows that you must take time to look after your health and daily routines. It is a card of paying attention to the smallest detail and at the same time having a reality check. Are your circumstances really improving, or are you deluding yourself?

*You are blocking this card today by:*

1. Not paying your bills
2. Not making fixed appointments
3. Not planning the week ahead
4. Not being fully prepared for an activity

## Connect to Your Card

Make a new step of any kind, whether a speculative venture or exploration. Send an email.

## The Page of Pentacles Says

"I am the Page of Pentacles, and I am the youthful ambition that never grows old. I am the voice from deep within that urges you to carry on and follow your destiny. You need to examine carefully what strengths you possess and how to turn every possibility into gold. I advise you to 'speculate to accumulate.'"

## Keywords

Speculation, starting work, perseverance, planting seeds, slow, steady, duty, realism, method, interest, diligent, careful, thrift, attention, sense, student, scholarship, reflection, realistic aims, focus.

# —Day 2: Page of Swords—
## Surveying the Scene • Drawing Back the Curtains

### Resonances

*Numerology:* 54/9

*Astrology:* Aquarius

*Kabbalah:*
Malkuth (Kingdom)

*Elemental:*
Earth of Air

*Perfume:* Storax

### Quick Connections

*Affirmation:* With every breath out, my mind becomes clearer and I can see what is in front of me.

*Meditation:* "The sword of criticism has two edges; the judgement of others and your judgement of yourself."

## The Lesson of the Page of Swords
### Entering into a Card

With today's introduction to another of the pages from the court cards, the Page of Swords, we'd like to introduce a new way of interacting and learning the cards which is a meditation. Whilst most of us don't get on with Zen-like meditation methods ("still the mind…think of nothing…I have to take the car in for service soon…"), we can actually use the tarot as a proactive meditation tool.

We're not going to say anything about the Page of Swords yet. Just take a look at your version of the card. Free yourself up for ten minutes, and imagine with each exhalation the image of the card pushing away.

You can hold the card and move it slightly one way and the other in front of your eyes whilst you do this, as if in a hypnotic manner.

With each breath in, the card comes back towards you. When you breathe out, it moves back away. Backwards and forwards…backwards and forwards…Do this for a couple of minutes, slowing your breath each time.

When you are ready, take a huge deep breath and either swallow the card (in your imagination!) or be swallowed into it. You can even move it towards your forehead and slap it right there!

Enter into the card, as a feeling, colour, or a full 3-D interactive environment. Perhaps you'll just hear sounds. It's important not to try and force any particular representation or visualisation. Just let the card surround you, or try to surround the card and feel what happens.

Then stay in whatever is happening for some time, just a few more minutes. You may even meet the Page of Swords personally in the experience.

Whenever you are ready to hear it, a phrase will come to your mind or be told to you, or you will read it in your mind like a script. It may sound like a riddle, a mantra, or a quote from something. Make a note of it in your journal and gradually ease back out of the experience to your everyday situation.

Now you can compare your experience with our introduction to Sam of the Swords.

### Sam of the Swords

When it comes to tarot, Sam is pretty sharp. It's all about the correspondences to Sam. He knows that in the great scheme of things, there are secret correspondences between everything; between big and small, the lowest and the highest—even plants correspond to the mighty planets. So Sam knows that the sunflower corresponds to the Sun, and a sword corresponds to air. Sometimes these associations are obvious, sometimes obscure, but to Sam, a true thinker, these are the real mysteries.

So when Sam is reading the cards, he sees a vast map of the cosmos. In the swords, he sees Air, thought, and knowledge. In the cups, he sees the emotions in their full range. In the pentacles, he sees pictures of everyday, life and in the wands the highest spiritual teachings of our inner life. It is likely Sam will be a student of Kabbalah, alchemy, astrology, and magick, where all these things are taught—even down to the Hebrew alphabet.

***Where you might meet Sam***: The library, laboratory, travelling, and unusual sites.

***What people say about Sam:*** He's pretty much in his head most of the time.

# The Card in Your Life/Reading

*Careerwise & Financially* this card indicates the writing of your résumé before making any further steps and doing thorough market research. It shows a holding back of any discussions and words, preparation for interviews, and practice rather than action.

"Although you may feel ready, the Page of Swords should show you that you must hold back and take a good, clear look at the battlefield before you commit your forces."

*Healthwise* this card indicates researching the whole situation and getting as many opinions as possible. It shows that having a clear overview is essential to a holistic management of your situation.

In *Relationships* this card indicates that it is time to withdraw a little and appraise—coolly and rationally—exactly what is going on in the relationship. It may be time to get a little air.

"Take a big step back out of the situation so you can see it clearly. What do you see?"

In *Travel & Lifestyle* this card indicates the mapping out of the whole journey and a critical gaining of knowledge, insider information, and experience. It shows that you must be aware of the whole landscape before you travel so you can uncover any obstacles and use your time wisely.

"The Page of Swords means that you should really know the landscape before travelling. This will allow you to have smooth travel and easy passage—you'll have the lay of the land."

In *Education* this card indicates a good look at the options and reevaluation of a course. It is a stock-taking of what you have learnt and where you intend to go with it. It can indicate time for a mentor session, study-break, or supervision session, plotting your route ahead. You may need to look more widely at your options—particularly if you might travel further afield for your studies.

In *Spiritual Awareness & Self-Development* this card symbolises the intellectual rigour and discipline of starting a new outlook—a new focus. It shows the change of mind that comes from taking a good stance on your own decisions, owning them, and accepting full responsibility for your actions. Certain clarity is shown by taking a moment to review your journal, life, and experiences.

*You are blocking this card today by:*

1. Not watching what you say
2. Protesting
3. Being irrational over decisions and making snap judgements
4. Being foolish in distinguished company

## Connect to Your Card

Say something clear and decisive today. Make an announcement. Read the news.

## The Page of Swords Says

"You should choose your words craftily and wisely, as they are a very sharp tool that when executed with this consideration can make or break a difficult situation."

## Keywords

Poise, concentration, alert, obedience, grace, dexterity, diplomacy, spying, observation, logic, constructive criticism, circumspection, investigation, vigilant, wisdom, strength, guile, defensiveness and agility, intellect, triumph without violence, awareness, sparring, deceit, rival, authority, a dilettante, surprises, examination.

# —Day 3: Page of Cups—
## The Dreams of Youth • The Art of Conjuring

### Resonances

*Numerology:* 40/4

*Astrology:*
Pisces/Scorpio

*Kabbalah:*
Malkuth (Kingdom)

*Elemental:*
Earth of Water

*Perfume:*
Indigo

FANTE DI COPPE  KNAVE OF CHALICES
VALET DE COUPES  SOTA DE COPAS

BUBE DER KELCHE  BEKERS SCHILDKNAAP

### Quick Connections

*Affirmation:* With every breath in, all the possibilities of creation become more available to me.

*Meditation:* "The dreams of youth are neither contained nor banished, the dreamer wakes by the river."

## The Lesson of the Page of Cups
### Working with the Card as a Scene

Today we take a first look at reading cards as if they were a scene in a story, ready for some later exercises where we take our cards for a walk and talk! You will also see that we are approaching each of the four pages very differently, according to their nature. By allowing the cards themselves to teach us in their own character, we become more immersed in their living wisdom—something we call *Tarosophy,* from combining the word "tarot" (whose source is still not quite known, but likely from variations on the Italian word for "triumph") and the Greek *sophia,* meaning "wisdom."

So here today we have the Page of Cups. We might say we really doesn't get on with this character—he has been drinking too much (in the WST), and so much so he believes he is seeing a fish leaping out of his cup. On the other hand, this could be a symbol of creativity! The card is often associated with thinking outside of the box, being open to new emotional content, a surprise from our own unconscious, and other aspects of the deeper self.

Have you noticed in the WST that many of the cards are drawn with a horizontal line across the bottom third of the card? It's as if there was a set and a stage on which the character was standing. It might come as no surprise then that Pamela Colman Smith was a theatrical designer!

Have a look at this Page of Cups—he is on stage with a backdrop of painted waves. We wonder what his line is…what his motivation might be in this scene. What stage directions do we give the Page—or the fish?!

When the Page of Cups stands in our reading, in our spread (which is indeed a stage, whereupon we are all players), what lines does he announce? What is his monologue?

Bonus points for anyone writing this in their journal in iambic pentameters!

### Charlotte of the Cups

With Charlotte, it's all about feelings. The cards are an intuitive channel for those deepest feelings that find themselves hard to express in words alone. In the images of tarot we can tap into that deep well of emotions and draw up the real heart and soul of the world. By laying out spreads, meditating and contemplating upon the cards, and dreaming about them and visualising them, we can dive into a world of emotions, the unconscious, and deeper layers of the self.

Charlotte doesn't teach, but she is a good example and role-model, reflecting on the way in which life goes by so fast we do not often take a moment to refresh and replenish ourselves in deeper wisdom. When she reads cards, she takes time, often only using one card which opens a vast floodgate of information from the sensitive, empathetic side of herself.

*Where you might meet Charlotte:* Dancing, singing, partying. At the beach.

*What people say about Charlotte:* She's a fun-loving girl with plenty of character.

## The Card in Your Life/Reading

*Careerwise & Financially* this card indicates totally unexpected opportunities and creative release. It can signify artistic direction and a new impetus or influence in your place of work. It can sometimes advise out-of-the-box thinking.

"It is time to take a creative leap and accept the consequences—be open to surprise."

*Healthwise* this card often indicates a birth, whether of a new baby or a new beginning to a health situation. Often surprising results and new information may be at hand, and there is openness to novel or unique suggestions.

"It is time to be creative and do something new in the situation. Rebirth will come."

In *Relationships* this card indicates friendly fun, surprises in store, and a relationship that creates a lot of energy. It is a young card with much potential, so be ready for the ride.

"When the Page of Cups is about, there's fun to be had in relationships—be ready for surprises!"

In *Travel & Lifestyle* this card indicates a willingness to be flexible and creative, experience new vistas, and be totally spontaneous. The Page of Wands is responsive to the situation as it unfolds about her and allows that to be a natural delight rather than stressful.

"This card shows that you can be open to spontaneous and new experiences in your life."

In *Education* this card indicates creativity and the enjoyment of new thinking, knowledge, and experience. You are advised in the card to remain uncritical and non-judgemental of your new learning or experience, until you have had time to experience it fully.

"Be open for a while to what is unfolding, no matter how surprising. It is time to experience. Reflect upon it later."

In *Spiritual Awareness & Self-Development* this card signifies the release of old patterns and habits for a new creativity to emerge. It can signify a willingness to perceive a new current, flow, or tide in your life, and whilst not yet being ready to respond to it, being aware of it.

"There is a growing recognition that change is coming, no matter what may follow."

### *You are blocking this card today by:*

1. Being crude and boorish in polite company
2. Behaving insensitively to those closest to you
3. Withdrawing your care and attention from those you love
4. Being very extrovert during a social gathering

## Connect to Your Card

Write poetry or create art. Think outside the box. Do something outside your usual routine.

## The Page of Cups Says

"Enjoy life; make the most of living it to the full. Savour the thrill of flirting and throwing caution to the wind. Behave like you only have a year to live! Court the unexpected in the most unusual of places, embrace surprise, let your emotions be your guide, and savour being the centre of attention."

## Keywords

Jaunty, mesmerising, active listening (counselling), sophistication, gentleness, kindness, news of birth of a child, intuition, inspiration, introversion, artistry, sensitivity. Intimacy, sentiment, emotional, curiosity, birth of an idea, indolence, confidence, discretion, integrity, good news, messages, taste, application, reflection.

# —Day 4: Page of Wands—
## Being Packed and Prepared • Ready to Step Out

### Resonances

*Numerology:* 26/8

*Astrology:*
Sagittarius

*Kabbalah:*
Malkuth (Kingdom)

*Elemental:*
Earth of Fire

*Perfume:*
Red Sandalwood

### Quick Connections

*Affirmation:* In between each breath, the Fire of my soul burns and radiates growing passion.

*Meditation:* "Harness the force of your passions and the force will carry you forth."

## The Lesson of the Page of Wands
### The Journey of Life in Tarot

Each of the tarot cards represents a snapshot of our life and the events of the world. Furthermore, the major arcana represent the archetypes that underpin our lives. With the four pages we see the starting of our journey in different ways: the Page of Pentacles represents our material concerns and the journey; the Page of Swords represents our learning and knowledge; the Page of Cups is our emotional sphere; and the Page of Wands is our values and spirit.

As we progress through our seventy-eight days we will seek to fulfill each of these journeys through the tarot. It is important that we see the cards in our real life, and whilst we learn such esoteric ideas as correspondences we should also respond to our feelings as we work with the cards. It is also important to use the cards to question our values and beliefs about the world in order to fully engage their power to transform our life.

Take a moment to review the previous four days and make comparisons between each of the page cards. We will return to court cards during our journey ahead, and you will see how they represent important markers in our life journey.

You might also take a moment to consider how people around you fit into the four families of the courts. Is there anybody you know who is entirely material and would be at home with the pentacles family? Is there somebody you know who is entirely studious and would love to meet the swords family? Whilst we divide the world into just these four fundamental elements, we can see how this allows us to make sense of our daily experience.

And do not forget that our aim as tarot readers is also to balance these four elements in ourselves so we can give wise readings from a range of experience. Tomorrow we will look further into exploring the tarot in our daily life.

### Wanda of the Wands

When Wanda comes along, you know it! Bright, vibrant, sometimes a bit flashy, Wanda wants to know all about the cards—she lives and breathes them—they are a way of life to her. Wanda is a born teacher, she tells us that tarot is all about living life to the fullest, experiencing it, travelling with the deck as if it were a constant companion. She talks to her cards and they talk right back at her—Wanda is a born communicator and traveller.

Wanda sets a good example: she engages tarot as a way of living and uses the cards to frame her experience of life, discover imbalances, create positive solutions, and generally use the deck as a toolkit. Whilst she looks at the cards as fortune-telling, she wants to find out more about how they teach us about time itself. When she looks at them as self-discovery, she wants to know about the self. When Colin of the Coins comes along and says they're just seventy-eight cards, she wants to know about their history. Wanda uses the cards to learn life.

*Where you might meet Wanda:* Teaching, leading, in the boardroom. In charge anywhere.

*What people say about Wanda:* Bossy and no-nonsense, she's one tough cookie.

## The Card in Your Life/Reading

*Careerwise & Financially* this card indicates the beginning of a fulfilling task, project, role, job, or career. In every way the Page of Wands is a good card to have in career questions, signifying the alignment of your life purpose to the tasks in hand.

"The setting off on a new job which fulfils you and is aligned totally to your ambitions."

*Healthwise* this card indicates the need to draw back to your core values and seek out what is most important in your life. Whilst not indicating any particular health issue, the card is one of energy and fire, showing rapid movement in any direction. It counsels holding on to what is most valuable.

"Take a moment to gather that which you personally find most rewarding and hold on to it."

In *Relationships* this card indicates a meeting of your values, although this can be seen as somewhat selfish. You may need to look beyond yourself to truly fulfill the promise of passion indicated by the appearance of the Page of Wands. What does the other person think is best about the relationship?

"Whilst you are enthusiastic about the relationship, you might take a moment to see if this is reciprocated."

In *Travel & Lifestyle* this card indicates a fulfilling journey ahead, one full of excitement and adventure. It is something that will give you experience that will be life-changing and close to your core values. In terms of lifestyle, this is a powerful card which initiates a re-alignment and sets you back on track.

"The Page here shows a return to your core values and lifestyle in the journey ahead. Enjoy!"

In *Education* this card indicates learning which is for its own sake and completes something in you. It symbolises a valuable and affirming journey beyond the lessons themselves.

In *Spiritual Awareness & Self-Development* this card is the journey of life and the seeking of higher values. It shows the seeker on their path to realisation through the trials of life. In a reading it can indicate that your self-development is taking a new path which may yet seem uncertain.

"You are about to commence a new initiation—a new journey awaits you in life."

*You are blocking this card today by:*

1. Non-reaction when roused to anger
2. Hiding your brilliance
3. Not owning your ambition

4. Being cowardly and not taking action when wronged

## Connect to Your Card

Do something just for yourself and what is important to you. Donate to charity. Take time.

## The Page of Wands Says

"Be like me, burst out and be proud! Focus on the good things that are in your life and conjure more brilliance."

## Keywords

Analytical, focus, rousing, coveting, innovation, entrance, sudden in anger, bearer of tidings, brilliance, reactive, courage, extroversion, daring, vigour, arousal, eagerness, messenger, awakening of passion, satisfaction, confidence, good news, burning, announcements, inspirations, creative.

### WAYSIDE LESSON: COURT CARDS

As many students and professionals will testify, the court cards are the most troublesome to learn and interpret in a reading. It seems that everyone asks the same question—do I read this card as a person, an event, an energy, or part of the personality of the querent?

There are whole books written on the subject: Kate Warwick-Smith's *The Tarot Court Cards* (Destiny Books, 2003) and Mary K. Greer and Tom Little's *Understanding the Tarot Court* (Llewellyn, 2004). The popular beginner books devote sections to the court cards, noting they may be read in as many as seven different ways, even as a time of the year (see Anthony Louis, *Tarot Plain and Simple* [Llewellyn, 2003]) without giving much indication of how the reader is to know which of those seven ways to choose.[9]

In Joan Bunning's *Learning the Tarot* (Weiser, 1998), an example is provided where the Queen of Pentacles may be the environment of a house, another person in that house group, or yourself. Bunning calls this the "subtle play of the Tarot" but offers no real conclusion as to which interpretation to follow in this example or any other reading where a court card appears.[10]

The court cards are also certainly an area where we may project our own opinions of our fellow creatures. In Sally Gearhart and Susan Rennie's *A Feminist Tarot* (Persephone Press, 1977), we see the Knight of Swords as "heavy police or military action repressing minority elements."[11]

They are also particularly time-fixed and culturally-relative, both in their hierarchical nature and in their possible interpretations as roles and relationships; in a 1930s cartomancy book by Zodiastar, *30 Different Ways of Card Fortune-Telling* (Universal, 1936), we read that the advice for a Queen of Hearts person-type is "you ought to marry a strong-willed person, since you need guidance."[12]

## People Are Strange

It's as Jim Morrison sang, isn't it? When we are presented with the court cards, we immediately see a person, and more so a person in a role. These are not just anybody—they are people in positions of power or service. Here we see an immediate issue: how do you personally relate to hierarchy? The rigid structure of the court is defined by notions of control, rulership, and in many cultures, divine right. You cannot look at the king without having to access your own unconscious associations with kingship. So you may wish to take a moment to think of what comes to mind when you think of a king (or queen). To which periods of time do you travel?

If you were a king or queen, how would you feel? What would you feel about your role in society? How would it influence your actions as a person? These are some of the many immediate yet consequential thoughts that arise when we are presented with this apparently simple and straightforward image.

But people are strange. We know that from our section on the major cards, cards such as the High Priestess and the Hermit are not people or **the** archetypes but **arising images** constellating from an unknowable archetypal field. Thus they remain ultimately indefinable and it is in this that resides their power to offer multiple interpretations within a reading. This is essential for tarot to work.

The same goes for the court cards. They are **not** the pictures that are depicted. They are not roles, and they are **not** people. They are symbolic place-holders for energies in relationship. They are examples—or more specifically, **exemplars**—of how the Universe holds together and reflects itself through our perceptions and awareness. However, because they are easily depicted as people in roles, our attention is held by this presentation and remains at that level. We must learn to look deeper—this is what Tarosophy teaches us.

When we look at a person, especially ourselves, we access the whole realm of the archetypal. We function in the *mundus imaginalis* of Henri Corbin, the imaginal world. It is here that true divination originates, if such could be said. The whole spectrum of experience is accessible to us—and anyone else. So when we look at a court card depicting another human being, we cannot help but wonder what the Knight of Wands does on his day off—whether he lays down his wand and takes up his cups, perhaps? We cannot and do not see them fixed in their role. This is why we cannot read the court cards. We try to fix them and they cannot be so fixed whilst we maintain them as people in roles.

At least the minors depict tableaus we take as applying universally and the majors as images of archetypal patterns that cascade into our reality in any manner of different fashions. With the court cards we immediately get locked into seeing them as personages, roles, even personality-types. And given that people are strange and infinite, we bounce between simple limitations; the King of Swords "is personified in successful investors or business persons…" (Paul Quinn, *Tarot for Life* [Theosophical Publishing House, 2009]) and their infinite possibilities as people within the archetypal realms.

## Infinite Strains of the Loom

If we go to the highest and most universal reading of this set of sixteen cards arrayed in a four-by-four loom, we can see that they are composed of a warp and weft created by four levels in four worlds. This is particularly appropriate to a Kabbalistic correspondence of four elements in four worlds as used by the Golden Dawn and subsequent esoteric groups such as the Ancient Mystical Order of Seekers (AMOS), whose Path of Light teachings, vol. VII cover the tarot. The Rosicrucian teachings of AMORC and BOTA also make this correspondence between the court cards and the Kabbalistic model.[13]

So we should perhaps consider the nature of these sixteen cards as primarily an elemental nexus—a knotting of raw energy in a particular form, held in a tapestry of sixteen squares. As this energy is in motion, it strains against the other knots, pulling our array out of shape. We might think of this like gravity—a number of objects in space all invisibly shaping what passes between their influences. When a court card or two turn up, they are like gravity wells in your reading, bending the other cards around them.

As the four levels of energy also have their elemental correspondences, we can further follow the Golden Dawn (and Crowley) in creating a matrix of elemental mixtures. The suits have their standard elemental correspondences, such as Earth corresponding to Pentacles, and the four levels have their correspondences of Fire (king), Water (queen), Air (knight), and Earth (page). Thus we start with the Page of Pentacles being the earthy part of Earth, all the way to the King of Wands being the fiery part of Fire. You might like to fill in the gaps below with your own analysis, reflections, and keywords for these elemental nodes:

| | Earth (Pentacles) | Air (Swords) | Water (Cups) | Fire (Wands) |
|---|---|---|---|---|
| Earth Level of (Page) | | | | |
| Air Level of (Knight) | | Bright, clear, empty... | | |
| Water Level of (Queen) | | | | |
| Fiery Level of (King) | | | Steam, pressure, extinguisher | |

These will give you the elemental essence of these sixteen cards whether they manifest that essence through a person, event, or characteristic. You may also now be able to make sense of the Golden Dawn titles of these cards, such as the Knave of Pentacles (Page of Pentacles) being entitled "The Princess of the Echoing Hills: Rose of the Palace of Earth," as she is the earth of Earth. The Knave of Cups (Page of Cups) is called "The Princess of the Waters: The Lotus of the Palace of the Floods," being the earthy part of Water.

## What Would We See in the Elemental Courts?

I would personally redesign the court cards as more ethereal or abstract images to reflect those elemental essences. In a sense, the work of Ithell Colquhoun on her tarot deck mirrors perfectly how I would cast the court. The card illustrated here is the Ace of Pentacles. The colours and shapes would refer to the correspondences of the elements; for example, a simple key of red for Fire and blue for Water would give us a King of Cups card merging those two colours.

Working within the colour correspondences of the Golden Dawn, I would have the Air suit of swords drawn as blue/yellow rays, in patterns according to their level:

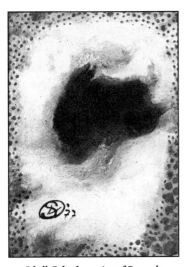

*Ithell Colquhoun Ace of Pentacles*

- Page: Unformed blue/yellow swirls, as unmixed gases, layered
- Knight: Directed rays as if sunlight through clouds
- Queen: Long uniform curves of curling shapes and morasses
- King: Stable lines and shapes, fixed in position like lasers ("coherent light")

This would then prevent reading the cards as people or being stuck with outdated notions of courtly hierarchy. However, I would still be interested to know if I should read this energy as coming through into manifestation as a person, a part of myself or my querent, or as a general summary of a particular process or complex situation.

## Knowing How to Read a Court Card

If we accept the sixteen court cards as dictating the nature of forces and their levels in a reading, we can use experience to determine how they are most likely making themselves manifest. A *single* court card in a spread would indicate that energy taking centre stage, bending the cards around it, influencing and affecting them. Likely a **particular individual** then! A *large* number of court cards for me signify a tension of energies, particularly if they are varying suits, indicating the levels are also widely variant. This more often than not signifies **aspects of the querent's personality** in conflict.

*Just two or three* court cards in a typical spread tend to indicate the **environmental forces** for me—the levels and energies at work in a project, relationship, or ambition taken as a whole. This system makes it far easier and more accurate (in my experience) to read the court cards—if it is just one card, you will be seeking to identify a person who fits that nature; if two or three, it is a summary of the events taking place. If more, they are aspects of the person involved, making it more practical to explore with the person present.

## Court Cards, Old Style

Another older method of interpreting the court cards may give you an interesting variation in your spread reading. This is from the time of Papus and Etteila. Whilst they certainly confused the origins of the tarot, making links to ancient Egypt and beyond, they were adroit at making systems of divination based on correspondences. More so, they were fond of systems that "weary not the memory," something I am also keen to attain in my own teaching! They built up from simple principles and the same goes for the court cards.

In Papus, we read that the court cards stand for man, woman, young man, and child.[14] These correspond to the nature of—and here I have rephrased slightly for contemporary usage—**Creativity**, **Union**, **Conflict**, and **Transition**. We can then apply these correspondences in the world (element/suit) in which they find themselves expressed.

Thus a Page of Swords would simply represent transition in the world of finances and material matters—a very uncertain position! A Queen of Swords would be union in the world of intellect and knowledge—perhaps a sudden insight, new item of information, or agreeing to learn. The Knight of Wands shows a conflict in ambitions and lifestyle choices—perhaps even a sudden overturning of values. You may like to complete the table here with your own interpretation and experience of these keys.

|  | Material, Career, Health | Intellect, Learning, Education, Ideas | Emotions, Feelings, Desires, Needs | Values, Spirit, Ambition, Lifestyle |
|---|---|---|---|---|
| Transition in...(Page) | | | | A new outlook in life, unsettled. |
| Conflict in...(Knight) | | | | |
| Union in...(Queen) | An agreement of practical terms. | | | |
| Creativity in...(King) | | | | |

## Are You Lookin' at Me?

Finally, buried in Etteila is an interesting idea we have used successfully for many readings which seems to work very well. The rule is simple: the kings and queens are other people, and the knights and pages are how those other people see (or respond to and project onto) the querent. It's a nice, simple idea loaded with psychological implication when used in a reading. If you have a few court cards in a spread, this is a fascinating exercise, as you identify the people involved, and then divine how they are responding to the querent from their own positions in the situation, represented by the spread itself.

Thus you may have a Queen of Pentacles and a Knight of Swords in a reading for a male querent. The former is in the "crossing" position of a Celtic Cross reading, and the latter is in the "resources" position (see section of the **Celtic Cross** for these terms). The

Queen would represent a real person, obstructing the querent in some way, and the Knight would show how she was viewing the querent—as being too ruthless or quick to make decision perhaps—not as a "resource" then, but as a threat.

## Reading Methods Using Only the Court Cards

Sometimes the question may be about a family situation or complex workplace environment and hence the court cards may all represent actors in that dynamic. In this case, we would be tempted to do a reading with the court cards alone, to place them in relationship to each other and explore how they relate.

You could also perform an interactive reading where the cards are split into majors, minors, and court cards. The querent selects out the court cards to represent the people involved, and lays them out in the most appropriate pattern.

You then shuffle the majors and place a major card against each court card on the table to divine which archetypal force that player is working through (or being worked through). You can then shuffle and place from the pile of minors to divine what the relationship is between each player—and even better, another card for how to resolve that relationship.

The following illustration is an example free-form spread using this method, which we call "All the World's a Stage." You may wish to explore it and determine your own interpretation.

Current Relationship

Resolving Relationship

**The All the World's a Stage Spread**

## All the World's a Stage Reading

In this reading, the querent selected the court cards and placed them in the positions illustrated in the spread. The Knight of Wands was riding away!

The majors were shuffled and selected, and placed above and below the court cards. Next, two cards were selected from the minors to divine the relationship and its resolution between the King of Cups and the Knight of Wands.

These minor cards were the Three of Swords (showing the current relationship) and the Two of Pentacles (showing a means of resolution). What do you think those two cards suggest together?

Whilst there are many interesting aspects of this reading, what might you also make of the Hanged Man working through the Page of Coins?

## Conclusion

The court cards are a powerful and elemental set in themselves, and should not be taken as troublesome, but rather as powerful significators and portents of elemental energy at work across different levels. The nature of the universe to allow such patterns to manifest in an infinite variety of ways is complex for sure, but we should—as Francis Bacon remarked—endeavour to expand our awareness to comprehend the mysteries, not narrow the mysteries to the limits of our mind.

# —Gate One—

# The Outer Courtyard

# Elemental Spread—For Finding Your Place

*It is dawn and you are in the courtyard. Four flags flutter lightly in the breeze of a new day, one to each quarter of the compass, emblazoned with the symbols of the four elements. You are prepared for your journey and yet hesitate to take the first step. How will you come to find your place in the world?*

## Soundtrack for the Journey
### *"Whatcha Waiting For?" (Gwen Stefani)*

In this first gated spread we use just the four cards we have encountered so far, the pages. We describe these as the *channelers* of each of the four suits from whose family they come. The four suits are the families of tarot, and they live in the Palaces of the Four Elements, one at each quarter of the compass in the world of tarot:

- Pentacles: Earth
- Swords: Air
- Cups: Water
- Wands: Fire

The pages are the representatives of that family, for better or worse, like any child. The Page of Wands is born of fire; the Page of Cups is of the water family. The Page of Swords is a child of air, and the Page of Pentacles nothing more or less than the son or daughter of earth. These elemental characteristics are so basic you can probably work out a great deal from them even now:

- Which Page is likely to be found drunk under a table?
- Which Page is likely to get into a fight?
- Which Page is likely to invest money more carefully than any other?
- Which Page has a cutting wit?

Because you already know people, because you are surrounded by them all the time, even on television, you probably know more than you realise about the court cards already.

The thing with the pages is that they can all grow up. They all symbolise the possibility of that family to take their place in the world. So the Page of Cups represents the possibility of bringing culture and art to society, perhaps as a poet or designer. The Page of Swords is the chance of invention and ideas—and in a reading would mean potential for new insight.

So, we must now decide which is your family. When you have read the descriptions of the four pages, consider which you identify with most. Whilst we are always a mixture of the four elements, for now, choose the one which most clearly embodies most of your everyday character.

When you have decided on your card, which is now your *significator*—a card which represents the person asking the question—shuffle all four cards face-down and lay them out as follows:

1. Earth Position
2. Air Position
3. Water Position
4. Fire Position

This is the Outer Courtyard and a representation of your current position in terms of the elements. To continue to the next gate, you must make a better arrangement of these elements in your life so you can present yourself at the Clockwork Museum and gain entrance.

To fulfill this gate, notice firstly in which element your significator has been placed. If it is the same element of your suit, i.e., you are the Page of Wands and that card is placed in the Fire position, this means that you are being called to totally engage yourself in actions suited to your nature.

This element indicates your current position and strength. In the case that your card is not in its own element, your work of the week ahead is to balance that element with the other three by performing activities which engage the three other elements. The activities you can select include:

1. Earth: financial matters, organisation, management, gardening
2. Air: speaking, presenting, experimenting, discussion, contracts, education, reading
3. Water: poetry, arts, culture, enjoyment, emotional satisfaction, luxury
4. Fire: Energetic actions, exercise, starting new things, spontaneity

If you would like to try the exercise with an optional extra rule, avoid doing any of the things associated with the element of your significator whilst you concentrate on the other three. These are not the only activities, of course; you can divide all human activity into these four general areas quite clearly in most cases.

Notice over the next seven days how you move in and out of your comfort zone and how acting in fundamental and elemental ways divides the world up into these four aspects. You will really experience the elements in daily life which will make you a great tarot card reader as you continue to build your skills and experience. In learning this way, every day teaches you more about tarot and tarot teaches you about your every day—and the days of others.

# —Day 5: Ten of Pentacles—
### Finding Yourself at the Beginning (Returning) • A Place to Return

### Resonances

*Numerology:* 78/6

*Astrology:*
Mercury in Virgo

*Kabbalah:* Malkuth
(Kingdom)

*Sabian Symbol:*
Virgo III—
An Automobile Caravan
(The Gypsy Soul)

### Quick Connections

*Affirmation:* Every
movement I make has a
place in this world with
the movement of the stars.

*Meditation:* "Wealth
and prosperity do not
come cheaply."

## The Lesson of the Ten of Pentacles
### Applying the Tarot to Your Daily Experience

The Ten of Pentacles teaches us to be structured and keep the outcome in mind at all times as we work towards it. In our lessons ahead we will always try and bear the Ten of Pentacles in mind as we build a good, solid understanding of the cards.

For today, you should simply take time to go over the detail of this card in readings, and imagine the sorts of situations you are in during your daily life where the Ten of Pentacles would be a good image. We will start off with straightforward observations.

Make a note in your mind or record in your journal of the things in your life that are very "10P-ish." It could be that you see a shop window full of family items, a poster that looks similar to your version(s) of the card—anything. It could even be the feeling after eating a good meal. You may even experience a strong and meaningful coincidence— a synchronicity.

By engaging the powers of the cards in our daily life, we come to connect to the invisible knots that bind the universe with often magical results.

## The Card in Your Life/Reading

*Careerwise & Financially* this card indicates a good solid job-for-life situation, where everything is fixed and a status quo has been established. This is not always a good thing for the rebel or those with new ideas. It shows the importance of making good connections with the established order of things.

"Establish yourself in the existing structure and work within it; this is not a time to rock the boat."

*Healthwise* this card indicates solid family support, the cycle of life, and structure. It is time to establish a regime and bow to the obvious. Everything is as it is, and the time is yours to see how one thing passes to another.

"Establish a good regime, no matter how traditional or boring. Reduce surprises and shocks."

In *Relationships* this card indicates family, domesticity, and a completion. There are many relationships beyond the couple, from one generation to another. We must also note when this card appears that we may be carrying on old habits from our parents, or teaching them to our children.

"The Ten of Pentacles symbolises the wealth of a good family and bodes well in all things."

In *Travel & Lifestyle* this card indicates family holidays, whether that is a traditional family or a family composed of like-minded friends. It can also indicate a cross-generational situation, where different ages are all involved in the travel, or in your life. Boundaries are suggested to ensure everyone gets their own requirements met.

"It is a time where different ages are all present in one big relationship, so get a good structure."

In *Education* this card indicates structure, established wisdom, and tradition. It is a learning which is passed on from generation to generation. Learn to see the valuable role you play in passing on whatever you learn, and learning from those with more experience.

"With this card we are shown the importance of structure and relationships across time. All knowledge is passed through time, and when this card appears we are called to play a role in that transmission."

In *Spiritual Awareness & Self-Development* this card shows the importance of structure and family in the most basic sense of security and support. It is a card which denotes that we must develop a firm basis and roots in the everyday world before aspiring to higher things.

"Take a good look at your life and ensure it is stable enough to support your highest aspirations."

*You are blocking this card today by:*

1. Being miserly and not treating yourself to the finer things in life
2. Not working and cancelling important meetings
3. Not visiting close family and friends
4. Not dressing to impress

## Connect to Your Card

Connect to your family, friends, or colleagues today. Have a gathering at your place.

## The Ten of Pentacles Says

"Good fortune is all around you; after much work, you have arrived at a place of security. You have many friends who want to share this with you; you must take care that those are true friends. You need to slow down now and take it easy. Let others take more responsibility—you need to delegate now."

## Keywords

Industry, cohesion, developed, solid, security, the card of finding yourself settled, windfall, gaining, good dividend, good returns, stability, prestige, property, tradition, lineage, earthing, inheritance, wealth, riches, success, agreement, assignations, arrangements, inhabitation, economy, marketing, exchange, possessions, reaping, gain, organisation, family, community.

## Resonances

*Numerology:* 64/1

*Astrology:*
Sun in Gemini

*Kabbalah:* Malkuth
(Kingdom)

*Sabian Symbol:*
Gemini III—A Cafeteria
(The Choice Is Yours)

## Quick Connections

*Affirmation:* I can take my time and my turn to decide whatever I need to decide.

*Meditation:* "The shock of the final conflict brings with it a sense of calm."

## The Lesson of the Ten of Swords
### *Reading Difficult or Negative Cards*

Is this a card—the Ten of Swords—that immediately makes you go "oh"? Is it one that you think querents (those who come to your readings) will frown at and then spend the whole reading not listening to anything you are saying because they are fretting and waiting until you explain the "bad card"?

As a card in itself, we see this as the world of "thought" (swords) in the densest possible place (10). And thoughts don't like to be there! A fixed mind not open to possibilities is not a happy mind. This is the end of the road and where you believe you can least be surprised, but—bang! There is a surprise! You get stabbed in the back.

It is a card of the "least expected."

In *Tarot Flip*, we call this card "distress." However, reversed it is "delight." When you hold the card upside down, what sort of feeling does it generate for you?

Here are a couple of questions—what is the significance of the ten swords being arranged down the spine of the body, and what is with the hand gesture in the WST?

If your card differs in detail from another deck, would it still carry the theme of "fixed thoughts/rigid thinking" or does it show some other theme?

How do you explain this card to a querent? We usually refer to the trope of "At least everything is now known and out in the open. You know the ground when you're face down in it."

And who did it? Who killed him? And what was the killer's motive?

## The Card in Your Life/Reading

*Careerwise & Financially* this card indicates a sudden end to whatever has gone before. A certain betrayal of your principles, ideas, and expectations. It is a dire card to receive during any project, as it means that the concept will be tested to its limits and may be declared obsolete.

"It is time to pin everything down and ensure there is no room for change."

*Healthwise* this card indicates invasion and surgery. On a lighter note it can indicate the world's worst acupuncture specialist. It is a warning to ensure clarity in everyone's opinions and ideas about treatment or recovery. This card shows no remorse for confusion or uncertainty.

"Whilst this card appears most dire, it is a caution to ensure clarity and absolute certainty."

In *Relationships* this card indicates that ideas about the relationship are not up-front and in the open. There are harsh words about the relationship, even if they remain unsaid. These will ultimately lead to the death of what stands at present.

"Ensure that in your relationship everything is up-front and stated in the open otherwise it will come to no good result."

In *Travel & Lifestyle* this card indicates a rigidity of ideas and lack of adventure. You may need to be kick-started from your regular way of thinking and expectations and do something most unexpected to find release and freedom.

"With the Ten of Swords in the context of travel (or lifestyle), we see that you have become fixed by your own expectations. You are using the past to foresee your future and this should not be the case."

In *Education* this card indicates an overwhelming set of ideas and concepts that keeps you from moving forwards. It may indicate the end of what you can usefully learn before starting again.

"It is time to move on and leave this study behind you."

In *Spiritual Awareness & Self-Development* this card symbolises the manner in which our rational thinking can never be comprehensive or complete. Sometimes we allow our logic to limit and constrain us. This card shows that we must use thought on its own level whilst remaining open to inspiration, imagination, and the unconscious mind.

"You cannot think your way out of yourself. You must realise the conclusion of logic is the recognition of its own constraints."

*You are blocking this card today by:*

1. Not looking on the bright side of life
2. Not aiming to succeed in everything you do
3. Not treating yourself to a healing remedial massage
4. Not recognising the joy of being a sentient being

## Connect to Your Card

Settle an argument or put something away that is long overdue. Tidy. Sort. Settle. Rest. •

## The Ten of Swords Says

"There is no more battling to do; you have come to a point in your life where you have to concede your way of doing things has just not worked. However, you will find that from this state of acceptance comes a sense of relief, in that the worst is over. Now you have a fresh slate and can start afresh. It is time for a significant rethink! Look at how your words/ thoughts have been destructive in your life. The wheel has rotated full circle!"

## Keywords

Caught out, stuck, inevitability, grounding, distress, ruin, defeat, pain, tears, failure, emotionally cut off, devastation, desolation, delusion, reason divorced from reality, jealousy, affliction, karmic justice, karmic results, grief, sorrow, madness, catatonia, martyrdom, enlightenment.

# —Day 7: Ten of Cups—
## *Imagining Happiness • The Creation of Life*

### Resonances

*Numerology:* 50/5

*Astrology:* Mars in Pisces

*Kabbalah:* Malkuth
(Kingdom)

*Sabian Symbol:*
Pisces III—A Table Set for
an Evening Meal
(Ultimate Satisfaction)

### Quick Connections

*Affirmation:* The joy of
the world is limited only
by my capacity
to surrender to it.

*Meditation:* "Joy can be
yours, if you only look
beyond the material and
glimpse the light there."

## The Lesson of the Ten of Cups
### *Meditating Yourself Deeper into the Tarot*

For today, we will learn to drop ourselves into our tarot cards with a basic meditation. To perform the visualisation, we have provided one of many techniques that we use in Tarosophy which are from NLP. It is a visualisation exercise taking us into deep states of awareness where we can then enter the card itself.

### *Visualisation Method: Multiple Frames*

This method is a quick relaxation technique that works with overload and the brain's ability to nest stories.

You can have a lot of fun with this and see how many frames you can open and close again—or work with a partner to do the same by guiding them.

This technique takes about twenty minutes to perform and should be done whilst sitting comfortably.

THE METHOD

With your eyes closed, visualize a mirror and see a scene inside the mirror which is one of perfect tranquility or calm. Many people have memories of holidays, of beaches, of a favourite place in their yard, or as a child.

Step inside the mirror and explore the scene in your imagination, seeing what you would see, hearing what you would hear, and feeling what you would feel.

Now imagine that you find a picture frame on the ground, or see it on a wall, within that scene, which has a picture painted within it of an even more peaceful, restful place. When you can see that scene, step into the painting and explore it a little further.

Now find a book on a table or other ledge within that scene, which is titled "PEACE," and open it to find an illustration. Step inside that illustration.

You can keep going through frames for at least seven to nine scenes, relaxing deeper in each one. You can also choose the titles of the books or labels on the paintings for other states, such as "Concentration" or "Focus."

At the point of deepest relaxation, picture the tarot card itself and enter into that. You may explore it, enter into dialogue with the figures, or just simply let it melt around you in a general sense of well-being. Explore the card or experience for several minutes, and allow yourself to bring out of it whatever you wish.

When you complete this method, you can find a mirror in the scene which takes you straight back out, or return through each frame and scene if you can recall them!

## The Card in Your Life/Reading

*Careerwise & Financially* this card indicates the harmony of an ideal work-life balance, where there is freedom to enjoy the fruits of your labour. It shows the benefits of working for a long-term goal, retirement, and security. In a predictive reading it is a good card to receive.

"All will be well in the choices ahead, and will lead to the best outcome for all involved."

*Healthwise* this card indicates cause for celebration and the concentration of blessings from above. It indicates a peaceful and harmonious outcome for the good of the body and general health. In most circumstances it counsels a time of rest with the close family.

"It is important at this time to count your blessings and enjoy moments with the family."

In *Relationships* this card indicates pure bliss and domestic happiness. All is achieved in perfect ease. There might be unexpected opportunities and a new life revealed when this card appears.

"All that you desire will become available, and celebration is ahead."

In *Travel & Lifestyle* this card indicates open possibilities to enjoy a shared lifestyle or travel with others, in ease and without work or hardship. There is no need to strive; simply rest and enjoy the rewards that will be made abundant.

"Abundance breeds abundance."

In *Education* this card indicates the deep passion and happiness that comes with satisfying study. It counsels that we must look to the long-term reward of study rather than anything material it may bring us. Often this card appears in a study reading as a card of an artist who has found his or her true calling. Whatever you are studying, this card means it will come to fruition and your desire will be met. Keep your thoughts on the big picture, and aspire to the highest heights.

In *Spiritual Awareness & Self-Development* this card indicates the beauty of a life well-lived. It shows a harmony of one's inner life and outer world, and a perfect happiness of the soul. In living to one's highest values, and manifesting them in every decision, this card illustrates the reward of spiritual integrity. As John Ruskin, founder of the Arts & Crafts movement, said, "only connect." In connecting all aspects of your emotional world to your spiritual life and basing your decisions on this simple connection, only good will flow.

*You are blocking this card today by:*

1. Being miserable about everything and everyone, being a commitment-phobe
2. Wallowing in a state of discontent
3. Creating ill-feeling and finding fault with your home life
4. Falling out with those close to you

## Connect to Your Card

Celebrate something that you have attained by taking a moment to enjoy it fully.

## The Ten of Cups Says

"Enjoy and appreciate your life now. You are where you are supposed to be, and you deserve the happiness that is all around you. All is perfectly balanced in your life, and you have a solid foundation for the future!"

## Keywords

Glee, pride, openness, welcome, ecstasy, happy family, lasting happiness, inspiration from above, joy, tranquility, bliss, rapport, unity, spiritual happiness, homecoming, peace, harmony, safe haven, family, contentment, satiety, friendship.

# —Day 8: Ten of Wands—
## *Working Towards the Goal • The Expression of Effort*

### Resonances

*Numerology:* 36/9

*Astrology:*
Saturn in Sagittarius

*Kabbalah:* Malkuth
(Kingdom)

*Sabian Symbol:*
Sagittarius III—Men
Cutting Through Ice
(Making a Difference)

### Quick Connections

*Affirmation:* I have
in front of me all the
resources I require to
get where I am going.

*Meditation:* "You will
always be alone when
you carry too much."

## The Lesson of the Ten of Wands
### *Reading a Card in a Spread*

Perhaps you already feel at the moment a little bit like the Ten of Wands—struggling to keep all your ideas together, manage your time and responsibilities, and generally push forwards in your studies even if you cannot see the end in sight? Well have no fear, for this card signifies an end will indeed be attained, because it is a ten card, and our values will be realised, because it is a wands card.

When we see a ten card, we always recall that the cards loop back on themselves, so the next card is an ace, a new beginning. The tens show us how to deal with the end so we can make a new beginning. In this card, we see that the figure should simply lay down his load (responsibilities), bind them all together in the same direction (align their values), and pick them up again. They will now be a single bundle—an ace!

At least the card signifies we are getting somewhere, even if it feels that we are not!

Here is your work for today's card. We can divide questions into general categories, for which there are an infinite variation of questions; so how do we read this card in each of the categories below? We have done this already for every card; however, have a go yourself, to show how any card can be re-interpreted in any way for any category of question.

1. Relationship
2. Career
3. Travel
4. Lifestyle
5. Education
6. Family
7. Legal
8. Health
9. Spiritual

You don't have to do all of them, or in detail, just something like:

• Ten of Wands/Lifestyle: "You are not looking at your work/life balance."

Then compare your answers with those we have given below or for any other card.

## The Card in Your Life/Reading

*Careerwise & Financially* this card indicates overworking and a loss of focus. This card shows how we can take on too much and lose sight of what is most important to us. As an advisory card, it indicates that we should immediately take stock of our situation and divest ourselves of our load. Only then can we bring things together and carry our responsibilities with ease.

*Healthwise* this card indicates a depression and anxiety which comes from an overwhelming of one's thoughts and feelings. In terms of physical health, it indicates that we have approached the limit of our capacity to recover in the present manner and must stop what we are doing and take a fresh approach.

In *Relationships* this card indicates that we have taken on the projections of another to our detriment. By seeing too much through other people—a problematic ploy in itself—

we have allowed ourselves to be blinded to our own goals and ambitions. At worst, this card shows a total abandonment of our own values.

In *Travel & Lifestyle* this card indicates a journey made under difficult circumstances. The road ahead may not be clear and yet the card indicates progress towards the destination. In life this card often appears when we already know what must be left behind yet somehow are not quite ready to let go.

In *Education* this card indicates too many priorities and the need for clarity, particularly in revision and research. It is time to take a break and reevaluate the goals of the course upon which you are set. Often this card indicates progress faltering towards the end of a course of study.

In *Spiritual Awareness & Self-Development* this card signals a collapse of values is about to take place, resulting in new energy and initiation. It is the result of the work you have carried out so far, even though it may not be clear and due to the distress of the change you may not even see that it is for your own good and self-willed.

*You are blocking this card today by:*

1. Being lazy
2. Avoiding responsibilities
3. Saying no to projects and workload
4. Dropping tasks you do not like

## Connect to Your Card

Take on every task offered. Move things onward. Move furniture. Go collect something.

## The Ten of Wands Says

"You have shouldered too much responsibility and burden in your life. It is time to figure out a more efficient way of going about your work/responsibilities, and it is time to delegate and pass on some of your passion for the project on to others."

## Keywords

Possession, earnest, determined, work load, complete failure, work inter-related stress, responsibilities, pressure, over-extension, demand, burden, cover-time, overload, struggle, limitations, oppression, cruelty/malice, revenge, injustice, intrigues, duplicity.

## Resonances

*Numerology:* 21/3

*Astrology:* Saturn

*Kabbalah:*
Yesod and Malkuth

## Quick Connections

*Affirmation:* This world is as much mine as anyone else's and I will give it a treat to remember.

*Meditation:* "The only world we truly call our home is the one within."

## The Lesson of the World
### *Reading a Spread's Outcome*

The World is our first major arcana card on the journey to the source of the tarot. We will today discuss the difference of majors and minors and also look at the card itself, which we consider close to everyone—it is the world itself.

We often describe to querents that the minors are like a still river, where one can paddle one's canoe wherever one wants, and the majors are like a strong current where it is more advisable to go with the flow. A mixture of these cards in a reading is like white-water rafting! A large number of majors is a time when "the force is strong," and a majority of minors is very much a "do as you will" time.

Now, the World. That's sort of *everything*. In some decks it is called "the Universe."

We say the WST image is like a mirror—a reflection of all things. This accords with its position on the Tree of Life, where this card is attributed to the path connecting Yesod, the foundation, (our own psyche) and Malkuth, the kingdom, the unknowable world of action which we only perceive through our senses and mental image of it. The World is an image of that interface—it appears to be the "world" but it isn't at all, it's our mental experience of an unknowable event.

Whilst that's all very mystical, in a reading it can signify that the card is showing where the querent and the "event" are most closely linked, most projected and introjected—most is connected and at stake in that position in a reading. So if the World card shows up in the "others" position of a Celtic Cross for example, it's showing that how the person sees "others" is most important in the whole situation.

We can also look at the WST image as an axis, in time and space—the symbol of a woman dancing, poised, is the axis of the universe, delicately balanced. The card symbolises in this regard a completion, a synthesis, a perfect equilibrium in events (as contrasted to the more abstract equilibrium in the Justice card).

So it is a card of completion, the all, the image reflecting reality, and everything!

What do you make of this card when it turns up, say, as an outcome in a reading?

## The Card in Your Life/Reading

*Careerwise & Financially* this card indicates a successful conclusion and new beginning of a career. It shows work coming together and a good team, project, or organisation working together. The World card indicates global responsibility and the need for an interconnected outlook, taking all aspects of the situation into consideration. It is a very earthy card symbolising success.

*Healthwise* this card indicates a whole body response to the present circumstances, and awareness that all things are connected, mental, psychological, physical, and environmental. You may be advised with this card in a reading to take a wider view of your circumstances and get a better balance in your life.

In *Relationships* this card indicates a realistic attitude and wholeness to the relationship. All things are for the good, and it is a relationship which has real connection. It can indicate in some positions that the relationship has become too mundane, and its advice would be to spice things up a bit!

In *Travel & Lifestyle* this card indicates a positive and successful journey with a new perspective. It can relate to a new way of seeing the world through your experiences and also the opportunity for those experiences to take place. If you remain open to the possibilities, this card indicates growth.

In *Education* this card indicates the need to be realistic about your studies and to apply them to real-life situations. Do not get carried away but keep your feet on the ground. There are novel ways in which you may benefit from your studies if you look about you.

In *Spiritual Awareness & Self-Development* this card shows that the world is indeed your oyster. There are new openings and opportunities ready for you if you, like the Fool, are willing to step into the world and take risks. The World is open to you and will respond accordingly at this time.

*You are blocking this card today by:*

1. Being narrow-minded and judgemental of people
2. Stopping yourself from doing what you want to do
3. Deliberately avoiding completing a task
4. Not cooperating with a team effort

## Connect to Your Card

Go for a walk or learn something about the world you don't yet know. Go to the zoo.

## The World Says

"The time has come to venture forth and become one with me. Come and discover the diversity that I embody. I have great hospitality to offer if only you would venture forth and share in my great bounty."

## Keywords

Diversity, experience, example, beginning, triumph, fulfillment, reward, arrival, liberation, synthesis, culmination, completion, conclusion, ending, prize, wholeness, oneness. Integration, accomplishment, involvement, completion, success, victory, unity, understanding, realisation, achievement, creation, cycles. New beginnings, endings, perfection, voyage, route, permanency, triumph, freedom.

# —Day 10: The Last Judgement—

*The Calling from Above • Awakening to a New Day*

## Resonances

*Numerology:* 20/2

*Astrology:* Pluto

*Kabbalah:*
Hod and Malkuth

## Quick Connections

*Affirmation:* In every day I will only answer those calls which are to my very soul.

*Meditation:* "You have to be listening keenly to hear sound of the call."

## The Lesson of the Last Judgement
### Interpreting a Card

Today we begin to look at how we interpret a card in a position in a reading. We will then explore different spreads beginning with simple three-card spreads before building up to the Celtic Cross and Opening of the Key methods to complete our seventy-eight-day exploration in tarot.

When we learn the Celtic Cross spread or many other spreads, we often have a position in the reading called the "outcome." This is sometimes termed simply "what will happen." We tend to see it as "what everything is currently moving towards given no other changes" (i.e., changes made in response to the reading).

So—let us consider that we have pulled Judgement for this position.

This is card XX (twenty) of the majors, and represents the following keywords: awakening, renewed energy, work well done, rebirth, end of an era, and resurrection.

It can also be equated with the symbol of the phoenix and in a deeper sense, a "calling." It is an entirely relevant and powerful card to receive in the outcome position for a reading! It indicates a powerful revival of creative forces and—after doubts and fears are overcome—a vast potential to live up to one's calling. Although somewhat daunting or challenging, this is such a great card to end any spread.

One interesting thing about this card in the WST is that the figures in the forefront of the card are positioned so they make signs of letter-shapes with their arms. They actually make (reading from right to left, as in Hebrew) L—V—X. This is the Latin LVX or *lux*, meaning "light," and they are the three gestures used in a Golden Dawn ritual called the Rose-Cross. In fact, the LVX can be seen as a Rose Key to open the soul. As Pamela Colman Smith and A. E. Waite were both members of this Order and steeped in its rituals, it is of no surprise this—and many other secrets—are presented in this deck.

So any querent for which this card appears in a reading as an outcome will surely see the light. What other symbols do you see on this card in your deck that denote the conclusion of a reading for a querent as being positive?

## The Card in Your Life/Reading

*Careerwise & Financially* this card indicates an appointment or interview (or other calling) will lead to new opportunities—a total rebirth of your career. It is certainly time to consider your true calling and to align your purposes to what means most to you. Make new appointments and call up old friends—it is time to make those connections.

*Healthwise* this card indicates a complete resurrection of your situation. It may be that you receive new information with regard to your situation. This card also indicates the importance of family support and the influence of higher forces on mundane situations.

In *Relationships* this card indicates a situation where one person judges another and finds them wanting. It is important to recognise in this card that all relationships are part of a higher calling and can be redeemed with a little bit of effort.

In *Travel & Lifestyle* this card indicates new opportunities and a complete broadening of your horizons. It symbolises a complete reboot of your life if you take opportunity to take immediate action. It is a card of doing rather than being. When this card appears in your reading, it indicates the nature of action you must take as indicated by its position.

In *Education* this card indicates new impetus and an awakening to the higher purpose of your course of study. It shows that the work you have put in will result in a higher calling. This is an extremely positive card to receive in an education-based question, for it shows that your work has brought the attention of higher forces.

In *Spiritual Awareness & Self-Development* this card signifies rebirth and new awakening. This card is very powerful in a reading's future or present position. It shows the light of the new day and a passing of all that has gone before.

*You are blocking this card today by:*

1. Succumbing to exhaustion, and not tackling your responsibilities and duties
2. Sticking to old habits that keep you where you are
3. Not heeding good advice
4. Not answering/responding to communications

## Connect to Your Card

Call someone. Get out of bed early. Respond quickly to a message. Jump to it. Decide.

## The Last Judgement Says

"The time has come for you to respond to my call. This is a time of endings and new purpose; it is the time for you to be receptive to change. You must embrace all the opportunities that will be coming your way."

## Keywords

Accountability, appraisal, summoning, renewed energy, work well done, rebirth, end of an era, resurrection, phoenix, calling, judgement, transportation, renewal, outcome, awakening, resolution, completion, confrontations, sentence, deliberations, rebirth, absolution, assessment, examination, perspective, aspirations, transformation, ascent, freedom, liberation, union.

# —Day 11: The Moon—
## All That Is Unknown • Steps in the Dark

## The Lesson of the Moon
### Creativity and the Tarot

In today's lesson we consider the Moon card. As it is often associated with a range of meanings including reflection, fear, the unconscious, confusion, intuition, etc., we will feel our way into the card through storytelling. Here's a piece that for us carries the Moon's meaning.

### The Discovery of Darkness

She had lived in this room since her eyes were opened and her voice gave forth words in which the room had found its description. It was a well-lit room, for which she was glad, and she made it so increasingly. There were many sources of light, it seemed, both within her control and not.

There were globes that spun lazily out of reach, with their dark green hue and random glimmers; candles whose flames burnt straight as hot spear-heads; lanterns and torches; bulbs that beckoned and beacons that bloomed; an array of incandescent shafts that cut through the still air. In such a room she came to be, and made her home. All in avoidance of shadows, which she feared and hated.

Oftentimes, should a source of light give up its fragile hold she would replace it with another. In this manner she came to understand that there could never be enough light in the room; once full, adding more light made no difference. In this there was revelation.

Finally, she came to see that the sources of light were never exhausted. Slowly, fearfully, she put out the lights, one by one; some by a mere whisper of her breath, and they fluttered out like bright butterflies; others took trials to reach and break. Others required subtle craft and trickery, puzzles in the making and breaking. Yet others went of their own accord, only to return later, renewed and resplendent.

So it came that there was only one solitary light left, one flame burning in the centre (perhaps, it was hard to tell in that final absence of other light) of the darkness. Surely she had made a mistake; the dark and the doubt assailed her. But she had come to a place of no choice; that light would surely not sustain her for long. She reached out and placed her hand on the flame, killing it before remorse or another sudden emotion could claim her. Once that last light was extinguished, it seemed as if her very life had gone with it. In that darkness was seen a light; a crack around a door. A door leading out.

What stories reflect upon the atmosphere of this card for you?

## The Card in Your Life/Reading

*Careerwise & Financially* this card indicates the uncertainty of a difficult job ahead. You must come out of your shell further to take on the challenges and gain the rewards ahead. In a time of reflection it may be that there is competition baying at your heels—the only way forwards is to face your fears and make progress.

*Healthwise* this card indicates that turning inwards, a reflection upon the past, and all that follows. The fears of the night may soon be past; however, the journey will be long. This card can also signify a trusting of the natural instincts of the body itself.

In *Relationships* this card indicates the unconscious projections and fears onto another. When this card appears in a relationship reading, it may indicate that whatever is unknown and feared are in fact projections from your own unconscious. It is time to examine yourself, not others.

In *Travel & Lifestyle* this card indicates a journey into the unknown. There will be little support and it may be that you hesitate even before you have commenced. The moon will guide you if you trust your own instincts. In terms of lifestyle this card signifies a change which may be constant and will require vigilance.

In *Education* this card indicates deep and profound learning which may take some time. The moon is an uncertain teacher, constantly changing; however, the tidal flow of information can soon take us into new discoveries. This is a card of unusual learning and more may be going on than meets the eye. We can learn from our fears—it is how we make progress.

In *Spiritual Awareness & Self-Development* this card signifies a return to the deeper parts of yourself and trusting your own embodiment. It signifies the importance of dreams, the unconscious, and may also predict the appearance of the dweller on the threshold. This is a fearful experience that precedes most initiation.

*You are blocking this card today by:*

1. Doing a task that is very analytical, such as bookkeeping
2. Reading the *Financial Times* front to back
3. Not believing your horoscope in the newspaper
4. Joining the James Randi Educational Foundation

## Connect to Your Card

Practice your tarot. Go for a swim. See the ocean. Have a bath. Go look at the moon.

## The Moon Says

"Keep in synch with me, for I am the source of your emotional sustenance; I share with you my life force. I am all that is dreamy. Within my realms you learn secrets from beyond the veil."

## Keywords

Escape, dreams, mystery, astral projection, ignorance, deception, intuition, psychic instinct, tides, netherworld, animal, atavistic, fear, self deceit, illusion, uncertainty, fluctuation, danger, darkness, terror, error, imagination, denouncement, trickery, feelings, sentiments, ignorance, deceit, fraud, flux, emotions, fantasy, fear, confusion, lies, secrecy, distraction, enchantment, romance, flirting, seduction, bewilderment.

—Gate Two—

# The Clockwork Museum

# Rainbow Spread—For Changing Your Pattern

*A week has passed since you set forth on your journey into the realm of tarot. You are truly on the path of return. Already you are seeing how your experiences of tarot can change you and your view of the world. Ahead of you is the fabled Clockwork Museum, a place of intricate workings and exhibitions, mirroring the world of habit and illusion. Whilst it offers endless fascination, you must not get lost in its endless capacity for amusement. If you wish to go beyond its machinery, you must break free yourself.*

## Soundtrack for the Journey
### *"Here I Go Again" (Melanie C)*

As the tens are at the end when counting from the aces onwards through the number sequence, they are often seen as the completion of that elemental energy or suit in the world. So the Ten of Pentacles, corresponding to Earth, is the most final card of all the deck, the bottom of the pile. This also explains why the Ten of Swords, representing Air and Thought, is usually depicted as a negative image, with ten swords placed in a body. The spirit of thought does not like to be fixed and finished when it gets to the Ten.

Luckily, tarot is an endless world and the tens are also the *returners*. In these seventy-eight days, we too are on the *path of return,* so we commence with the tens and move up through the deck. Whilst this may seem strange for those of us who have learnt to count from one upwards, it is the perfect way to approach matters both divinatory and divine.

In this spread we look at shaking our patterns up so we can break out of the Clockwork Museum.

Take the following cards from your recent days; the World, Last Judgement, and Moon. Lay them out left to right in this order: Last Judgement, World, and Moon.

Take your significator from the previous gate and place it below these three cards.

Take the remaining three page cards and the four tens. Shuffle these seven cards and lay out one card from this mini-deck face-up against each of the three majors above your significator.

*The Clockwork Museum Spread*

Using your knowledge of the cards from your previous days, read them as follows:

*Last Judgement Position:* The card here shows an ACTION to break you from your patterns. This is often related to the card in the Moon position.

*World Position:* The card here shows you a new way of looking at the world which will help you see through the traps of the Clockwork Museum.

*Moon Position:* The card here shows you a HABIT which stops you making progress and escaping the Clockwork museum. If it is a ten card, it shows the area of that habit (pentacles/physical, cups/emotional, swords/intellectual, wands/lifestyle); if it is a page card, it shows the character area of that habit in yourself. For example, the Page of Swords might indicate over-analyzing or speaking too much.

You now have seven days to continue on with the workbook whilst using the results of this gated spread to unlock a bad habit or pattern in your life. The next gate will take you further into the labyrinth, so you must approach it with a broken pattern to enter the spread.

# —Day 12: Nine of Pentacles—
## Finding Yourself Kept Inside • A Place of Possessions

### Resonances

*Numerology:* 77/5

*Astrology:*
Venus in Virgo

*Kabbalah:*
Yesod (Foundation)

*Sabian Symbol:* Virgo
II—Two Heads Looking
Out Beyond the Shadows
(Troubleshooting)

### Quick Connections

*Affirmation:* The world is
wise to have provided me
these challenges.

*Meditation:* "Security
is a prison of your
own making."

## The Lesson of the Nine of Pentacles
### Using your Response to the Image

When Samuel MacGregor Mathers talks about this card, he sees it in terms of "discretion."
With Waite's text, it is "prudence, safety, success, accomplishment…" Crowley has "good
luck attending material affairs, favour, and popularity."

It's interesting that Waite describes the image as "…a manorial house. It is a wide
domain, suggesting plenty in all things. Possibly it is her [the woman in the garden] own
possession and testifies to material well-being."

We have always seen this card as more like the "kept woman"; the restriction of a situation which is controlling, though not totally unpleasant. It is perhaps the Waite-Smith
image of the hooded bird on her wrist that speaks of this restrictiveness. The wild bird is
not free, although it is well looked after.

This card is interesting—the text and the image may trigger a different reaction for everyone—are there any cards that do this for you?

Now suppose this card came up in a spread for a position called, "What to Learn." What might you think this card signified we could learn from the day ahead today?

## The Card in Your Life/Reading

*Careerwise & Financially* this card indicates a right and fair balance of responsibilities and attribution of reward. All those involved in any project will receive their fair share and entitlement. If you are managing your own affairs, you must carefully balance how you reward others. This card can also indicate a donation from a sponsor.

*Healthwise* this card indicates a weighing up of all that has passed before. It may indicate the requirement for new information and the assistance of others. There is unlikely to be significant progress at this time.

In *Relationships* this card indicates a need to write off domestic responsibilities and a fair division of labour. Both parties must share equally from the rewards of the relationship itself. This is not a time for overdoing charity, and it may be that you need to make harsh decisions.

In *Travel & Lifestyle* this card indicates the requirement to be self-sufficient and fully funded, no matter what the source of the funding may be. It can indicate the need to budget carefully and to be realistic about one's resources. Even the most visionary plan requires a constant stream of funding, whether it be your time, energy, or finances.

In *Education* this card indicates the ability to make careful decisions about one's learning plan. It may be that you have taken on too much in terms of your experience and abilities. It is time to take a good hard look at what you can realistically accomplish. You may also have to consult others in order to gain insight from the outside.

In *Spiritual Awareness & Self-Development* this card signifies a new current of excitement and enthusiasm led by somebody else. You will benefit from the grace of others in what they can share and teach you. This is not a time for false pride; rather, it is a time for being open to others.

*You are blocking this card today by:*

1. Downsizing, giving all your worldly possessions away. Going backpacking.
2. Doing a dextox—depriving yourself of your favourite treats, such as chocolate, coffee, beer, a glass of wine, or other pleasures of life.
3. Not letting yourself go for the day, avoiding grooming and lounging around in sweats. Saying to yourself, "I don't care what anyone thinks of me!"
4. Looking into starting a whole new career and adopting a whole new lifestyle; taking a risk for a change.

## Connect to Your Card

Meditate in the garden. Pick or buy flowers. Dress well. Pamper yourself. Luxuriate.

## The Nine of Pentacles Says

"I want for nothing and I am content here within the gardens of bounty, I am secure in the safety of my haven. However, my security comes with a price, a lack of thrill and risk."

## Keywords

Security, weighed down (bound) by security, captive, favoured, blessed, held to ransom, hostage, selfishness, caution, solitary enjoyment, comfort, attainment, success, fruition, completion, safety, accomplishment, impotence, prudence, retirement, independence.

# —Day 13: Nine of Swords—
### Expecting the Worst • An Examination of Fearful Thoughts

### Resonances

*Numerology:* 63/9

*Astrology:*
Mars in Gemini

*Kabbalah:*
Yesod (Foundation)

*Sabian Symbol:*
Gemini II—An
Aeroplane Falling
(To Take or Not
Take Control)

### Quick Connections

*Affirmation:* This too
will pass.

*Meditation:* "When we
live in fear we distort
reality; we allow darkness
to block our light."

## The Lesson of the Nine of Swords
### *Using the Detail of the Card*

As we learn to read each card, we will find different ways to use the symbolism and art of the card to access our knowledge and intuition through an experience in order to provide relevant readings.

One approach to learning the cards is to examine the detail in each card, which is particularly useful when you are exploring a new deck. When we look at this card, the Nine of Swords in the *Shadowscapes* deck, we see a range of detail from which we may draw.

If we break the card down into its detail, we can see such items as:

- storm crows
- a sword (sheathed)
- sword tattoos

***Shadowscapes
Nine of Swords***

- wings
- a storm funnel
- clouds
- light

These are all containing potential points of reading from this card. When you compare these elements to the meaning of this card today, you will see how each of these components illustrates the meaning of the card. You may wish to compare details in your deck in a similar way.

## The Card in Your Life/Reading

*Careerwise & Financially* this card indicates a troubling time when the road ahead may not seem clear. The decisions of the past have led to a point where the future is uncertain. You may experience regret; however, it is important to realise that you are just approaching a critical turning point. Look forwards to a sudden change of events indicated by any other card in the spread.

*Healthwise* this card indicates a time when the concerns and worries of the body outweigh the ability of the mind to make clear decisions. This card suggests that you are allow the passing of time to heal your wounds whilst having more patience to endure that passage. Whilst this is a card of grief, it indicates that "this too will pass."

In *Relationships* this card indicates the concerns and worrying thoughts that can plague us from past relationships. It does not in itself indicate the need for these fears in the present time; however, one should consult other cards in order to determine the exact nature of this anxiety.

In *Travel & Lifestyle* this card indicates failure to achieve realistic goals and outcomes. Your ideas have not been able to manifest in the real world. Rather than dwell on this, you should allow time to pass so that new plans may be made.

In *Education* this card indicates the burdensome anxieties of having to manage information. It symbolises the overwhelming nature of learning when it is not applied to practical use. It is time to take what you have learnt, and go out and practice.

In *Spiritual Awareness & Self-Development* this card shows the necessity of having a point to your ideas. It shows that one must make real all the visions and ideas that populate the mind. It can also show the limitation of logic to guide us forwards when emotions are strong.

*You are blocking this card today by:*

1. Celebrating with all your friends because you are so damn happy!
2. Booking that dream holiday you have put off for far too long.
3. Volunteering to do charity work.
4. Being carefree and seeing the best in everyone and in everything. It's a wonderful life!

## Connect to Your Card

Say you're sorry. Sit in bed and eat chocolate. Write a confessional poem. Watch or read a tear-jerker.

## The Nine of Swords Says

"Listen attentively to yourself, your inner voice, your greatest wisdom and resource. Take time to be kind to yourself, and act upon the cries for attention that arise from the inner workings of the deeper recesses of your mind. Ask what issues have you been avoiding, that have grown so that they wake you in the night?"

## Keywords

Pessimism, suffering, desolation, doubt, loss, misery, worry, despair, anguish, depression, anxiety, cruelty, unconsciousness, tribulations, martyr, pain, conscience, shame, failure, suspicion, senility, overwhelmed.

# —Day 14: Nine of Cups—
## Imagining All Your Dreams Fulfilled • The Creation of Satisfaction

### Resonances

*Numerology:* 49/4

*Astrology:*
Jupiter in Pisces

*Kabbalah:* Yesod
(Foundation)

*Sabian Symbol:*
Pisces II—An Aviator
in the Clouds
(Poor Visibility)

### Quick Connections

*Affirmation:* I take
pleasure in all I have
accomplished in my own
way and know the future
can differ from the past.

*Meditation:*
"Contentment and
happiness are the
rewards of dedication
to a purpose."

## The Lesson of the Nine of Cups
### Using the Attraction Point of the Card

When reading any card, you might consider the "attraction point." Place your finger in the physical centre of a card. Notice what the artist has decided to place in the centre.

Now look at the card again and decide where the emotional centre of the card appears to be. This may be very different from the attraction point.

You can also consider where your attention is first drawn in the card—perhaps to a particular element of the card, a colour, or a figure within the scene itself. All of these attraction points give you access into the interpretation of the card. Moving between them can offer the tarot reader flexibility.

# The Card in Your Life/Reading

*Careerwise & Financially* this card indicates the emotional satisfaction of a job well done. In a future position it indicates a satisfactory outcome to any new career or project. One has to be careful to avoid overindulgence; however, overall this card is entirely positive. It can sometimes indicate a compromise just before the completion of the project.

*Healthwise* this card indicates comfort and stability in the situation. Whilst it can signify a stationary attitude, it at least represents a positive outcome. With the appearance of this card one should take comfort in the accomplishment of the past and support from those around oneself.

In *Relationships* this card indicates fulfillment, sensual pleasure, and all good things. Whilst it is important not to be too smug about the state of the relationship, the card usually indicates all wishes have come true.

In *Travel & Lifestyle* this card indicates a happy environment, although it can be prone to stagnate. For those seeking the high life, this is an annoying card because it means that you have to count your current blessings rather than make exciting progress forwards. In terms of lifestyle, this card indicates success and stability.

In *Education* this card indicates complete comfort with the application of learning and the emotional satisfaction a new education can bring. It shows an experienced teacher or class in whose company one learns very well indeed. This again is an entirely positive card to receive in questions of education.

In *Spiritual Awareness & Self-Development* this card indicates a need to connect with one's emotional past. It often signifies the potential for stagnation which requires a new impetus to break free. When this card appears in terms of spiritual questions one should ask where the querent feels fulfillment because that may be what is attaching them to their current block.

## *You are blocking this card today by:*

1. Feeling dissatisfied and finding fault in all that is around you. You're one miserable dude today!
2. Being a miser today and keeping your hands in your pocket. Let others pay the cheque!
3. Not sharing your giant bar of chocolate with friends.
4. Being cold and standoffish.

## Connect to Your Card

Feast. Show people what you have got. Buy something that appeals to you. Display. Strut.

## The Nine of Cups Says

"I am pleased with myself; just look at all I have achieved and surrounded myself with at all time. I do not do anything by half; I live for abundance. You too can have all you desire too, if you have a wish or vision of a better life. I love to entertain and be the life and soul of the party."

## Keywords

Self-satisfaction, complacency, fulfillment, sensual pleasure, get your wish, well-being, contentment, smugness, comfort, happiness, satisfaction, wish fulfilment, sensuality, pleasure, satisfaction, material success, stability, complete success, loyalty.

# Day 15: Nine of Wands
*Working Towards Your Own Ground • The Expression of Security*

### Resonances

*Numerology:* 35/8

*Astrology:*
Moon in Sagittarius

*Kabbalah:* Yesod
(Foundation)

*Sabian Symbol:*
Sagittarius II—A Golden-
Haired Goddess of
Opportunity (The World
Is Your Oyster)

BASTONI BATONS — 9 — WANDS BASTOS
STÄBE — STAVEN

### Quick Connections

*Affirmation:* I can take
heart from any opposition
for it tells me I am
moving forwards.

*Meditation:* "Often
our resistance to new
ideas is because we are
holding on to an outworn
one, ourselves."

## The Lesson of the Nine of Wands
### *The Four Levels of Reading a Card*

Today we are going to ask a question, for which this card is the answer, as if we were doing a single-card reading. Let's ask "What do I need to know to be successful in my forthcoming trip to Paris?"

Now take a look at your card and answer in these four ways first:

1. Literal—describe something in answer by referring to a literal object, event, or person on the card. I might say, "Don't forget to pack a staff and bandage."

2. Symbolic—answer in a way that is implied by the symbols on the card. As an example, taking the bandage (in the WST) as a symbol of past emotional wounds, I might reply, "You need to be wary of repeating the pains of the past."

3. Extended—use your connections to real-life events in your own past or experience that relate to this card to tell a story. This card reminds me of when I

struggled to convince a project team of the problems in their proposals. I might say then, "Your trip is going to be most successful when you convince others of your own ideas about which you feel sure."

4. Secret—in the fourth level of reading the card, we read it as it inspires us. Simply watch the card, go through the other three levels of response, and then wait for something to strike you. Write that down or say it out loud. I look at the card and what comes to mind … "See things on a different level, get more involved. Your trip will tend to make you feel removed from people, so ensure you take time to connect. Take a gift to your hosts."

These four levels of reading are based on an area of Kabbalah. However, we don't need to go into that here, just take the levels as Literal, Symbolic, Extended, and Secret. These are four ways of reading any card.

## The Card in Your Life/Reading

*Careerwise & Financially* this card indicates the necessity to have a solid review. One really needs to know who is standing with you and who is standing against you in projects you have in hand. It may appear that people are fighting against you or blocking you; however, it could be that they are trying to protect you from taking on too much. The card indicates a time of caution in your career.

*Healthwise* this card indicates resistance to all that afflicts you. It shows that you must have the stamina to stand against constant attack. In general the card shows stamina, strength, and good health; however, there is a cost in maintaining such a defence.

In *Relationships* this card indicates a form of defensiveness that has come about by preaching one's own values to another person. It can show an argumentative attitude and suggest that the barriers must come down before further progress can be made. Do not hold on to your own values so strongly that you neglect to see what the other person positively intends by their behaviour.

In *Travel & Lifestyle* this card indicates the need for order and organisation in one's values. In terms of travel, this card can indicate difficulties crossing borders. Sometimes it may indicate the inability to appreciate another culture or be fully open to the experience of others.

In *Education* this card indicates a potential resistance to taking new ideas on board even if those new ideas are stacking up. You might feel the need to defend yourself, but this is just a matter of opening up to new learning. The more you resist taking the new leap, the more difficult it will become.

In *Spiritual Awareness & Self-Development* this card may speak to us of the need to hold true to our values despite the blocks of other people. It is only because we have chosen such a strong principle to hold to that other people appear to resist us. This should serve to strengthen our resolve and not to break it.

*You are blocking this card today by:*

1. Giving in to difficulties at the first hurdle
2. Being very forgiving of trespassers
3. Taking a duvet day
4. Relaxing and letting others worry about possible threats

## Connect to Your Card

Get your friends together. Check your insurance. Get assurance from somebody close.

## The Nine of Wands Says

"Surround yourself with reliable support and draw upon your life experience to gain well-deserved territory. Is there something you have worked hard towards which you are very protective about maintaining as your own creation? If this is the case, you probably feel resentful of others coming after you and reaping the benefits. Therefore, try and trust in the natural process more; you are protected better than you may think."

## Keywords

Paranoia, shifty behaviour, self-sufficiency, care, stout defence, good health, obstinacy, preparedness, protection, territoriality, resistance, last stand, perseverance, defensiveness, stamina, strength, threat, mishap, order, discipline, disposition, displeasure, teaching, preaching.

# —Day 16: The Sun—

*The Enlightenment of the Self • Seeing Things Clearly*

## Resonances

*Numerology:* 19/1

*Astrology:* Sun

*Kabbalah:*
Hod and Yesod

## Quick Connections

*Affirmation:* The light of every dawn brings a new day of possibilities and creation to me.

*Meditation:* "The very act of expressing happiness and joy brings its own rewards."

## The Lesson of the Sun

*Reading a Major Card and a Court Card Together*

Today's card is the Sun, one of the astronomical/astrological major cards. It is a very bright and cheerful card to receive and usually bodes well. It speaks of expansion…the Sun of course being a large nuclear bomb exploding in slow motion! In a reading we say that this card embodies innocence, openness, wholeness, and well-being, so it is a brilliant card to get in an outcome or future position. In the past position, however, it can signify that someone is now "burnt out."

If we take a major card with a court card, we get an archetypal energy pattern—a fundamental pattern of human experience coming through a particular level of activity into our life.

So if we take the Sun and the Page of Cups, we see these two cards as showing an expansion of brilliance in the level of creative openness. It is the exact description of a young and gifted graphic designer being given his or her first project, perhaps!

What other real-life situations can you consider which would be an example of the Sun coming through the level of energy of the Page of Swords?

## The Card in Your Life/Reading

*Careerwise & Financially* this card indicates bright new beginnings and success. It is a card of joy and celebration in all respects. In the outcome position, this card shows complete accomplishment. It is also a card of demonstration, so it may indicate you need to walk the talk in order to show what it is you are capable of.

*Healthwise* this card indicates new beginnings and creative solutions. It is a card of youthful energy and excitement symbolising steady progress towards health. In a very literal sense, it can indicate the need for exercise and an outdoor activity. Further to this it also shows we can reconnect to the activities we enjoyed when we were young.

In *Relationships* this card indicates openness and delight. The relationship will be a perfect unity and realise new creative actions. It is time to make hay while the sun shines! The sun card dispels all doubt and speaks of a bright future. In terms of timing questions, the sun indicates a one-year period.

In *Travel & Lifestyle* this card indicates new opportunities and liberation. It shows a freedom to enjoy one's own self and creates new beginnings. It is a time of bright blessings and forward movement.

In *Education* this card indicates an openness to the honest truth of the learning experience. At this time one must simply bathe in the light of new learning rather than try and grasp any particular thing.

In *Spiritual Awareness & Self-Development* this card is a card of spiritual radiance and the open awareness that is true attainment. It is a time of spiritual fulfillment whilst we remain open and innocence to the present moment. A new day will indeed dawn when this card appears in our readings.

*You are blocking this card today by:*

1. Being a pessimist
2. Being lethargic and very lazy
3. Being excessively cynical and negative
4. Suppressing any enthusiasm and joy you feel

## Connect to Your Card

Laugh. Smile. Be happy. Find something to do with childlike enjoyment. Express yourself.

## The Sun Says

"Retain your sense of childlike wonder! Get up and go out into that brilliant world and have fun! Think positive thoughts and see the best in everyone and share your newfound radiance. You are full of energy, vitality, and life—now is the time to think about expanding your horizons. Are there things you are always putting off? Most likely these are things that are for you only, the things you consider to be selfish. So go on and put yourself first for a change, treat yourself. Life is to be lived to the fullest!"

## Keywords

Fearless, unencumbered, enthusiasm, outstanding, brilliant, pride, genius, "bling," razzle-dazzle, showy glory, demonstration, attainment, liberation, success, achievement, fulfilment, blessing, affirmation, exuberance, optimism, radiance, clarity, integration, accomplishment, involvement, completion, victory, unity, understanding, realisation, creation, cycles, new beginnings, endings, perfection, voyage, route, permanence, triumph, freedom, evolution, growth, enlightenment, truth, honesty, source, saviour, ascension, illumination, improvement, earning, expanding horizons, awareness, greatness, vitality, assurance, demonstration, triumph, riches, contentment, cheerfulness, prosperity, energy, optimism, creativity.

# —Day 17: The Star—
## *The Vision of the Soul • Future Pacing*

### Resonances

*Numerology:* 17/8

*Astrology:* Aquarius

*Kabbalah:*
Netzach and Yesod

### Quick Connections

*Affirmation:* Every man and every woman is a star and I will discover my own orbit today.

*Meditation:* "The importance of fulfilling a divine purpose and being part of an ongoing process."

## The Lesson of the Star
### *Vision in the Tarot*

The two most attractive cards to most tarot card readers are the High Priestess and the Star. Perhaps this is because the High Priestess represents the mysteries and the Star represents a vision of the future. Some people call the Star the card of hope; however, it is best considered a card of vision in a reading.

We later see the Star appear in the lamp of the Hermit—someone has taken his or her vision and is living up to it. The Star presents as a lesson that whilst we may have the imagination of future success, it is not useful unless we are walking towards it.

On this day make a realistic note in your journal of what your vision is for your tarot practice.

# The Card in Your Life/Reading

*Careerwise & Financially* this card indicates that while one has a vision, it is not yet realised. It is important not to waste energy in projects or pursuing interviews that are unlikely to result in real work. This card demands a more realistic attitude to one's career. It can also signify a past time that was successful which creates a new vision for the future.

*Healthwise* this card indicates new hope for a positive outcome. It also indicates the necessity to balance one's energies, both physical and spiritual, in order to achieve a comfortable balance in the circumstances. The Star can symbolise new hope and prospects for rejuvenation.

In *Relationships* this card indicates potential so long as one's vision is aligned to that of one's partner. This card symbolises the requirement to both contribute different things to the relationship in order to create a perfect blend. Unlike the Temperance card, the Star shows that we should let "the winds of heaven dance between us" rather than merge into one whole.

In *Travel & Lifestyle* this card indicates a compelling vision which can be achieved by taking measured risks. The appearance of this card suggests we keep true to our ultimate goal and take steps towards it at all times. The Star card is our very own self calling to us and when it appears, we are reminded to keep that one star in sight.

In *Education* this card indicates the requirement to balance different types of learning in order to accomplish the goal of the course. It indicates the need to balance carefully the streams of learning we are accessing and not to become overbalanced by any particular one.

In *Spiritual Awareness & Self-Development* this card indicates our true individuality. The star is at our very core, the course that burns brightly within us. It is the star of our self that guides is most truly, and the appearance of this card shows the need to reconnect to that very self within us.

*You are blocking this card today by:*

1. Keeping your good ideas to yourself and not sharing
2. Not supporting your work colleagues
3. Repressing your creativity
4. Expressing your inner glum

## Connect to Your Card

Give away something old and buy something new. Go to an inspiring talk. Encourage someone to achieve something.

## The Star Says

"Be reassured that all is how it should be and that your potential will be fulfilled. Take a look around you and see the wonder that is creation, be full of purpose and be part of the process of making a difference in the world. Take pride in your work and achievements and be assured that fulfillment and prosperity will come from doing what you do best!"

## Keywords

Service, conservation, environmental care, enlightenment, hope, inspiration, health, insight, promise, charisma, refreshment, astrology, replenishment, devotion, guidance, potential, fulfillment, dreaminess, harmony, satisfaction, expectation, prospects, healing, rejuvenation, reflection, recuperation, release, guidance, optimism, luck, good fortune, success, renewal, inspiration.

# —Day 18: Temperance—
## The Alchemy of Creativity • Becoming Yourself on the Way

### Resonances

*Numerology:* 14/5

*Astrology:* Sagittarius

*Kabbalah:*
Tiphareth and Yesod

### Quick Connections

*Affirmation:* Every moment today has the potential to be changed.

*Meditation*: "Focusing on the divine and in doing so facilitating transformation."

## The Lesson of Temperance
### Using Alchemical Symbolism in the Tarot

Today we look at another major card and the issues of metaphor and application.

One of the things worth noting with the Temperance card is that there are two very different depictions of it between the WST version of the "angelic figure" and the Thoth version of the ART card of alchemical combination. The former is very tranquil, the latter very active. It seems we all have our own perspective when it comes to what we can cope with, what our thresholds are in life—for this is indeed a secret "threshold" card.

On the Tree of Life it is an initiatory card, for it connects Yesod and Tiphareth, corresponding to the psyche/ego/identity and the true self/awareness/consciousness. The angel is the connection between these two aspects of our experience of the world.

A little secret with this card too…have a look at the flower—it is an iris. Now look up the goddess Iris; you'll see that she is the goddess of the rainbow (a mystery too deep to examine here) and also depicted often as "a winged woman bearing two jugs." That's right, it's not an angel on this card, it is a goddess!

Now, we like the initiatory nature of this card because it indicates in a reading that someone has the opportunity to make a change, if they get the timing right. They must combine and recombine their experience perfectly—and then go for it! In this, it is quite alchemical…like Crowley and Harris's Thoth version of the card.

So take a close look at the actual process of *tempering,* and see what we can learn in our own lives from this process, and then make a metaphor of the tempering process. What does it teach us about life? What tempering have you experienced in your life? Let's use this major arcana card (as we can all the other images of archetypal patterns in our lives) as a teaching card.

In other words, for this card, "I am glorified by suffering and trail. This is no part of me that is not of the gods" or… "what does not kill me makes me stronger."

## The Card in Your Life/Reading

*Careerwise & Financially* this card indicates the need to cooperate with others to achieve your goals. Whilst you may have to make some compromise, the overall results will be to everybody's benefit. This card is also a card of the good manager who can take everybody's opinions into account.

*Healthwise* this card indicates moderation in all things. It shows that all aspects of your health must be taken under good management and be fully assessed. This card may also indicate that higher forces are involved in the situation.

In *Relationships* this card indicates a perfect blending of what may appear to the opposite temperaments. You can indicate the ideal relationship where two personalities come together to create a harmonious unity. Temperance also symbolises the need to adjust to another person's way of communicating.

In *Travel & Lifestyle* this card indicates a time of economy. You must carefully measure all your efforts to ensure they are adequately rewarded. The card also demonstrates the need to have a perfect balance between your work and social life.

In *Education* this card indicates a highly creative and energetic blending of experience and theory. The card shows you are learning lessons that will take you to a more elevated perspective. This card shows experimentation and the alchemy of practical life. Your experiences will serve to make you a stronger person.

In *Spiritual Awareness & Self-Development* this card is a signal of the communication between the higher and lower realms. It also shows a union of the conscious and unconscious forces. At this time there are likely to be powerful influences that serve to change you. The Temperance card is an initiatory card leading to expanded awareness.

*You are blocking this card today by:*

1. Going on a binge of self-indulgence
2. Being very intolerant
3. Being very flirty
4. Shopping till you drop

## Connect to Your Card

Cook something. Create something from what you have. Be good all day. Be diplomatic.

## Temperance Says

"Any workings or projects you may have been developing may now have reached a 'proving point' which is ideal for materialising success. However, this stage needs to be handled carefully, otherwise it could easily be spoiled. Focus on being emotionally and physically balanced and poised to achieve a state of being that will assist you in this endeavour."

## Keywords

Catalyst, prospecting, timing, discipline, assessment, adaptation, coordination, self-control, combination, blending, prudence, compromise, discretion, creativity, moderation, virtue, cooperation, mixing, mingling, manipulation, flexibility, economy, frugality, management, accommodation, distillation, reduction, conformation, uniting, augmentation, tempering, economy, balance, health, assessment.

If you would like to create a magical incense or oil for your tarot readings, you can use the following table to create a mixture of two essences from the court cards and their corresponding perfumes.

Choose the two or three energies you require for your reading space and consult their relevant cards for their perfumes. Blend these perfumes as oils for an oil burner (or if they are the same, choose that one) for an appropriate energy to be released in your reading space.

- Practicality: Page of Pentacles
- Observation: Page of Swords
- Creativity: Page of Cups
- Energy: Page of Wands
- Confidence: Knight of Pentacles
- Insight: Knight of Swords
- Connection: Knight of Cups
- Assertiveness: Knight of Wands
- Nurturing: Queen of Pentacles
- Wit: Queen of Swords
- Clairvoyance: Queen of Cups
- Drama: Queen of Wands
- Assuredness: King of Pentacles
- Judgement: King of Swords
- Compassion: King of Cups
- Passion: King of Wands

# —Gate Three—

# The

# Labyrinth

# Escape Spread—For Finding Hope When Lost

*With the Sun, Star, and angel now guiding your way, you enter the labyrinth of the lost. This is the first of the trials on your path of tarot—the confusion of learning a new language, over-interpreting the symbols and signs, until all seems an endless maze of connections leading back to each other. To escape the labyrinth we must invoke assistance from the powers above.*

## Soundtrack for the Journey
### *"Here Comes the Flood" (Peter Gabriel)*

Take all the cards you have encountered so far: the pages, tens, and nines, the World, Last Judgement, Star, and Temperance. Shuffle whilst considering your experiences since leaving the Clockwork Museum and ask your cards the question, **"What path can I now see after having changed my old patterns and habits?"**

When you feel ready, lay the mini-deck face-up and carefully go through it until you find the Star card, the card of vision. The two cards either side of the Star are the answer to the question and the path out of the labyrinth.

Make a note in your seventy-eight-day journal about the actions you will take in the week ahead to follow the direction of these two cards. Ensure these are reasonable, realistic, and timely activities. Without taking these actions, you will not be able to escape the labyrinth and proceed to the Garden of Delight!

*NOTE: You can use this method when using a full deck in response to a question where there appears to be "no hope." Shuffle the whole deck, find the Star, and the two cards either side provide the vision and hope required to move forwards. You can perform alternate readings using the Sun card in a similar way where clarity is lacking, the Devil card where you need to know how to manifest something, or locate the two cards on either side of the Blasted Tower card to find out how to make a great change in your life. There are twenty-two possible variations of this method using the major cards.*

# —Day 19: Eight of Pentacles—
## Finding Yourself Working • A Place of Work

## Resonances

*Numerology:* 76/4

*Astrology:* Sun in Virgo

*Kabbalah:* Hod (Glory)

*Sabian Symbol:* Virgo I —A Man's Head (The Importance of Identity)

## Quick Connections

*Affirmation:* I will take comfort in my work and see in it that I give myself to the day.

*Meditation:* "Working towards a goal."

## The Lesson of the Eight of Pentacles
### Hidden Sets in the Tarot Deck

Today's card is the Eight of Pentacles. Let's compare this card to some of the others in its suit to see how it is different and unique in itself.

If this card represents someone working for the sake of it, without necessarily having any audience or market (whatever that work may be), then we could call it the Journeyman card. We have an Apprentice card in the pentacles/coins/disks…what do you think it is?

And if that is the Apprentice card, and today's Eight of Pentacles card is the Journeyman, which card would be the third of these Guild cards—the Master?

# The Card in Your Life/Reading

*Careerwise & Financially* this card is the journeyman or craftsman card. You can compare it to the Three of Pentacles (the apprentice) and the Ten of Pentacles (the master). In this card we see the craftsman at work. At this time you should work in the faith of achieving recognition or a market or audience even if none are apparent yet.

*Healthwise* this card indicates small gain. Each stage in your health program will require absolute attention, and it must be taken in small steps. This card shows steady progress that requires patience and commitment at all times.

In *Relationships* this card indicates a modest acknowledgement of your own part in building a relationship. It shows that you must continue to work on the small things of everyday life in order to craft a fulfilling and rewarding union.

In *Travel & Lifestyle* this card indicates devolution and patience to achieve your destination. You may have to work longer and harder than at first you expected. As a lifestyle card, this card signals self-sufficiency and the ability to take responsibility for your actions.

In *Education* this card indicates that discipline and devotion of maintaining concentration on the task in hand. At this time you should continue to work hard on the smallest details and corrections in your work to achieve final recognition. The devil really is in the details at this time.

In *Spiritual Awareness & Self-Development* this card is a picture of how our work reflects our inner nature. You should spend time to recognise the attitude you bring to all things you create. This spirit lives in your creations. This card also shows how we are a cocreator with the divine spirit in the world itself.

### You are blocking this card today by:

1. Performing an important task in a shoddy way
2. Being very careless
3. Not being reliable
4. Paying somebody else to come and decorate

## Connect to Your Card

Work hard. Concentrate on getting jobs off the list. Do some D.I.Y. Get on with it.

## The Eight of Pentacles Says

"Keep going with the path of training/ learning you have been following; it may have been a hard slog and you may have invested substantial amounts of money and precious time. However, the new skills you have acquired will serve you well in the future. You will have a good grounding and you will be well rewarded for your talents."

## Keywords

Productivity, work ethic, precision, coordination, self-confidence, learning a trade, skill, handiwork, small gain, talent, craftsmanship, meticulousness, prudence, artfulness, economy, modesty, devotion, work, commission, proficiency, diligence, discipline, knowledge.

# —Day 20: Eight of Swords—
### Expecting Rescue • An Examination of Trust

### Resonances

*Numerology:* 62/8

*Astrology:*
Jupiter in Gemini

*Kabbalah:* Hod (Glory)

*Sabian Symbol:* Gemini I
—A Glass-Bottomed
Boat in Still Water
(Insight through
Calm Transparency)

### Quick Connections

*Affirmation:* Whatever
binds me today tells
me where I can cut
myself free.

*Meditation:* "Your words
and thoughts can be your
worst enemy, so be wary."

## The Lesson of the Eight of Swords
### Using Astrological Correspondences in Tarot

Today we have the Eight of Swords. We'll return to a little astrology here with the Thoth deck, if we may, using the late Hajo Banzhaf, in his book with Brigitte Theler, *Keywords for the Crowley Tarot* (Weiser, 2001). This is also in Crowley's original *Book of Thoth* of course; Banzhaf and Theler lay it all out more clearly.

If we trace this card from the Golden Dawn teachings, we see there in in the Book of Thoth that the Eight of Swords is termed "The Lord of Shortened Force." It is seen to correspond with Jupiter in Gemini. So we have the expansiveness of Jupiter within the detail-obsessed Gemini—not a good combination. This gives the card meanings of "too much force (Jupiter) applied to small things (Gemini)."

By the time Waite and Smith came to design their Eight of Swords, it became "a woman, bound and hoodwinked, with the swords of the card about her." Waite goes on to say, "Yet it is rather a card of temporary durance than of irretrievable bondage." So we have that same idea again of short-term obstruction as the Jupiter force works through the Gemini focus.

We then come to Crowley some years later and see that he has the card as "Interference" which Banzhaf and Theler refer to as "High Goals (Jupiter) that are threatened by doubts and inner conflicts (Gemini)." Crowley sees this as good fortune (Jupiter) attending weakened efforts (Gemini) plagued by accidental interference. It's the annoying telephone call that comes with good news just when you are trying to finish something else with a deadline. The news is great, but we wish it had come at another time, as we can't stop what we're doing. We know that one!

See if you can do the same—trace the evolution of a card—from the Golden Dawn, through Waite to Crowley—using the astrological correspondences (pick a minor card numbers two through ten in any suit). Or simply take one card, find its astrological correspondence, and see if it helps you make sense of the card itself.

## The Card in Your Life/Reading

*Careerwise & Financially* this card indicates criticism either by yourself or by others. However, this criticism is usually undeserved and if you take time you will see a way through it. Although there may appear to be many restrictions in your path, this is perhaps just a test of your ability to think through to a new solution.

*Healthwise* this card indicates blockages which inhibit further progress. You may have reached an apparent limit in your ability to think through the situation. However, this card is not as despairing as it may first appear; there is still an open option for you to take. It may just be that you are not yet ready to accept the consequences of your own decisions.

In *Relationships* this card indicates both vulnerability and disquiet. There may be a bit of a blame game being played by one or both parties in the relationship. It is time to take the blindfold off and move on from this no-win situation.

In *Travel & Lifestyle* this card indicates a situation where debt has built to such an extent that it is now restricting you. You must clear all outstanding issues before you will be able to make progress forwards, even if this means facing up to difficult decisions.

In *Education* this card indicates a refusal to take in new information. You may feel isolated and surrounded by those who know better. It is important to release your own unique capacity to learn in the best way possible. You must make a stand for your own methodology.

In *Spiritual Awareness & Self-Development* this card symbolises our own capacity for self-sabotage. It can indicate a situation where we have unknowingly blocked ourselves even where there is no need to do so. We must look within myself to find the avenue of escape from at present situation. This is not a time to blame others or the ideas of others for our current circumstance.

*You are blocking this card today by:*
1. Being highly motivated
2. Finding solutions to ongoing problems
3. Getting out and about for a long walk or a cycle ride
4. Getting together with your nearest and dearest friends

## Connect to Your Card

Stay silent. Keep yourself to yourself. Don't go out. Conserve your energy. Avoid arguments.

## The Eight of Swords Says

Be wary of being restricted by your own self-destructive thought patterns and refusing to see where you can change your life for the better. You need to ask yourself whether there is part of you that needs to feel helpless and victim. Do you have a desire to be rescued by another, rather than you liberating yourself? Stop telling yourself you cannot cope; stop creating obstacles that are of your own mental creation."

## Keywords

Petrified, denial, obstinacy, self-loathing, trust, restriction, censure, prison, blockage, inhibition, oppression, crisis, interference, criticism, blame, obstacles, debt, disquiet, treacherous, self-sabotage, isolation, vulnerability.

# —Day 21: Eight of Cups—

*Imagining Somewhere Different • The Creation of a Calling*

## Resonances

*Numerology:* 48/3

*Astrology:*
Saturn in Pisces

*Kabbalah:* Hod (Glory)

*Sabian Symbol:* Pisces I—
A Public Market
(Meeting Ground)

## Quick Connections

*Affirmation:* The Universe has created me as a sum of many parts, and I am completely self-sufficient in the world.

*Meditation:* "Only seek what is worth finding."

## The Lesson of the Eight of Cups
### Surprising Interpretations

Today we look at the Eight of Cups. Let's compare it again with the Ten of Cups, covered in the first week of our journey. How do we know they are different cards? We know it seems an obvious question, but it may provoke a bit of "beginners mind" for some us! Obviously the number is different, as is the illustration.

We can suggest that the Eight of Cups is an "approaching a plateau" card. The eight stage is difficult, as it is "almost there" but not nearly enough. We think this is made even more troublesome and challenging in the cups, the suit of emotions, which usually like to be in a stable state!

However, not all is gloom and doom in this card—we know the illustration on the WST is somewhat solitary compared to the family group on the Ten of Cups, but at least there is movement—and the eclipse signifies transience and a rarity—perhaps like the rainbow in the Ten, another natural phenomenon with its own symbolic interpretation.

So what do you make of this card? I once had this card come up frequently at a bad time, and I kept thinking it was doom and gloom. However, a magical event led to a move of the family into the mountains and a better life—just as the card suggests, literally!

## The Card in Your Life/Reading

*Careerwise & Financially* this card indicates the need to withdraw from your current circumstances no matter how emotionally attached to them you feel and make your own way into an unknown situation. Whilst you may feel despondent, you are being called to a different place and you must follow that calling.

*Healthwise* this card indicates despondency and misery. Though it is an entirely negative card with regard to health, you can make progress, but it will be long-term and not lead to the expected results.

In *Relationships* this card indicates abandonment and a rejection of the deeper feelings within the relationship. It could be that there is a lack of attention to the direction in which the relationship is developing. It is time to shake yourself out of your current weariness and move forward, even if you feel as if it is all down to you.

In *Travel & Lifestyle* this card indicates a change of house. It can also signify a complete change of circumstances which at that time may feel oppressive; it is essential to move to higher ground. When referring to a lifestyle question, this card indicates that *you* must take the higher ground and be true to your own feelings.

In *Education* this card indicates a quest for the deeper meaning of what you are studying or the need to move to a place where your studies can be fulfilled. Whilst this can often be a long and lonely journey in your studies, it is always worthwhile.

In *Spiritual Awareness & Self-Development* this card signifies your search for meaning and a desire to leave the attachment of the mundane world for higher principles. It also shows an eclipse of your unconscious fears by conscious concerns. This card symbolises your deeper quest in life and should be taken as extremely important when it appears in a spiritual reading.

*You are blocking this card today by:*

1. Looking at where you are presently and making the most of all the positive aspects of your life.
2. Tackling a relationship issue directly, stop avoiding!
3. Making the effort to reinvigorate old friendships/relationships from the past.
4. Not moping around and expressing some joy!

## Connect to Your Card

Go somewhere new by yourself. Turn your back on something or someone.

## The Eight of Cups says

"You may feel you have a calling to respond to, or an urge to change your life. How you have been living is not working for you anymore, and the things that once made sense to you, now leave you puzzled. Know that change is needed for growth so it is of importance that you must avoid a state of stagnation."

## Keywords

Emotional thirst, forging on, quest, attending, rejection, abandonment, disappointment, misery, desire to leave material for higher, withdrawing, looking inward, leaving home, "man's search for meaning," changing direction, moving on, weariness, deeper meaning, downsizing, ennui, shyness, timidity, honour, modesty, despondency.

# —Day 22: Eight of Wands—
## Working Towards the Unknown • The Expression of Movement

### Resonances

*Numerology:* 34/7

*Astrology:*
Mercury in Sagittarius

*Kabbalah:* Hod (Glory)

*Sabian Symbol:* Sagittarius I
—A Grand Army of the
Republic Campfire (The
Spirit of Reunion)

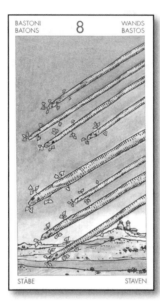

### Quick Connections

*Affirmation*: I am on
my way always with
the divine drive of the
entire cosmos.

*Meditation*: "Action is
self-replenishing; the
more you do, the
more you can."

## The Lesson of the Eight of Wands
### *Going Beyond the Obvious*

Today's card, the Eight of Wands, is a good example of a card which may have multiple meanings. The tarot cards are *multivalent*—they have many possible meanings for the same symbol. Here we often see a representation of eight wands or staves flying through the air.

What are we to make of this? Perhaps we can see a journey, news from afar, or acceleration or imminent landing of our projects.

Going beyond the obvious, we can perhaps determine that, as wands represent our values and spiritual path and the eight is well established towards the ten, this is the point of divine inspiration when our own energy is aligned with the divine.

When this card appears, it could be that everything which follows is inevitable. We must always go beyond the obvious with each card to allow flexibility of reading to any question that is asked of us.

## The Card in Your Life/Reading

*Careerwise & Financially* this card indicates good management and progress in your ambition. It is a powerful card to receive in a career question, for it demonstrates the pursuit of your vision. Also this card shows that news is on its way and there is inevitability to all the things you have set in motion. One way of saying this is that your chickens will soon come home to roost.

*Healthwise* this card indicates urgent news which must be taken into consideration. Often this news comes from far away or from someone not directly involved in your current circumstances. The card indicates a new impetus in the recovery process.

In *Relationships* this card indicates the growth of the relationship at a faster pace. However, it is important to understand in which direction the relationship is moving so that it does not get overtaken by the furious pace of the present moment. It can also signify that you will soon receive information with regard to the relationship that is presently on its way to you.

In *Travel & Lifestyle* this card indicates an extremely positive forward movement where your dreams will be realised and your travel requirements fulfilled. It shows in itself a flight, movement, and a fast and easy journey, so it is entirely advantageous to receive in a travel or lifestyle reading.

In *Education* this card indicates a swift activity to ensure that your plans are all moving in the same direction. It is time to take a quick review of your resources and your goal. As related to a course, this is a time of realignment so that you can attach yourself to the important things which will result in a positive outcome.

In *Spiritual Awareness & Self-Development* this card signifies the way in which we align to our own values to achieve forward movement in our life. It symbolises the speed of life which is attained when we are truly cocreating and aligned to the universal flow. It provides and the ease of life where there is always time to achieve one's true spiritual goals.

*You are blocking this card today by:*

1. Meditating
2. Slowing down
3. Sending a letter by snail mail rather than by e-mail
4. Taking a gentle approach to communication, avoiding heated discussion

## Connect to Your Card

Send a message. Surprise someone with a visit. Go flying. Try archery.

## The Eight of Wands Says

"The momentum is there, so use it to your advantage and keep up the pace. You can achieve so much now after all the effort you have put forth to get to this significant point. Keep focussed on the resolution that is at hand and be ready to start making new plans; be ready for the impact that this will have on your surroundings. You will find yourself freshly grounded."

## Keywords

Growth, morale booster, strategy, upwards and onwards, teamwork, management, approach, journey, swift action, news, fast pace, frenzy, urgency, progress, motion, flight, movement, quick action, news, conclusion, action, activity, swiftness, stabilising, observation, discord, interrogation, misgivings, conscience.

# —Day 23: The Hanged Man—
## The Sacrifice of Being • Fastening Yourself to Your Highest Principles

### Resonances

*Numerology:* 12/3

*Astrology:* Neptune

*Kabbalah:*
Geburah and Hod

### Quick Connections

*Affirmation:* I will connect to my highest values and see the world through my own eyes.

*Meditation:* "From the place of humility comes inner strength when the brash ego has faded."

## The Lesson of the Hanged Man
### Life Lessons and Personally Difficult Cards

Today's card is one I never really understood. For the first ten years of my tarot studies, I just didn't connect with the Hanged Man. I got that it was about "suspension," "hanging around," things being held without activity, and so forth, but it just didn't resonate with me.

Is there a card you have a similar relationship with, a card you just don't understand?

One day, I realised that the Hanged Man is fastened to the "higher" and suspended above the "lower." His sacrifice is one of awareness and values—he represents someone who has chosen to be fixed to his or her own values rather than whatever the world expects. This can sometimes turn life upside down, and there is never any way others will understand this behaviour.

For me, I learnt the Hanged Man when I became him…it just took ten years!

What lessons have struck you in life about a particular card?

For the next few days we will deepen our studies again by looking at how the tarot can assist us in self-development and understanding. These questions are a useful starter.

## The Card in Your Life/Reading

*Careerwise & Financially* this card indicates a suspension of your duties in order to meet the requirements of others. You may have to bite your tongue or hold back from judgement in order to let things pass at this time. You should, however, stick to your principles and realise that losing a battle may not lose the war.

*Healthwise* this card indicates a necessary sacrifice of your resources and freedom in order to make the best recovery possible. It shows the state of limbo in which your best response is to learn as much as possible given your constrained circumstances. The patience with which you endure the present moment will define you in the future.

In *Relationships* this card indicates a unique situation where you can abandon yourself to the relationship itself and allow it to take you to an expected insight. This relationship will recover deeper parts of you than you currently realise and is extremely transformative. It may also indicate an unusual relationship.

In *Travel & Lifestyle* this card indicates a suspension of activity so you can learn before making further advancement. It may also indicate that your plans will be turned literally upside down. You may find yourself facing situations for which you are unprepared, but it is important to remain true to your own self. Doing so will guide you through any challenges and result in illumination.

In *Education* this card indicates a sudden insight that comes after a lot of learning. You may not understand where this insight comes from; however, it should be recognised as a breakthrough moment. Sometimes this card can show a renewal of your studies in mysticism, philosophy, or divination.

In *Spiritual Awareness & Self-Development* this card symbolises a necessary sacrifice when we hold to the divine principles above those of the mundane world. In doing so, we bring that light down through our awareness so that others can see—even if it appears upside down to them. This is a powerful card for spiritual initiation; for example, symbolising the sacrificed god.

*You are blocking this card today by:*

1. Standing up for yourself
2. Moving onwards and upwards towards your objectives
3. Taking life too seriously
4. Being very possessive of your material belongings

## Connect to Your Card

Stand firm on your principles. Don't commit to anything. Hold your place. Bungee jump.

## The Hanged Man Says

"You are placed in a position where you have to look at life from a whole new perspective; think about why you are here, how you got here, and what events and actions have shaped your life so far. What can you take forward from this, and what do you need to sacrifice? You need to be brutal in your assessment, and not be fearful of letting go!"

## Keywords

Revelation, ecstasy, altered consciousness, surrender, spiritual growth, prophesy, reversal, limbo, uniqueness, suspension, sacrifice, transition, readjustment, limbo, paradox, salvation, renewal, upturn, suffering, mysticism, philosophy, religion, descent, surrender, initiation, wisdom, circumspection, discernment, trials, intuition, divination, living to your values, reframing, release.

# —Day 24: The Devil—

*The Traps of Attachment • Facing the Unknown*

## Resonances

*Numerology:* 15/6

*Astrology:* Capricorn

*Kabbalah:*
Tiphareth and Hod

## Quick Connections

*Affirmation:* In every connection I add to the world I am myself connected.

*Meditation:* "Keep wanting and you will always be in need."

## The Lesson of the Devil

*Using Reversals (Upside-Down Cards)*

We today introduce (briefly) the idea of reversed cards. We cover this more in our book *Tarot Flip,* and there's a lesson on our website's Citizen Streets by Mary K. Greer herself on reversals—when you want to explore these further, her book *Complete Book of Tarot Reversals* is a must!

The Devil itself is read most often as withholding, attachment, or ignorance. So when it is reversed, it may indicate the possibility for learning to come from a dark situation or the feeling of release from a prison. If the Devil is material attachment, we might consider what happens when taken to its extreme. It is from this we get meanings of perversion and disorder of natural principles. When reversed, it could be that this card tells us we can draw energy from our natural instincts when applied to higher principles.

If you're using reversals, then this is good practice for any card—"What happens when [Card meaning] goes wrong?" Although there are many other ways of considering reversals, this is a reasonable place to start.

## The Card in Your Life/Reading

*Careerwise & Financially* this card indicates that your position is being oppressed and deliberately restricted. It is possible that somebody seeks your downfall and will do everything to ensure you look your worst. It can also be possible—as related to, say, a job interview—for this card to indicate that not everything has been revealed to you all truthfully told. When this card appears, it is time to have full disclosure.

*Healthwise* this card indicates a dark shadow in your life. The Devil card traditionally means obsession and addiction. It therefore indicates an unhealthy attachment to things that do you no good. Our "demons" must be overthrown and faced in the light of day.

In *Relationships* this card indicates an entirely physical level which is not necessarily healthy in itself. The card signifies a form of bondage which does not give the necessary freedom for the relationship to develop. It can also indicate that one partner has turned the rules upside down to the detriment of the other.

In *Travel & Lifestyle* this card indicates a form of materialism born out of desire which is not fulfilled. It shows that your travel or lifestyle will not satisfy you under the current circumstances despite it being full of attraction.

In *Education* this card indicates the extremes of ignorance and revolution. It can show that you have become attached to old and outworn ideas—even superstition. It can also, on the other hand, show a time of revolt and an upturning of ideas from the past.

In *Spiritual Awareness & Self-Development* this card is a warning not to be bound to the attachments we make to the material world. The Devil card shows that whilst there can be light in the darkness, we must build from our ego state and transcend it.

*You are blocking this card today by:*

1. Not wanting results
2. Being open about your desires
3. Being tolerant and forgiving
4. Being generous and flexible

## Connect to Your Card

Do something slightly naughty. Just for today, give in to temptation. Indulge. Treat someone.

## The Devil Says

"They say 'better the devil you know than the devil you don't.' So get to know me better and all will become much easier. Stop avoiding the situations in your life that hold you in a state of fear and control and 'just do it!' The more you resist my charms, the more you will be tempted to give in with total abandonment, with no limitations!"

## Keywords

Beholden, enthralled, beguilement, attachment, withholding, bondage, domination, perversity, revolution, fascination, illness, limitation, darkness, lust, oppression, repression, obsession, addiction, restriction, fear, shadow, bondage, compulsion, materialism, ignorance, hopefulness, mystery, desire, lust, struggle, weakness, fatality, greed, anger, descent, crisis, shadow, vicious cycle, bad habits, inhibitions, temptation.

# —Day 25: The Blasted Tower—
### Communication • Shocking your System

**Quick Connections**

*Affirmation:* This day provides me the power of speech to change everything.

*Meditation:* "After the climax of the drama comes the state of resolution."

## The Lesson of the Blasted Tower
### Introducing Kabbalistic Symbolism

This is another of those cards (like the Ten of Swords from earlier) for which every querent makes the pantomime "oh no!" the moment they see it.

There are, however, particularly in the WST version of this card, a profound number of spiritual and Kabbalistic symbols:

- Crown: Kether, the top Sephirah in the Tree of Life (*kether* means "crown" in Hebrew)
- Lightning: The *Ztimzum*, the Lightning Flash of Creation down the Tree of Life
- Three windows: The Upper Sephiroth, the Holy Trinity
- The cloud line: The Abyss, separating the divine with the material
- The two falling figures: The Fall

- The ten Yods and the twelve Yods: The shards of the divine manifesting as the Sephiroth and the Zodiac
- The three tongues of fire: the Shin, the Divine Spark of communication

It is interesting in terms of symbolism that the Tower of Babel (where we get "babble" from) is about communication—well, actually "pride" and communication. Man thought he could get to God by just building a big tower, and in our pride we fell—and were made unable to communicate with each other. So we read this often as a card of mixed communications, a downfall brought about by misunderstanding and miscommunication… often in a dramatic fashion.

The best thing about this card as a "change" card (we'll cover the other "change" cards as we come across them) is that it is sudden, obvious, and quick. And it clears the ground, making new horizons possible for the first time. It is an end to restriction.

What do you think? When in life is the Tower a desirable card to draw?

## The Card in Your Life/Reading

*Careerwise & Financially* this card indicates a complete and sudden change. This can be as abrupt as bankruptcy, redundancy, or the close of business. However it usually indicates the need to overthrow all that has come before and start afresh. Whilst the tower card may be swift in its action, what is left can be built upon in confidence. It also allows you to see a clearer horizon once the smoke has cleared.

*Healthwise* this card indicates a breakdown of your situation, leaving only what is strongest. Whilst this may be a traumatic time, it ensures that what is weakest is released, leaving only the strength to continue.

In *Relationships* this card indicates surprise and disruption to the stability that has been building thus far. If you are not currently in a relationship, this card may indicate a sudden change of that status. The Blasted Tower is a necessary card in all healthy relationships to revive and spice up what could otherwise stagnate and become boring. It may indicate a need for you to introduce new things into your relationship.

In *Travel & Lifestyle* this card indicates an acceleration to your plans. You may be surprised how quickly things can change in both travel and lifestyle when this card turns up in a reading. It often indicates the introduction of something entirely new to your situation which is indicated by the cards immediately surrounding the Tower.

In *Education* this card indicates a revolutionary insight that changes the conceptions and patterns of the past. This card shows that whatever you have done to date has not worked and needs shocking and surprising change. It is a card that tells us to think entirely outside of the box and to not fear an attack on outworn ideas.

In *Spiritual Awareness & Self-Development* this card signifies the fall of the Tower of Babel. It shows is that on our spiritual power pride does come before a fall and that fall is necessary for others to learn what is most important to us. It is also a card that shows when we are closed to the divine principles; the divine principles have a way of contacting us.

*You are blocking this card today by:*

1. Making long-term plans, consolidating what you have built so far
2. Keeping to your routine, ordering the same latte you order every day
3. Not making rash decisions or changes
4. Staying in bed with the duvet over your head

## Connect to Your Card

Totally wipe away something outworn. Sort something top to bottom. Make a dramatic statement.

## The Blasted Tower Says

"The time has come and it is now! All those best-laid plans are going go to the wall literally, and you are going to have to start all over again. This is not necessarily a negative thing; it can be just the thing that we need in our life. A forced change that will put us on a new track towards a better future, the one we should have been on in the first place. This is effectively a wake-up call, so get up and get out and turn your life around!"

## Keywords

Arousal, shock, eviction, spiritual emergency, acceleration, overthrow of ambition, conflict, catastrophe, collapse, modification, surprise, upheaval, rupture, confused communications, disruption, breakdown, freedom, release, crisis, destruction, crumbling, toppling, fall, loss, change, misery, distress, adversity, calamity, deception, ruin, overthrow, bankruptcy, reorganisation, downfall, revelation, surprise.

The ace of each suit provides the seed concept which grows into the remaining cards of that suit. We have reflected this by giving the theme of each suit's ace the identical theme of the suits themselves.

The Two of Pentacles reflected strongly the nature of the twos in all suits, i.e., organisation. This we take to indicate that the pentacles manifest the processes of the other suits. The pentacles are the making real of the other ideas found throughout the deck. When a pentacle is present, things will be happening in the noticeable world of events! You'll also notice the twos are organisers and the sevens are reorganisers. You may compare the twos and sevens of each suit and see if this fits for your deck and your appreciation of it.

Threes and fours are activating and applying cards. While they seem fairly close together, the three is like the motor running after ignition and the four the pedal being depressed to make it move!

The fives represent the transition boundary of the theme of the suit. They are difficult only when this transition is resisted. The fives in each suit are truly "calling cards."

We also found the sixes reflecting the theme of their suit. This is very appropriate in Kabbalah, where each Tree of Life in the "four worlds" grows out of the sixth Sephiroth of each Tree. When a six is present, we see a "flip" in the energy of the situation—things are being taken to another level when these cards appear.

The sevens are the re-organisers after the flip of the sixes. They put everything back into a new pattern and usually fairly quickly because they are quite advanced in the 1 to 10 process.

The eights are directive cards, which can particularly be seen in the wands, the suit of ambition.

The nines represent the theme resting, its final phase until the ten shows it returning to the start of the cycle.

Thus, ambition when fulfilled (Nine of Wands) is always incomplete until the return to the original impulse of the activity (Ten of Wands) leads to completion and frees us for a new beginning (Ace of Wands).

—Gate Four—

# The Garden
# of Delights

# Escape Spread—For Escaping Temptation

*Immediately after escaping the labyrinth, we appear to reach our destination. Yet this is another alluring trap set on our way. The Garden of Delights can bring about a devilish downfall, as we can now see from the cards of the Devil and the Blasted Tower. You must make your escape from temptation!*

## Soundtrack for the Journey
### *"Dark Therapy" (Echobelly)*

Take your significator (a page) and place it face-up on the table. Take the two cards you worked with (from either side of the Star) last week and place them either side of your significator. Consider the actions you took in the last week with response to these two cards.

Take out the Devil card and place it over your significator sideways.

Take out the Temperance (Angel) card and lay it above the Devil.

Take all the other cards you have covered so far as a mini-deck; the pages, tens, nines, eights, and the majors (World, Last Judgement, Moon, Sun, Star, Hanged Man, Blasted Tower).

Ask the question, **what is my temptation?** Pull a card, place it below the Devil and interpret it.

Ask the question, **what can I call upon to transcend this trap?** Pull a card, place it above Temperance and interpret it.

Write down your thoughts and any resolutions you may take to respond to this gate in your journal. Over the next week, you may encounter this challenge and you should draw upon your knowledge of this reading in order to make a good response. It is this action or decision that will carry you through the Garden of Temptation and up towards the Mountain of the Sun.

# —Day 26: Seven of Pentacles—

*Finding Yourself Waiting • A Place of Cultivation*

### Resonances

*Numerology:* 75/3

*Astrology:*
Saturn in Taurus

*Kabbalah:*
Netzach (Victory)

*Sabian Symbol:* Taurus
III—Wind, Clouds, and
Haste (The Transitory)

### Quick Connections

*Affirmation:* Wherever I
find decrease there is the
space for increase.

*Meditation:* "Be wary of
thinking and not doing,
for in a moment doubt
can sow its seeds."

## The Lesson of the Seven of Pentacles
### *One Card Narrative (Day 1)*

During the next few days we will begin to build up our narrative skills to interpret the cards as we draw them out in a reading. We will then start to look at weaving cards together and then place them in fixed position spreads to assist our reading.

If you'd like another way of looking through a card, take the "shifting perspective" method and answer the same question, "What do I need to know to be successful in my upcoming trip to Paris?" by first imagining you are in the card, looking out through the person's eyes. He is very close to that bush isn't he, when you are in his shoes! What advice would he offer?

This multiple-frames-of-reference approach can be very powerful for gaining "out of the box" insight into a question and is a useful skill to practice for all oracles!

We'll see you tomorrow after this one-card break, where we'll take a look at a few more spreads and bringing our learning together.

## The Card in Your Life/Reading

*Careerwise & Financially* this card indicates that a plateau has been reached and a time of reevaluation is called for. It may be that whilst things have grown, other aspects of your life have not been taken into account. It is time to pause and assess where your work has been most rewarded. From there you can make further decisions.

*Healthwise* this card indicates that nurturing is required even if this also requires your patience. It is time to evaluate where you are most healthy and tend to where your work is most beneficial.

In *Relationships* this card indicates the need to cultivate only those things which give you benefit in the relationship. You may have to reassess your position that this can be done from a position of strength when you consider all that you have contributed to build the relationship.

In *Travel & Lifestyle* this card indicates the need for attention to detail. It is important to take a moment to assess what is most rewarding about travel or your lifestyle before taking advantage of the offers at hand.

In *Education* this card indicates assessment and evaluation—it is a time of testing of what you have built in your knowledge to date. This card is a card of revision and attention to detail after your previous hard work. You are beginning to build up your knowledge such that it must be tested to ensure future growth.

In *Spiritual Awareness & Self-Development* this card tells to consider all that is positive and beneficial in our life and concentrate on nurturing those aspects alone. Whilst we may consider that life does not always provide what we appear to need, it may be that we have exactly what we need.

*You are blocking this card today by:*

1. Taking a day off work
2. Just getting on with the task at hand
3. Not doubting your abilities and having self-belief by the spade full
4. Cancelling the appointment with your bank manager

## Connect to Your Card

Review your finances. Live within your means. Service your car. Check your house.

## The Seven of Pentacles Says

"Look at your business plan and assess what is working and what is not; you may have worked hard and have achieved your objectives so far, but you must not take it for granted that you are now secure. Think about nurturing aspects of your life that are giving you a good return. Make a decision about whether to uproot and discard those aspects which are becoming a drain on your well-earned resources."

## Keywords

Expectations, deliberation, accounting, need to re-invest, bank money, risk of wasting money, cultivation, re-evaluation, pause, growth, patience, plateau, attention, nurturing, assessment, dissatisfied, honorary work, indecision, greed, inertia, worry, melancholy, impatience, apprehension, evaluation.

# —Day 27: Seven of Swords—
## Expecting Exchange • An Examination of Support

### Resonances

*Numerology:* 61/7

*Astrology:*
Moon in Aquarius

*Kabbalah:*
Netzach (Victory)

*Sabian Symbol:*
Aquarius III—A Big
White Dove, A Message
Bearer (Glad Tidings)

### Quick Connections

*Affirmation:* I can
collect my thoughts
before speech, and speak
before action.

*Meditation:* "Be wary
of taking the unguarded
words of others and using
them against them."

## The Lesson of the Seven of Swords
### One Card Narrative (Day 2)

You can also involve your querent in the reading itself should you choose to adopt this particular approach. Some readers favour involving the querent, whilst others do not factor this in at all. When looking at a particular card such as today's seven of wands you would ask the querent what this would illustrate in their life at the moment.

You can then use your reading skills and interpretive ability to apply that card to their situation with its meanings and its reflection of any other cards in the spread.

If we ask the querent about the seven of swords and they said it looked like somebody was stealing something, we could then suggest that the card showed the stealing of ideas behind somebody's back. If we looked and saw the King of Cups, for example, in the reading it is entirely likely that a character answering to the personality of that card is the one doing the stealing!

Involving the querent in the reading can be an exciting step for any tarot reader to take and opens up new possibilities for your own learning.

## The Card in Your Life/Reading

*Careerwise & Financially* this card indicates the need to cover your bases and ensure that no one is about to betray you. Before heading into any meeting or discussion, you should ensure that everybody is on your side. In the case of interviews, this card requires attention to ensure that no trick questions catch you. It also advises a lot of careful preparation.

*Healthwise* this card indicates the need to understand exactly all aspects of your present condition. It may be that whilst your attention is drawn one way, other aspects are slowly taking away your resources. Take a moment to check with everybody involved that all is well.

In *Relationships* this card indicates potential dishonour and the need to uncover any uncertainty in what is thought about the relationship. This is a card of trespass and betrayal so it is important to be discreet in how you handle conversations and discussions.

In *Travel & Lifestyle* this card indicates the need to escape. However, you must only take the ideas that serve you well and leave behind anything that has proven troublesome or quarrelsome in the past.

In *Education* this card indicates uncertainty and the need to gain a more comprehensive understanding of the situation. It is a card of partial learning, and whilst you may avoid this being found out, it warns that you cannot carry on in this state for much longer.

In *Spiritual Awareness & Self-Development* this card tells us of the limits of our logic. Whilst we may think we understand things clearly in our mind, we can never know something fully. This card speaks of the paradox of life when considered in the mind. If there are things that currently confuse you, leave them behind.

*You are blocking this card today by:*

1. Being open and honest with all your transactions
2. Not reacting badly to a person who is annoying you
3. Letting go of old grievances
4. Facing a problem person head-on instead of contriving and plotting behind people's backs

## Connect to Your Card

Destroy and delete old information and papers. Read up on conspiracy theories.

## The Seven of Swords Says

"Be wary of sharing delicate information with others. Are you sure your communications will not be divulged to a third party? Be particularly wary of being too trusting when embarking on a new business venture. It could also come into play in your workplace environment—be wary of sharing your ideas with others, as they may take these innovative ideas and pass them off as their own. You have been warned."

## Keywords

Trespass, unreliability, betrayal, insolence, spying, dishonour, guile, escape, discretion, evasion, uncertainty, appeasement, courage, cunning, cowardice, vacillation, schemes, attempt, tricks, quarrelling, slander, babbling, dishonesty, stealth, deception, subterfuge.

# —Day 28: Seven of Cups—

*Imagining the World in your Image • The Creation of Vision*

### Resonances

*Numerology:* 47/11

*Astrology:*
Venus in Scorpio

*Kabbalah:*
Netzach (Victory)

*Sabian Symbol:*
Scorpio III—A Woman
Drawing Two Dark
Curtains Aside (Fate
Revealing the Truth)

### Quick Connections

*Affirmation:* I am able to
look beyond the obvious
and see hidden delight in
the world.

*Meditation:* "It is within
your rights to create pie-
in-the-sky ideas, just do
not expect anyone else to
feast on them."

## The Lesson of the Seven of Cups
### *One Card Narrative (Day 3)*

Let's kick back a little today, shall we? Let's have some fun and let our intuition ride out to play! We're also going to expand a card rather than contract it (i.e., with a single keyword).

We have before us today the Seven of Cups. What we'd like you to do is simple. Get in front of your computer or journal, find somewhere where you can type or write freely, and do this …

1. Look at the card, the Seven of Cups.
2. Play some stirring music in your head that suits the card.
3. Now let the card change in brief snapshots of movement, as if you were watching a movie trailer.
4. Practice your movie trailer voice and narrate what you see.
5. Type out what you hear for this card, about ten sentences at most!

Have fun, don't pause, and just see what happens—no editing!

## The Card in Your Life/Reading

*Careerwise & Financially* this card indicates that although your ideas may appear to you most worthy, they are in fact unrealistic. You have allowed yourself to believe your own hype and have not considered the input of others. This card tells you to get a reality check before you are drowned in your own illusion. It can also indicate unrealistic expectations of your job, in which case it is perhaps time to move on.

*Healthwise* this card indicates self-indulgence and altered states that may not be to your benefit. Whilst the attractions which have captured your attention may appear exciting, they are not doing you any good at all. If you feel like merely a shadow of yourself, the solution to reclaiming your persona lies in the dangers of what is most consuming your time at present.

In *Relationships* this card indicates a form of escapism and a lack of clear decision making that leaves the relationship empty. It is most important to pull away from repeating arguments and concerns and simply move on. There is no need to dwell on the "what-ifs" or "maybes."

In *Travel & Lifestyle* this card indicates the impracticality of your current plans. You should most certainly take time to be realistic about what is available to you. This card is a warning that what appears to be an opportunity may in fact be a trap or pipe dream.

In *Education* this card indicates a need for clear thinking instead of overindulging your imagination and creativity. You must seek ways to apply your knowledge rather than dream of future success.

In *Spiritual Awareness & Self-Development* this card signals that our vision may sometimes overwhelm us and it is our *vision* which must serve *us* rather than ourselves serving our vision. It is a good time to seek external advice and counselling to get a second opinion of what is going on inside us.

### You are blocking this card today by:

1. Being practical and working towards completing deadlines.
2. Stopping talking about fulfilling your dreams and start living your life for real.
3. Looking at your financial in-goings and out-goings.
4. Having your eyes tested and cleaning your mirror—metaphorically and for real!

## Connect to Your Card

Go to the cinema, theatre, or other exhibition. Lose yourself in something. Dress fancily.

## The Seven of Cups Says

"In the realms of your imagination anything is possible; however, the imagination needs to be kept in check, as it does not always convert well to material reality. There is fanciful and there is downright deluded—you need to use your imagination in a practical way or it will use you, be more Albert Einstein than Walter Mitty."

## Keywords

Delusion, obsession, opportunities, spoilt for choice, emotional overload, release, dreaminess, dissipation, illusory success, fantasy, illusion, window-shopping, escapism, altered states, vision, yearning, impracticality, wishful thinking, self-indulgence, dissipation, options, abundance, ideas, designs, resolutions, lying, deceit, error, disappointment, sentiment, decision, thoughts, imagination, reflection, impressions.

# —Day 29: Seven of Wands—
## Working Towards the Higher Ground • The Expression of Confidence

### Resonances

*Numerology:* 33/6

*Astrology:*
Mars in Leo

*Kabbalah:* Netzach
(Victory)

*Sabian Symbol:* Leo III—
Zuni Sun Worshippers
(Creating Favour)

### Quick Connections

*Affirmation:* There is strength in my stance and I am able to stand up against all obstacles.

*Meditation:* "Through persistence comes mastery of the soul."

## The Lesson of the Seven of Wands
### Two Card Narrative

As we work through our sevens, we'll give a simple method to start reading tarot cards together by combining today's card with a previous card, the Eight of Cups.

Take a sentence for each card based on what you can generate with the keyword kaleidoscope and add the sentences together—just like learning a language! The symbols on each card are our "letters," the cards are "words," and the reading is our "sentence." This is a narrative way of reading cards, which we'll look at today—because we are going to create one big story from all seventy-eight cards as we go along.

So if we have the Seven of Wands and the Eight of Cups, we might suggest . . .

"During a time of great conflict"+"One man's quest begins"

That sounds like yesterday's movie trailer voiceover script already!

What might you create for these two cards?

For those wanting to delve deeper, here is an example for a three-card narrative reading: Ten of Cups + Eight of Cups + Four of Cups.

Let's keep it as a narrative first … ours might be "From happy beginnings he travels on a quest, but when resting he misses an important invitation."

Now let's also add in a "gestalt" reading of cards, taking them all together so we have to merge, swish, and overlay the three cards until one meaning arises. You can practice with two cards by placing them apart from each other, and switching your eyes from one to another, and then allowing a "third card" to appear in the middle with a single feeling or word on it in your mind's eye. So if we took: Ten of Cups + Eight of Cups and flipped looking from one to another, we might get a feeling of "insecurity" and all that arises from it—a fear of loss, exile, dissatisfaction, and so on.

Next, try it with three cards (you can pair the three together in three different versions of two cards and then merge all three arising words if you want): Ten of Cups + Eight of Cups + Four of Cups.

If you imagine these were three pictures illustrating a book, what would the title be? What would be the book's main theme? For the three cards in our example here, we get: *Selfishness or Independence*. Perhaps those are flip-sides of the same idea, shown when these three cards come together. Obviously, you can't learn every combination of two or three cards, but a little practice with how to read multiple cards means you will soon be able to read any combination.

A few more thoughts about the Seven of Wands, which is perhaps the "tipping point" in so many situations. Do we stand and fight or succumb to the inevitable, overwhelmed by opposing forces? Whilst we may feel that we have the high ground, perhaps we need to be knocked off our hobby horse.

The sevens of each suit are the first stage in the "last leg" of manifestation. They have the energy, direction, and weight of the history of the aces, twos, threes, fours, fives, and sixes behind them … but they're not quite there yet! A good book to read on this subject is *The Tipping Point* by Malcolm Gladwell.

In the world of wands—values, lifestyle, spirit—when this seven turns up, it calls for a rapid appraisal of the situation. Trying to hold steady in a "seven" state is very energy-intensive! It is trying to hold momentum but not letting it completely carry you away … or perhaps learning you can afford to give up on some battles (even given massive investment) and still win the war.

We like the fact that this is one of the cards in the WST which shows the "giant" perspective so clearly. Pamela liked drawing giants (and dwarves), as seen in the illustrations for *The Book of Friendly Giants* by Eunice Fuller. This for us adds the meaning that sometimes we need a sense of perspective in such times. That perspective is possible from the vantage point of the seven and of course, we at least by this stage can see all the challenges.

Now, for today, in terms of our exercise, perhaps we can take a look at the "7" as a number. We have the seven ages of man, the seven days of the week, etc. Choose one of the things in this world that has a seven structure and play with it in tarot terms, in any way you like.

We take this quote from Shakespeare's *As You Like It*, Act II, Scene VII:

All the world's a stage,
And all the men and women merely players;
They have their exits and their entrances;
And one man in his time plays many parts,
**His acts being seven ages.** At first the infant,
Mewling and puking in the nurse's arms;
And then the whining school-boy, with his satchel
And shining morning face, creeping like snail
Unwillingly to school. And then the lover,
Sighing like furnace, with a woeful ballad
Made to his mistress' eyebrow. Then a soldier,
Full of strange oaths, and bearded like the pard,
Jealous in honour, sudden and quick in quarrel,
Seeking the bubble reputation
Even in the cannon's mouth. And then the justice,
In fair round belly with good capon lin'd,
With eyes severe and beard of formal cut,
Full of wise saws and modern instances;
And so he plays his part. The sixth age shifts
Into the lean and slipper'd pantaloon,
With spectacles on nose and pouch on side;
His youthful hose, well sav'd, a world too wide

For his shrunk shank; and his big manly voice,
Turning again toward childish treble, pipes
And whistles in his sound. Last scene of all,
That ends this strange eventful history,
Is second childishness and mere oblivion;
Sans teeth, sans eyes, sans taste, sans everything.

## The Card in Your Life/Reading

*Careerwise & Financially* this card indicates the need to defend your position against the opinions and plans of others. You must take a firm stand and keep your ground—there is strength in adversity and you have a good chance of success by holding to the strength of your convictions. In meetings and interviews, this card bodes well if you stick up for yourself.

*Healthwise* this card indicates the need to be defiant and set clear contracts and boundaries in your own capabilities. Despite the advances of others, you know what it is that you must do and this is likely the healthiest option.

In *Relationships* this card indicates a conflict because what is important to you is not seen as important to others. You must clearly state your argument and hold your ground in order to resolve the issue.

In *Travel & Lifestyle* this card indicates the need to be forceful and take an advantageous position against the opinions of others. It is not a time to be shy or retiring, but rather you should hold your ground, which will result in success.

In *Education* this card indicates the need to form your own opinion from the different opinions of others no matter what their experience or knowledge. You can debate and discuss matters all you wish; however, it is your understanding of the matter that counts in the end.

In *Spiritual Awareness & Self-Development* this card shows the inner strength that comes from the practice of holding to our own values. Although the world and its unfolding events can challenge and change our values, there are times when we make advancement through holding true to our own course. When this card appears, this is one of those times.

*You are blocking this card today by:*

1. Getting off your soapbox and letting someone else have a go
2. Running away when the going gets tough
3. Throwing caution to the wind and being carefree
4. Not being too defensive and paranoid; no one is out to get you

## Connect to Your Card

Sign up for self-defence lessons or watch a martial arts film. Don't back down. Be obstinate all day. Don't change your mind.

## The Seven of Wands Says

"There are situations in life where you just have to stand firmly for what you believe in! So stand up and be counted; show your competition that you know you are in a strong position. Let them see the might of your force; you will not be manipulated and controlled by an inferior attack on your principles."

## Keywords

Independence, brazen, planning, preparation, exposure, stiff competition, energy, courage, keeping your ground, strength in adversity, advantageous position (holding the fort), forcefulness, aggression, conviction, defiance, competition, valour, violence, conflict, discussion, contract, measure, negotiations, perplexity, anxiety, caution.

# —Day 30: Death—

*Transformation • Not Recognising the Old You*

## Resonances

*Numerology:* 13/4

*Astrology:* Scorpio

*Kabbalah:*
Tiphareth and Netzach

## Quick Connections

*Affirmation:* The coal
becomes the diamond,
the seed the plant, and I
am constantly renewed in
every moment.

*Meditation:* "The whole
purpose of beginning a
journey is to reach
the end."

## The Lesson of Death
### Change and Learning Cards

The Death card is one of the majors which we see as a "set," that is, different types of a common theme. It is one of the Change set. These are:

- High Priestess—Intuitive or transcendental change (the sort you don't really recognise is going on)
- Wheel—Cyclic change
- Death—Transformative change (change that uses what you have, turning it into something else)
- Blasted Tower—Sudden change

So when the Death card turns up in a reading, we know there is a transformation implied, and we have to use the other cards to divine where this transformation will come from and what form it will take.

Here's a question for you—and it just might be a trick question—which cards in the majors are types of Learning/Teaching cards (or Education cards) and what sort of learning/teaching does each of those cards represent?

A clue... the Hierophant is "traditional teaching."

## The Card in Your Life/Reading

*Careerwise & Financially* this card indicates a gradual transformation of your job and role. It can also signifies a revolution of a project or complete turnaround in your fortunes. However, the card provides nothing new or unexpected so it is likely the answer lies in your current position.

*Healthwise* this card indicates a regeneration and transition in your life. Whilst the Death card may appear to be quite literal, it often signifies a gradual transformation and change in life rather than a sudden ending.

In *Relationships* this card indicates the need to regenerate the present situation so that out of it can be reborn a new beginning. The Death card indicates the end of one phase of a relationship and the commencement of another. Really, it doesn't indicate anything new or shocking but rather the need for change in what is already present.

In *Travel & Lifestyle* this card indicates a revitalisation that has long been worked towards. When the Death card appears in lifestyle questions, it is an entirely beneficial current which will take the person to new horizons and avenues. In terms of travel, it signifies a need to embrace entirely new environments and explore the unknown.

In *Education* this card indicates a slow learning process in which you are changed more than you realise. It can indicate a gradual dissolution of old ideas in favour of new ones which are not yet known to you. It is inevitable that this learning process takes place even if it may appear uncomfortable at the time.

In *Spiritual Awareness & Self-Development* this card is an initiatory change that signals the death of one state of life and the entry into another. It is a rebirth card that allows others to embrace what is currently unknown so that we can do so more in future.

*You are blocking this card today by:*

1. Making long-term plans
2. Hanging on to old habits
3. Cancelling your gym membership
4. Not going out or doing anything creative and productive

## Connect to Your Card

Clear away something old. Turn junk into cash. Remember the departed. Check out your family history or photos.

## Death Says

"There are some things in life that are inevitable and I am one of them, so embrace the positive aspects of the nature of inevitability and what I represent as death. I am the catalyst for you to eliminate the aspects of your life that are outworn and no longer required, which can include bad habits or simply routines that have become restricting in your life. Face up to the inevitable and stop avoiding living life to the full because of your self-imposed limitations."

## Keywords

New horizons, shadow work, life, change, rebirth, renewal, revolution, death of political figure, transformation, revitalisation, regeneration, reincarnation, dissolution, transition, ending, elimination, inevitability, change, destruction, mortality, corruption, mutation, cycle, season, decay, acceptance.

# —Day 31: The Wheel—
## *Cause and Effect • The Hub of Synchronicity*

### Resonances

*Numerology:* 10/1

*Astrology*: Jupiter

*Kabbalah:*
Chesed and Netzach

### Quick Connections

*Affirmation:* I am in the centre of the wheel of change, the hub of whatever spins about me.

*Meditation:* "The hands of time sweep our well worn past away."

## The Lesson of the Wheel
### *Narrative in Time (Day 1)*

To develop our narrative skills, let's stick to this one card but look at it in terms of past and future—and present! What does it mean in those three phases? Try different sentences using the following words highlighted in bold, with anything else you want to say with the card. You can also try this for any of the other cards.

For example:
- "I see with this card you **have been** going around in circles"
- "I see with this card **you are** in the middle of a revolution"
- "I see with this card **you will** experience ups and downs for some time"

Have a go at using the three tenses for the same card, and see how that little shift changes your perspective of the cards. They themselves are *a-temporal,* outside of time, particularly the archetypal cards, the majors.

## The Card in Your Life/Reading

*Careerwise & Financially* this card indicates that of the situation in your favour. You will be lucky and make progress if you take risks on the wheel. The appearance of this card may show that life is not in your hands at the present time so you can afford to wait for the wheel to turn your way.

*Healthwise* this card indicates the cycles of life and the changes that time brings. In health questions this card signifies that you must wait for inevitable change to occur. The situation is presently out of your hands and you must let time pass.

In *Relationships* this card indicates good luck and fortune if you allow things to move at their own pace. It signifies forward movement in relationships; however, it also shows the complexity that comes when many aspects are involved. You must let the wheel do its own thing and not interfere at this time.

In *Travel & Lifestyle* this card indicates exciting and comprehensive changes. The timing is right to take risks and trust your luck to fate. Your gambles will pay off and good fortune will smile upon you. However, one is reminded that the wheel can take life down as well as up, and you may wish to also use your good fortune to prepare for a later rainy day.

In *Education* this card indicates being in the right place at the right time to secure your success. It is time to take steps forward and trust to the revolutions of the wheel in order to put you on the right course to success. The only thing you can do at the present time is to take risks and live life as fully as possible. At the moment, life is out of your hands; however, good things are coming.

In *Spiritual Awareness & Self-Development* this card illustrates the nature of synchronicity. Its appearance tells is to be aware of those moments in life that transcend time and space and all known connections. It is a powerful card for the oracle to receive, for it tells that we are at the centre of the wheel and can be aware of the invisible knots that connect the world together. The wheel symbolises time and its mysteries. It is the card that lies underneath the world.

*You are blocking this card today by:*

1. Avoiding taking any chances or risks
2. Not wearing a watch
3. Not buying a lottery ticket
4. Over-planning

## Connect to Your Card

Look out for synchronicities. Check things more than once. Play a game of chance or challenge.

## The Wheel Says

"'Being in the right place at the right time' and 'it is all in the timing,' these things have been said. It all comes down to good old destiny and fulfilling it! You are heading one direction and it is inevitable that the wheel that is your life will turn and turn until it stops. So while you are riding this wheel of destiny, make it a good one, seize the opportunities as you pass them by, learn and grow, take risks if need be, and embrace good luck and bad luck the same."

## Keywords

Plan, *rota*, movement, fate, good fortune, favour, luck, progress, tao, karma, synchronicity, cycles, inevitability, timing, destiny, fortune, elevation, luck, felicity, risk, success, fate, chance, change/transition, gambling, movement, pinning, rotation, cycles.

—Gate Five—

# The Mountain
# of the Sun

# Solar Spread—For Opening to the Light

*Having escaped from the Garden, and now free from the Wheel of Death and Rebirth, you gain the path to the Mountain of the Sun. From here you can at last see the whole of your journey so far and even some of the journey ahead. All is clear in this place, and you can enjoy the beautiful light of the soul of the Sun, illuminating every step. This is the place of the Tarot Adept.*

## Soundtrack for the Journey
*"Send Me an Angel" (Scorpions)*

Take the Wheel card out of the deck and place it in the centre of the table. Place the Sun card on top of it. This represents the Mountain of the Sun.

Take all the tens, nines, eights, and sevens out of the deck. Place them in four piles—the tens in one pile, the nines in another, etc.

Take the World, Last Judgement, Moon, Star, Temperance, Hanged Man, Devil, Blasted Tower, and Death cards out of the pack and place them in a pile.

Shuffle the four tens face-down whilst considering the question, **"what is my light?"** Select one, placing it face-up above the Wheel.

This card indicates your light in the world of action and manifestation.

Shuffle the four nines. Select a card and place it face-up below the Wheel.

This card indicates your light in the world of your inner self and dreams.

Shuffle the four eights. Select a card and place it face-up to the left of the Wheel.

This card indicates your light in the world of your mind and learning.

Shuffle the four sevens. Select a card and place it face-up to the right of the Wheel.

This card indicates your light in the world of your emotions and heart.

Consider these four rays of the Wheel of the Sun.

7|16

Now, pick up the pile of the nine major arcana and shuffle them. Ask **"What blocks my light?"** and consider how you avoided the temptation indicated by the previous Gate reading of the Garden of Desires. Select one card. Place this on top of the Sun and Wheel cards in the centre of the table.

Take a moment to interpret how this major acts through your behaviour to block your light. Make a note in your journal of this reading and also write down at least one behaviour or attitude you will work on to free your light from this block over the next week.

Having seen your journey thus far in the rays of the Sun and a little of the journey ahead, we can make our way to the next landmark, the Ancient Coliseum, the sixth gate of our journey. However, be aware that you must work on your blocks—the next gate is a trial of spirit, and you will have to travel light to accomplish its task.

# —Day 32: Six of Pentacles—
### Finding Yourself Giving and Taking • A Place of Charity

## Resonances

*Numerology:* 74/11

*Astrology:*
Moon in Taurus

*Kabbalah:*
Tiphareth (Beauty)

*Sabian Symbol:* Taurus
II—A Red Cross Nurse
(Selfless Service)

## Quick Connections

*Affirmation:* In giving of
myself I receive blessings
from above.

*Meditation:* "It is not the
act of giving that counts,
but your motivation."

## The Lesson of the Six of Pentacles
### Narrative in Time (Day 2)

Today we consider the Six of Pentacles. We have seen already how we can analyse a card by looking at all the various symbols on it. Today we will look at how to weave a narrative whilst reading several cards together.

Firstly, we'll look at the Six of Pentacles as someone giving charity and receiving recognition. It is a card of resources.

Now let's take that idea and put it onto a flow of cards. Obviously, the word "resources" can be modified to "resourced," "resourceful," and "resource." This is one problem with Keywords—they teach people one fixed word, and the sentences they then try to create get skewed to fit the word, rather than the other way around!

So let us see this card in a few different locations in a spread and consider what we might say:

In the outcome: "So, in summary, you should gain **resources** from a benefactor."

In the past: "Having been **resourceful** in your affairs, you can now move forwards."

In the future: "You will find yourself easily gaining the **resource** you require."

Now let's combine the card with another in a sequence. Have a go at putting a sentence together for the Seven of Cups and the Six of Pentacles today. Do it in one or any of the below ways:

- [Seven of Cups] and [Six of Pentacles]
- [Seven of Cups] however [Six of Pentacles]
- [Six of Pentacles] if [Seven of Cups]
- [Six of Pentacles] so [Seven of Cups]
- [Seven of Cups] when [Six of Pentacles]

Example: if I were to do [Seven of Cups] if [Six of Pentacles] I would write:

You may be [beguiled by illusionary success] if [you take assistance from others].

## The Card in Your Life/Reading

*Careerwise & Financially* this card indicates the need to further your ambition by sharing with others. You may wish to delegate your work, share rewards, or allow other people to take some credit at this time. Your charity will be rewarded, and the scales will tip your way. The Six of Pentacles in a career question shows perfect balance in your favour. All is well. This card is also a card of grants and loans, and it may indicate the need to apply for such in order to further your work.

*Healthwise* this card indicates that necessary assistance will be received in fair measure. Although it may be slow and appear restricting, what is given to you at this time (no matter the source) is perfectly reasonable under the circumstances. This card shows a balancing of the scales to achieve an improvement or settling as related to your health.

In *Relationships* this card indicates the need to equally share the rewards of the relationship. It may be that the power balance in the relationship—particularly with regard to finances—has become upset. You need to ensure that your resources, whether they be time, attention, or finances, are equally shared. If you don't, the relationship will fare far worse than it needs to.

In *Travel & Lifestyle* this card indicates a need to ensure that you can stretch limited resources in order to secure the travel or lifestyle you expect. It may be that you will need to depend on the generosity of others in order to enjoy life at this time. The appearance of this card indicates that such outside help will be offered to you.

In *Education* this card indicates the requirement to sort your finances and put your house in order to concentrate fully on your learning. There will be no exciting developments at this time but rather a slow and steady pace.

In *Spiritual Awareness & Self-Development* this card demonstrates how the world always gives us exactly what we need rather than what we expect or desire. It is a card that shows we can learn from the experience of the world as it really is in order to learn more about our relationship to the world itself.

*You are blocking this card today by:*

1. Being selfish
2. Not sharing your good fortune with others
3. Not showing appreciation where it is due
4. Not spending

## Connect to Your Card

Donate to a charity. Support someone with a gift. Give some love.

## The Six of Pentacles Says

"Look at me: I have achieved status and wealth and am now in a position to give something of value to others. This something of value isn't just money; it can be delivered in many forms, such as scholarships, the sharing of experience, mentoring, or volunteering. What abilities do you possess that can be used in a positive way? The sharing of value could involve volunteering your skills to support a charity. It is important that you closely examine your motivations for wanting to do this—is it entirely for selfless reasons or are you trying to create a good impression? Are you trying to buy approval or acceptance? Are you just wanting to be liked?"

## Keywords

Welfare, compensation, return, resources, sharing, charity, gifts, gratitude, loans, grants, assistance, dispensation, philanthropy, material success, prosperity, gratification, ambition, aim, generosity, consideration.

# —Day 33: Six of Swords—
## Expecting New Horizons • An Examination of the Journey

### Resonances

*Numerology:* 60/6

*Astrology:*
Mercury in Aquarius

*Kabbalah:*
Tiphareth (Beauty)

*Sabian Symbol:* Aquarius
II—A Popularity That
Proves Ephemeral (A
Need for Self-Approval)

### Quick Connections

*Affirmation:* I can look to longer-term horizons at any point in my journey.

*Meditation:* "Wherever you go you take yourself along, so before you leave become a better you."

### The Lesson of the Six of Swords
#### Narrative for Two-Card Readings

Today we consider the Six of Swords and a simple spread for practicing a two-card narrative. If we have the Six of Swords in a one-card reading, the querent may want to know what to do as a result. We simply take the next card from the deck to answer this question.

So what does it take for someone to make that next step? Pull a card from your deck and use it to explore what it is that takes someone from the Six of Swords onwards.

Let's use the Six of Pentacles as an example. In order to make that step from the Six of Swords, someone has to know that his or her endeavours will be fairly rewarded—in a very real and practical sense.

# The Card in Your Life/Reading

*Careerwise & Financially* this card indicates the work required to make progress at this time. There is no immediate reward; however, it remains in sight. You must be prepared for a long journey in order to fulfill your ambition. You should also be prepared to make waves and expect the journey to be hard. That being said, do not change your course or plans midway, for you are set on the right path.

*Healthwise* this card indicates the need to make do with your present circumstances and make the most of what you possess. It can also signify more literally the need to move away from your current environment by taking a break or a holiday even if getting there will take hard work.

In *Relationships* this card indicates that you are struggling to take the situation forwards because it always appears that you are doing all the work. This can often go unrecognised by others so it might be a good idea to share your inner thoughts with those who are closest to you. They may be able to assist you and not work against you as is the present circumstance.

In *Travel & Lifestyle* this card indicates movement away from one situation to another which will be in your benefit. Whilst it is important to keep your goal in sight, you should be prepared to work hard for longer than originally anticipated in order to achieve your goal. If you are travelling with others, do not expect them to share the load.

In *Education* this card indicates a change of attitude to make the work less burdensome. You may be pushing the wrong direction and perhaps need to organise your revision or learning in some other way. However, it is important not to disrupt things too much at this stage so you may just feel that it is time to push on regardless.

In *Spiritual Awareness & Self-Development* this card shows that we make our own future from the thoughts and memories of the past. Whilst these cannot be removed entirely we can choose to create a better future by reframing the events of the past as learning experiences.

## You are blocking this card today by:

1. Giving in to circumstances that are not of your liking
2. Staying where you are and wallowing in your stuckness
3. Seeing things in the same old negative way
4. Believing the world owes you a favour

## Connect to Your Card

Travel over water. Take a trip. Let someone else drive—literally or metaphorically.

## The Six of Swords Says

"Moving on and being progressive in your thinking is the best possible solution at this moment in time. Use your good sense of reason to navigate yourself through these emotional times. Once you have covered the distance and are back on your feet, you can start afresh in a whole new world."

## Keywords

Holiday, passage, representation, transition, relocation, removal, change of attitude, recovery, earned success, merit, moving away from immediate danger, fleeing, labour, journey, stalemate, envoy, expedient, way, route, recovery, new perspective.

# —Day 34: Six of Cups—
## *Imagining Childhood Wishes • The Creation of Memory*

## Resonances

*Numerology:* 46/1

*Astrology:* Sun in Scorpio

*Kabbalah:*
Tiphareth (Beauty)

*Sabian Symbol:* Scorpio
II—A Fellowship Supper
(Kindred Spirits)

## Quick Connections

*Affirmation:* In every
way the day can be seen
through innocent eyes.

*Meditation:* "Childhood
is paradise lost, never
again will we experience
our life through such rose-
tinted innocence. We are
left with the remnants of
our childhood self in the
form of memories."

## The Lesson of the Six of Cups
### *Narrative for Eight-Card Reading*

Well now, eight cards together?! Don't forget that 8 is just 4 x 2. We know how we can ✳ try
compare two cards and come up with a "gestalt" in a single word. We can do that with two
pairs (four cards) and then combine the two words to make one word and so on with 4 x 2
cards. Let's try that with the eight cards we have, as pairs. Don't worry, this isn't how we
have to do it all the time, it's just a good way of learning!

- Ten of Swords + World = Finality
- Four of Cups + Eight of Cups = Doubt
- Ten of Cups + Three of Wands = Expectation
- King of Swords + Tower = Disaster
- Finality + Doubt + Expectation + Disaster = Turmoil (or Shock)

Another possible word might be "catastrophe." Interestingly, when we come to look that word up, it comes from two Greek words, meaning "to overturn." We can certainly see that in this reading!

## The Card in Your Life/Reading

*Careerwise & Financially* this card indicates a gift from the past, such as an inheritance or benefiting from the loss of another. You should receive any gifts with a carefree attitude and not gloat too much at others' misfortune. This card can also indicate the need to put money aside all into projects that bring you amusement and enjoyment. You should stop for a moment and enjoy the freedom that money can buy…without overspending.

*Healthwise* this card indicates a return to the past and the importance of our emotions in securing stable health. It often shows the need to return to those things we once enjoyed in order to gain (or regain) a positive outlook on life.

In *Relationships* this card indicates a childlike expectation of what the relationship can offer. You may be applying immature feelings and seeing the other person through rose-tinted spectacles. Whilst this may be a convenient position for the moment, it will not hold out in the long term. There may be deeper patterns from your own childhood at play that should be recognised.

In *Travel & Lifestyle* this card indicates new surroundings in old places. It can signify a return to the past and a reconnection to the enjoyment of the previous time. You may be surprised by just how easy it is to return to the patterns and places of your own childhood. In other circumstances this card can signify a blast from the past which surprises you in the present moment.

In *Education* this card indicates the importance of memory in your studies. It is a sort of halfway house in which you must consolidate all that you have learnt to date. Do not make plans to move forwards until you have absorbed your learning so far. You may wish to create something from your experience and gift it to another or make a presentation about your progress thus far.

In *Spiritual Awareness & Self-Development* this card is a profound reminder of how the past creates our future. Indeed, the past of the entire world shapes our own possibilities. Whilst it is a backwards facing card, it shows us that we must connect to our memory of the most pleasant things in order to positively shape our future. It can also indicate karmic ties between people.

*You are blocking this card today by:*

1. Being cold and clinical
2. Being ruthless in achieving your happiness
3. Being destructive and creating disharmony
4. Being afraid of commitment

## Connect to Your Card

Visit a place from the past either in reality or through old photos.

## The Six of Cups Says

"Take time out to be more childlike in how you relate to others. Try drawing on the simplicity of that time in your life when you did not have the responsibilities you have now. In regard to your a significant other, what attracted you to this person? What triggered that first flutter of attraction? Try to focus on this to inject more harmony into your relationship."

## Keywords

Appreciation, immaturity, gift, past, pleasant memories, new surroundings, innocence, karmic ties, sentiment, nostalgia, reminiscence, affection, playfulness, childhood, goodwill, harmony, memory, equilibrium.

# —Day 35: Six of Wands—
## Working Towards Recognition • The Expression of Victory

### Resonances

*Numerology:* 32/5

*Astrology:* Jupiter in Leo

*Kabbalah:*
Tiphareth (Beauty)

*Sabian Symbol:* Leo II—
Early Morning Dew
(Starting Afresh)

### Quick Connections

*Affirmation:* Today brings its own recognition of my accomplishments.

*Meditation:* "Remember, never rest on your laurels. It is when we flatter ourselves with our success that we go off guard and expose ourselves to threat. The Laurel leaves of victory shrivel and die; the glory of success is short lived."

## The Lesson of the Six of Wands
### Narrative for Eleven-Card Reading

Today we take a whole sequence of cards and weave a story, noticing how with additional cards our first cards may change meanings altogether, or some aspect of each card gets drawn into sharper focus. This is due to the *multivalent* nature of symbols—a blindfold can mean guilt in one instance yet refusing to see the obvious in another. It can mean lies in one case and hiding in another, and so on. All symbols have this nature, and this is essential for tarot to work! It is important not to learn a single symbolic meaning for any image or object, but at least two alternatives so you leave your mind free to create even more when reading in the context of different cards and questions.

- Ten of Cups
- Eight of Cups
- Four of Cups

- The World
- Ten of Swords
- Three of Wands
- King of Swords
- The Tower
- Five of Swords
- Knight of Wands
- Seven of Pentacles

That's eleven cards now, and from tomorrow we'll see how they change when we put them into positional reading spreads (with a meaning for each location, i.e., "future," "past") such as the Celtic Cross. We'll then have a break with looking at novel ways of reading individual cards for a few days, and then start to do some really interesting things with our deck.

Here's an example reading narrative for a new business question in terms of those cards:

The business commences well, doing well, providing a good service to the community (Ten of Cups). However, the people running it will become over-ambitious, becoming unhappy with their lot and the rewards (Eight of Cups). They don't feel rewarded for the work and things go backwards (Ten of Cups to Eight of Cups). They are offered an opportunity which will offer security but they hesitate (Four of Cups) because they don't want to lose sole control (the World). They find themselves in a fixed and stuck position with loans, stuck in a rut (Ten of Swords).

So they call in a business advisor (Three of Wands) who looks at the export market. He reasons with them from authority and advises clearly (King of Swords). They need to make sudden change and act immediately! (The Tower). They have to clear some of their loans first (Five of Swords) by selling some things of value (Knight of Wands). Whilst not entirely profitable, things hold fast whilst they take stock of the situation.

## The Card in Your Life/Reading

*Careerwise & Financially* this card indicates a position of victory and leadership. You can be assured that your team will follow you or your project will gain success. In finances this is a card of steady investment building on the success of the past. However one must be careful not to become too sure of oneself before the final gate is crossed. Ensure you have a contract in place.

*Healthwise* this card indicates the support of others, particularly in your home life. It is important to take advantage of the support of those who truly believe in you and your accomplishments. Whilst the battle may be over, the victory celebrations are still ahead.

In *Relationships* this card indicates that your own values are recognised by your partner or by those around you. Your friends support your choice. It indicates that you can make steady progress in your relationship but do pay attention to the opinions of those around you or you may get too carried away.

In *Travel & Lifestyle* this card indicates opportunities of amusement and recognition ahead of you based on all that you have done so far. However, it is important to keep an eye on what drives you because there is a slight chance it may shift underneath you and throw you from your position.

In *Education* this card indicates that your work is appreciated and people are supporting your progress. You must ensure that you keep a tight rein on your own drive and resources to ensure steady advancement towards your final goal.

In *Spiritual Awareness & Self-Development* this card shows the importance of holding on to values and bringing other people along in the spiritual journey. However, it can indicate falling into a position of false dignity or pride where we must be assured that our vision and values are still true. We might also need to be encouraged to hold on to those values.

*You are blocking this card today by:*

1. Behaving like a sore loser
2. Not having any ambition
3. Not taking the credit for an important achievement you have made
4. Failing to be rightfully assertive when the occasion requires you to be

## Connect to your Card

Go horseback riding. Polish your trophies. Get good feedback. Celebrate with others.

## The Six of Wands Says

"Times are pretty good at the moment, and you have achieved success in what you set out to do. You have to be wary, however, of experiencing a sense of dissatisfaction after experiencing the heady heights of success."

## Keywords

Elevation, dignity, amusement, victory, leadership, good news, triumph, acclaim, vindication, self-assurance, pride, domesticity, desire, disloyalty, efficiency, apprehension.

# —Day 36: Justice—

*Accuracy • Meeting Your Measure*

## Resonances

*Numerology:* 11/2

*Astrology:* Libra

*Kabbalah:*
Geburah and Tiphareth

## Quick Connections

*Affirmation:* There is a reckoning to the world which abides with me at all times.

*Meditation:* "One man's justice is another man's woe."

## The Lesson of Justice

*Three-Card Spread (Do or Do Not)*

Today we will take three cards and place them into fixed positions for a three-card reading. This one we will fix into an unambiguous spread for a clear-cut question. Perform the reading with the knowledge you have gained from the last few weeks, and simply answer the question, "should the person do it or not?"

It's a yes/no question. Even if either option has more detail from the reading, decide yes or no. The question is "I have been offered a job overseas. Do the cards say I should go?"

Here's the three-card spread and the cards in each position:

- What I should do: Three of Wands
- Safe bet/middle path: Blasted Tower
- What I should **not** do: Four of Cups

Try to boil it down to a yes or a no—should the person go or not?

# The Card in Your Life/Reading

*Careerwise & Financially* this card indicates the need for accountability, particularly in terms of gaining contracts, judgements, and legal settlements. It is a card that shows justice will be given as fairly as possible, but to some extent the matter is out of your hands. The card suggests you present your case as clearly as possible so that justice may be served.

*Healthwise* this card indicates a balance and harmony will enter in your life. Though you may have to adjust, it will be easily done. There is a sense of balance and settlement to the situation in hand.

In *Relationships* this card indicates a fair measure of understanding between all involved. Each person is taking proper responsibility, and there is a need for objectivity and disclosure in order to see the matter is settled.

In *Travel & Lifestyle* this card indicates that whilst there may be trials ahead, all will be judged in your favour should you be open and honest in your travels and dealings. This card indicates the need to be transparent in your affairs to achieve a full settlement.

In *Education* this card indicates the need to be fair to yourself and your own abilities to make progress in your course. You should weigh what you are gaining in both the short and long term of your studies to assess whether you should continue in this way or not. This is also a card of testing and examination; it shows a fair assessment will be reached.

In *Spiritual Awareness & Self-Development* this card teaches us that equilibrium is at the heart of the universe when considered over time. All things have their balance and it is up to us to learn to see that balance and the scales of justice in all human activity. This requires us to transcend our own boundaries of space and time.

## *You are blocking this card today by:*

1. Not being judgemental
2. Giving a biased response to something which should be entirely objective
3. Being unfair and unreasonable without giving the issue at hand proper consideration
4. Letting your emotions entirely rule your decision making

## Connect to Your Card

Make a decision one way or another. Watch a courtroom drama. Learn about the law.

## Justice Says

"It is crucial to be objective in regard to decision making, we must not let these decisions be clouded by our own personal agenda. It is easy to fall into the trap of responding in a knee-jerk reaction to a problem that needs solving. It is advisable to take a step back and evaluate the situation at hand."

## Keywords

Fair play, law, reason, debate, deliberation, accuracy, judgement, balance, well-balanced mind, equilibrium, harmony, fairness, accountability, contract, settlement, integrity, justice, responsibility, decision, accuracy, karma, trial, honesty, arbitrator, adjustment, equity, rightness, balance, retribution, punishment, truth, objectivity, impartiality, equality.

# —Day 37: The Lovers—
## Choice and Blessings • Every Moment a Decision

### Resonances

*Numerology:* 6

*Astrology:* Gemini

*Kabbalah:*
Binah and Tiphareth

### Quick Connections

*Affirmation:* I relate to the world in joyful choice.

*Meditation:* "By putting the well-being of your other half first you do not become second but one with the whole."

## The Lesson of the Lovers
### *Three-Card Spread (Simple Soul Mate Spread)*

Moving on, today's exercise is a simple three-card reading about relationships. Now that we have started to look at the cards and different ways of looking at them, we will do a few spreads, with all the cards—even those we have not yet looked at specifically…

Today's spread is called the Simple Soul Mate Spread:

• Card 1: What half of me does the other person complete?

• Card 2: What will we create together?

• Card 3: What half of the other person do I complete?

I wonder about the connection between the Four of Wands celebration and the Three of Cups celebration. They are both celebratory, and it seems several cards celebrate life in some way or another—such as the Ten of Cups as the most obvious celebration of domestic bliss.

The Four of Wands seems to belong to a celebration of lifestyle, values being rewarded—or living up to one's ideals. In fact, this reminds us of the root of celebration, to be "numerous" or "thronged," well known and celebrated, from which we get of course "celebrity." A celebrity should be someone who has lived up to his or her values so clearly that the person is instantly recognised and respected—this is the potential in the Four of Wands I think of when it comes up. The card suggests there is an opportunity of celebrity (rather than a celebration in itself) by living up to one's values and being true to oneself.

I suspect that later, wands cards will show the struggles that being true to one's values can bring!

## The Card in Your Life/Reading

*Careerwise & Financially* this card indicates the difficulties of choice and cooperation. However, it is often a card that signifies success in our affairs and an unexpected blessing from above. If we have to partner with others, this is a card that denotes a mutually beneficial relationship. It can, however, signify temptation, in which case one's career and finances will suffer accordingly.

*Healthwise* this card indicates the need to commit to a long-term relationship with one's own body in order to achieve a healthy situation. There are difficult choices to be made, and the temptation will be to take the easier path. However, we should consider the long-term implications of any decision at this time and also trust opinions of those closest to us.

In *Relationships* this card is of course the most positive card to receive in relation to this topic. It shows the ideal situation of love where two people are in perfect harmony and union. There is perfect attraction, love, and beauty. The union is blessed from above.

In *Travel & Lifestyle* this card indicates that each choice you make will lead you down a different road, and it is important not to succumb to the temptation of the most immediate choice. There are dangers ahead, and you must carefully choose what you feel is the right thing deepest in your own heart.

In *Education* this card indicates positive inspiration leading to a new connection to your chosen subject which will open your relationship in unexpected ways. There may be choices to make as to how you move forwards in your studies; you should ensure you take the longest term view possible.

In *Spiritual Awareness & Self-Development* this card represents the alchemy of relationship to the world and to the divine. In a harmony of the inner and outer worlds, a true connection can be created which is divinely blessed.

*You are blocking this card today by:*

1. Putting yourself first in every way
2. Relating from the head alone, not the heart
3. Avoiding communicating your needs to a loved one
4. Not listening to the needs of those close to you

## Connect to Your Card

Be a lover, not a fighter. Do something romantic. Go someplace where you might meet someone special.

## The Lovers Says

"We are aligned with unity and cooperation. We are at one, and can embody love and life. There is a need to be open and transparent in our relationships; nothing should be held back, even if emotional expression exposes us to feelings of vulnerability."

## Keywords

Union, harmony of inner/outer, inspiration, sharing, duality, ordeal, temptation, decision, blessing, attraction, cooperation, trial, choice, harmony, love, beauty, completeness, commitment, relationships, marriage, friendship, reunion, integration, separation, polarity, passion, alchemy, sexuality, bond, contrast, antithesis, divorce.

# —Day 38: The Emperor—

*Power • The Application of Force*

## Resonances

*Numerology:* 4

*Astrology:* Aries

*Kabbalah:* Chockmah and Tiphareth

## Quick Connections

*Affirmation:* I am in command of my own intentions and embrace my will in the world.

*Meditation:* "To rule without the might of power is like a ship with no wind to sail by."

## The Lesson of the Emperor
*Eight-Card Spread (Dawn Spread)*

Today we will put our knowledge into a new daily practice called the Dawn Spread. It is the ideal spread for learning to put cards together from your own experience on a daily basis. Its design replicates the shape of the sun on the horizon.

In the morning, shuffle your full deck and lay out the cards in the shape of a sunrise on the horizon as follows:

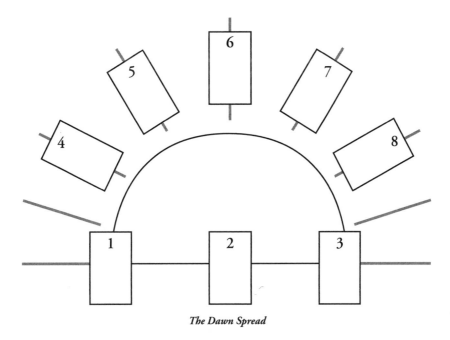

*The Dawn Spread*

You can see the positions:

1. Morning Influence
2. Afternoon Influence
3. Evening Influence
4. Friends & Colleagues
5. Finances & Rewards
6. Lesson of the Day (What to Observe and Learn)
7. How to Get the Best Day (Advice Card)
8. What to Avoid (Warning Card)

At the end of the day, review your day in your journal and compare it to the cards and what you originally interpreted in the morning. This way you will soon build up a feedback loop that creates a good "pre-telling" sense in your head. You'll know what the cards are likely to mean **at the end of the day in review** when you look at them in the morning! You'll be learning how to tell your fortune and install *a priori* intuition.

Today's card for our lesson is the Emperor. Let's have a quick look at the card in each of these eight positions, sort of like we only had a deck with that one card in it.

1. The morning will give you opportunity to get known as someone forceful.
2. The afternoon brings a strong current of which you can take advantage.
3. The evening requires that you have the right and appropriate responses at hand.
4. Your friends and colleagues will demand a lot of energy from you today.
5. There are impulse purchases and sudden decisions with regard to money ahead.
6. By the end of the day you will learn where it is best to apply yourself.
7. When in indecision today, always remember the Emperor would go for it.
8. Avoid getting into any dealings which require your energy.

## The Card in Your Life/Reading

*Careerwise & Financially* this card indicates energy and authority. You must take the initiative and drive your own ambitions forwards at this time. This is not a time to be shy or retiring—make bursts of energy happen. The trick with this card in career and finances is to put your best foot forward in as many different projects as possible until you find the one that meets your requirements.

*Healthwise* this card indicates both energy and structure. You must apply your energy to only those things that are under your control and authority. This may require you to withdraw from other activities which are under the rulership of others.

In *Relationships* this card indicates a passionate energy and drive that brings new levels of activity to the relationship. It can also signify domination by one person over another in a negative manner. If both partners are equally enthusiastic, this is an extremely positive and powerful card to receive a question of this kind.

In *Travel & Lifestyle* this card indicates an initial burst of energy and enthusiasm which may not be able to be sustained in the long term. It can signify leadership and taking charge of matters by bringing them under your own control. This is not a time to rely on other people to fulfill your ambitions.

In *Education* this card indicates status and structure. It is time to toe the line and fit within the established hierarchy in order to make progress. You must find your own position in the power structure and within the subject itself.

In *Spiritual Awareness & Self-Development* this card pictures the raw energy that creates the world in all its forms. This is the beating heart of the universe and the heart of every star. You are one of those stars. Your energy is boundless—the question is where are you going to direct that energy in your life?

*You are blocking this card today by:*

1. Not owning your power
2. Failing to delegate to those around you
3. Not being self-assured
4. Not being assertive

## Connect to Your Card

Take control and lead. Ask people to do something. Organise an event.

## The Emperor Says

"Exercise your authority and maintain your boundaries. Otherwise, you may find it difficult to maintain order and control. You must muster your drive and ambition, and always be the initiator of new ideas. Lead by example. Remember, you are the master of yourself first and foremost. If you cannot manage yourself, there is not much hope for managing difficult situations."

## Keywords

Rock solid, force, stubborn, endurance, authority, paternity, leadership, reason, self-mastery, martial arts, status, structure, society, regulation, domination, order, rulership, command power, stability, power, support, certainty, development, ambition, commanding, form.

# —Day 39: The Hermit—

### *Finding Yourself as Your Own Path • Becoming Your Own Lantern*

**Resonances**

*Numerology:* 9

*Astrology:* Virgo

*Kabbalah:* Chesed and Tiphareth

**Quick Connections**

*Affirmation:* I am guided by my own star, far from the voices of others.

*Meditation:* "You can be alone even in the company of others if you are lost to yourself. Withdraw and find the light within."

## The Lesson of the Hermit

### *Fourteen-Card Spread (Lucky Week Spread)*

As we expand our ability with the cards, for today's lesson we'd like to share a **new** method from an **old** book, *30 Different Ways of Card Fortune Telling* by Zodiastar. This book was originally published in 1936 and contains a wealth of methods for divination by using playing cards. We've taken inspiration from many of them and adapted them with a tarot twist to get even more information available from the spreads.

Here is one example of what we term in Tarosophy a **split spread**, in that it divides out parts of the deck for different parts of a reading/spread.

### *The Lucky Week Spread*

1. We use only the minor cards for this reading. Select out the minor cards (ace to ten of each suit) so you have all forty of them.

2. Take out the Nine of Cups (Nine of Hearts in the original method) and place it on the table. In effect, this acts as a significator for the reading.

3. Shuffle, cut (if you wish), and select out the top seven cards, placing them face-down in a semi-circle above the Nine of Cups.

4. Shuffle again, cut, and again select seven more cards, laying them on top of the cards already laid out, so you have seven pairs of cards.

5. Turn over each pair, either all together or a pair at a time, and read as follows. They stand for each day, so the first pair is the day following the reading, the next pair the next day, and so forth.

6. The rules are simple (in the original)—a pair of red cards is a good luck day, a pair of black cards is a bad luck day, and one of each red and black is a mixed day or neutral day.

7. That is to say, in tarot:
   - Wands = Diamonds = Red
   - Cups = Hearts = Red
   - Swords = Clubs = Black
   - Spades = Pentacles = Black

You can use your own correspondence system if you prefer. This is a typical one as used by A. E. Waite and others:

8. If you had the Seven of Wands and the Two of Cups, that would be a good luck day, whilst the Three of Swords and the Ten of Pentacles would signify a bad luck day. Having the Five of Cups and the Seven of Swords as a pair would be neutral.

9. Zodiastar advises us not to plan significant events on bad luck days, and plan our projects for the week around the foretold good luck days. Try it and see what happens!

10. For even better practice in our tarot, we can of course then read the pairs of cards as if in a normal reading, foretelling the nature of the good/bad luck (or the nature of a neutral day) and act to avoid the bad luck, mitigate it, or even repurpose it in some way, whilst making the best of the good luck.

# The Card in Your Life/Reading

*Careerwise & Financially* this card signifies your best option is to withdraw from others and find success in your own way. You may require privacy and seclusion in order to achieve the results you want all to see things clearly. This is also a card of coaching and mentoring as well as presenting your own vision to others so that they may follow your footsteps to success.

*Healthwise* this card shows that you must take time to meditate and contemplate on your own condition. You may wish to seek retreat to a place where you can have peace and quiet. This card shows that you must return to your own vision of health and lifestyle away from the opinions of others.

In *Relationships* this card indicates how important it is to remain true to yourself and walk in your own path. This card shows the relationship can succeed best if you share your vision with the other person and they agree to walk alongside you.

In *Travel & Lifestyle* this card indicates a powerful time when your own path will lead you to the places you need to be. This is a card of the inner quest and an important reminder that we can be self-sufficient and independent whilst still making our way in life.

In *Education* this card indicates the need to withdraw and protect yourself from the influences of others so you can remain open-minded to the learning available to you. This card signifies that you may know more than you think and your experience can guide you more clearly than you recognise. It is also a card that shows you can set an example to others by sharing your own light.

In *Spiritual Awareness & Self-Development* this card is a deep and profound symbol of how our own vision guides us on the path until we become the path itself. Staying true to our own values, we are led forwards by our quest for higher places in order to open the way for others. We must be assured that we be a good example.

*You are blocking this card today by:*

1. Being outgoing and leery
2. Being arrogant
3. Being tactless
4. Being very needy and possessive

## Connect to Your Card

Spend time by yourself. Go for a walk. Avoid invitations. Enjoy the peace and quiet. Stay silent.

## The Hermit Says

"Leave me alone. I need time away from the noise of the world to find answers. I cannot show you the way, your way is your own. It is for you to look within and find your own purpose in life."

## Keywords

Frugal, simplicity, shy, humble, solitude, wisdom, guidance, open-mindedness, contemplation, meditation, withdrawal, deliberation, study, patience, introspection, retreat, discretion, circumspection, isolation, quest, protection, prudence, loneliness, pilgrimage, searching, quiet, silence, privacy, detachment, acceptance, seclusion.

—Gate Six—

# The Ancient Coliseum

# Shadow Spread—For Facing Fears

*All light casts a shadow when something is placed in its path. You have journeyed far from the Mountain of the Sun and now come upon an ancient coliseum, a place of old battles, scarred with age. The ruins hold your memories and history and the ghosts of the past. It offers you a choice—dare you continue even if you will lose everything in the journey, or will you simply return to the Mountain of the Sun to forever bask in its beauty?*

## Soundtrack for the Journey
### "Understanding (Wash It All Away)" (Evanescence)

At this stage of the journey, you have learnt the most recent lessons of the cards of Justice, the Lovers, Emperor, and Hermit. The story of these cards might be considered as: aligning yourself to the cosmic scales, making the choice to take the path, claiming your own will, and living to your own standards. It is usually at this point in the journey that our fears and insecurities come to haunt us, and we must face them in order to proceed. It is also a crucial landmark in the spiritual journey because we can turn back at this point and return to the Mountain of the Sun. If you have experienced the energy of these gated spreads in your life so far, you may wish to consider whether you are ready to proceed—this gate is a trial.

Remove the Justice, Lovers, Emperor, and Hermit cards. Lay them in a row.

Leave a gap between each card for another card to be placed.

Take your significator card and place it to the left of this row.

Take the tens, nines, eights, sevens, and sixes. Shuffle this mini-deck of twenty cards.

Consider the question, **what do I now fear?**

Select out three cards and place the first between Justice and the Lovers, the second between the Lovers and the Emperor, and the third between the Emperor and the Hermit.

Over the coming week, consider how these cards represent your fears in the following ways:

*Card between Justice/Lovers:* Fear of making the right choices/Fear of being open.

*Card between Lovers/Emperor:* Fear of standing up for yourself/Fear of claiming your own power.

*Card between Emperor/Hermit:* Fear of others/Fear of self.

As you move through the week, move your significator along the row of cards as you believe you face, experience, or consider these fears in your life. Do not move the significator unless you truly understand the lesson of the cards. You may be surprised how observing these fears calls them into your life and gives you the opportunity to meet these trials and challenges.

When your significator has cleared the final pair of cards and is placed on the right side of the row, you have passed through the pillars and gates of the ancient coliseum and can move on, fortified by your ordeal.

You are now a tarot knight rather than a page—your progress continues!

# —Day 40: Knight of Pentacles—
*Proving Your Capability • Demonstrating Commitment*

## Resonances

*Numerology:* 67/4

*Astrology:*
Taurus/Capricorn

*Kabbalah:* Tiphareth
(Beauty)

*Elemental:* Air of Earth

*Perfume:* Asafoetida

*Timing:* Taurus
(April 21–May 21)

CAVALLO DI DENARI    KNIGHT OF PENTACLES
CHEVALIER DE DENIERS    CABALLO DE OROS

RITTER DER MUNZEN    MUNTEN RIDDER

## Quick Connections

*Affirmation:* Moving
patiently I pan for
the gold in every
moment of today.

*Meditation:* "Security
is jeopardised with the
weight of responsibility
and the fear of not being
able to maintain it."

## The Lesson of the Knight of Pentacles
*Four-Card Spread (Split Spread, Court Cards Only)*

In today's lesson, we look at a neat way of reading a situation with just court cards (much like the "All the World's a Stage" method we use elsewhere in this workbook).

Take the sixteen court cards and shuffle whilst thinking about a "dynamic situation" in your life, one which is currently undergoing a lot of basic change. As this is an "elemental" reading, the more earthy, fiery, airy, or watery the situation is—the better!

Take the deck and lay out four cards in a cross in any fashion, knowing each position is an element as follows:

1. Earth
2. Water
3. Air
4. Fire

Now look at the balance and mix of elements between the cards (as below) and their positions:
- Pentacles: Earth
- Cups: Water
- Swords: Air
- Wands: Fire

So for example, if we lay out the four court cards we have covered so far in our lessons, we would get:
- Earth: Knight of Wands (Fire)
- Water: King of Swords (Air)
- Air: Page of Wands (Fire)
- Fire: Queen of Wands (Fire)

Now we can interpret the dynamics (or dignities) of those combinations—or read intuitively what this mixture might mean—is it cement or dynamite?! We can see in the reading we have above, that it's all on fire, other than the Water, which is being "cooled" by the King of Swords (Air).

If we'd asked a question about a relationship going through lots of uncertain change, these cards in those positions above might be interpreted as too much male energy, the situation is way too "driven" and the King of Swords is "too much in his head" with the emotional aspects of the relationship.

We can also look at the levels of energy (such as the queen being the most "enduring") and see where they feature, to figure out where the stability can be gained, for example. Perhaps we can look at a page in a reading and see where a "spark" might be found in an otherwise dull situation, etc.

## The Card in Your Life/Reading

*Careerwise & Financially* this card indicates steady progress and gradual gain in your affairs. So long as you adopt a slow and serious approach to your work, you will see rewards. You may be tempted to rush into things; this is not advised at this time.

*Healthwise* this card indicates a solid basis from which to make a recovery or improve your health. It indicates the importance of attention to detail and sticking to a long-term plan. Even if you cannot see the way ahead, do whatever is at hand with all the energy you can muster at the moment.

In *Relationships* this card indicates a very practical outlook and a solid basis from which to build the relationship. You may have to be more patient than you feel and wait for the other person to fully open themselves to you. Their approach may sometimes annoy you, yet they complete a part of you that is lacking.

In *Travel & Lifestyle* this card indicates a good plan executed seriously and persistently. It is important at all times that you stick to the plan and make steady progress. Whilst your ambitions may not be immediately realised and life is not as exciting as you thought, you are building something for the future.

In *Education* this card indicates good solid work that will be rewarded in the future. You will be proven capable and trustworthy and as such be given further responsibilities. There is a slight warning to pay attention to details and ensure you present yourself as fully as possible.

In *Spiritual Awareness & Self-Development* this card indicates the energy of the alchemical process of calcination—a slow, steadily burning fire. It is this fire of energised enthusiasm that must be maintained for a long period of time in order to cause the changes desired.

*You are blocking this card today by:*

1. Being disorganised, not thinking things through
2. Behaving in an irresponsible way
3. Behaving in a rash manner
4. Giving up partway through an important task

## Connect to Your Card

Ensure something gets finished today. Check over something with detail. Collect money.

## The Knight of Pentacles Says

"I am reliable and dependable, and you could certainly rely on me in a practical emergency. My shortcomings are that in affairs of the heart I only go the extra mile…if it is in the opposite direction; I am quite commitment phobic!"

# Keywords

Insurance, loyalty, capability, methodical, trustworthiness, laborious, steady progress, industry, diligence, seriousness, duty, practicality, patient, trustworthy, utility, responsibility, responsible, hardworking, persistent, realistic.

# —Day 41: Knight of Swords—
### *Proving Your Agility • Demonstrating Responsiveness*

## Resonances

*Numerology:* 53/8

*Astrology:*
Aquarius/ Libra

*Kabbalah:*
Tiphareth (Beauty)

*Elemental:* Air of Air

*Perfume:* Galbanum

*Timing:* Aquarius
(January 21–February 18)

## Quick Connections

*Affirmation:* Moving swiftly I cut through all hindrance with speed.

*Meditation:* "You think a little and unwisely speak too much, so think more wisely and say little."

## The Lesson of the Knight of Swords

Today we meet the Knight of Swords. We also thought we would share a little tip about court cards from our experiences. Sometimes people have difficulties knowing whether to interpret a court card as a person, influence, aspect of a project, timing, etc. In fact there are at least eleven ways of interpreting a court card.

Here's a simple rule: because the court cards embody four levels of energy in four worlds, how they manifest can be determined in practice by how many cards there are in a (for example) ten-card reading:

- If there is only one court card, it is likely referring to a person
- If there are two or three court cards, they are likely referring to aspects of the situation
- If there are four or more court cards, they are likely referring to parts of the querent

So if the Knight of Swords is the only court card in an eight-to-fifteen-card spread, I would read it as a person, someone who has this Knight's qualities in his or her personality. If he was one of two or three court cards, I would read it as "the situation requires a new energy of forward-thinking and impetus." If the reading was awash with four or more court cards, I would describe this Knight's appearance as a part of the querent which is intellectual and on which he or she must draw.

Looking back through the court cards we have covered thus far with this in mind, you will see that it is fairly easy to read all  court cards; they provide essential "energy spots" within any spread.

Let's say we read the Knight of Swords in the future position, the Knight of Pentacles from yesterday in the past position of that same spread, and these were the only two court cards. How would you read them if the question is "How do I break out of my current situation at home?"

## The Card in Your Life/Reading

*Careerwise & Financially* this card indicates an urgency to skillfully press your case and pursue your goal. This card shows that you must throw yourself into battle and consider the consequences later. You may feel as if you are burning bridges; however, this card shows success will come from jumping into things immediately. The trick is having the energy to make rapid progress and to keep accelerating from a standing start.

*Healthwise* this card indicates a requirement for stimulation and excitement in your activities. It is time to shake off the cobwebs and make rapid changes in your life. This is a card that shows you must be more impetuous and spontaneous. It can suggest you will need courage to face the challenges ahead but have the resources to do so.

In *Relationships* this card indicates a lively situation, particularly if one is pursuing another. Whilst it can be very exciting, you are cautioned that the chase may be more thrilling than the catch. It can also indicate arguments or disagreements ahead, so be sure you know the lay of the land before being caught in such discussions.

In *Travel & Lifestyle* this card indicates a likely acceleration of your plans and sudden forward movement. You will be given a new impetus and should seize the moment, taking advantage of the new current in your life. This is not the time to hesitate!

In *Education* this card indicates skill and intellectual stimulation. This is the perfect card for all students and indicates success in the learning ahead. If you are waiting for news of a course, this card is very positive. It also shows the importance of throwing yourself entirely into your studies.

In *Spiritual Awareness & Self-Development* this card indicates the power of the mind to cut through the realms of illusion by clear thinking. There is a place for active thought, and this card symbolises that such mental effort must be used at this time. It is time to think clearly rather than trust to your intuition or heart.

*You are blocking this card today by:*

1. Being a total wimp/pushover
2. Being clumsy
3. Behaving like a total fool
4. Being slow to respond to verbal attacks

## Connect to Your Card

Debate or discuss something. Sign a petition or set one up. Make a statement.

## The Knight of Swords Says

"Always be alert and ready to defend yourself against those who disagree with you. Never take things at face value, always check out a situation well, and when you do make a move, do it swiftly. Take no prisoners. Be direct and speak your mind."

## Keywords

Rash, deft, responsiveness, engaged, pursuit, strong, brave, courage, skill, cleverness, impulse, assertiveness, rapidity, stimulation, active, clever, subtle, enmity, wrath, fierce, pushing, antagonistic, ready for a fight, skillfulness, avenging, defence, self–assured, assertive, incisive, impetuous, indiscreet, impatient, tactless, brusque, intellectual.

# —Day 42: Knight of Cups—
## *Proving Your Depth • Demonstrating Creativity*

### Resonances

*Numerology:* 39/3

*Astrology:*
Scorpio/Pisces

*Kabbalah:*
Tiphareth (Beauty)

*Elemental:* Air of Water

*Perfume:* Camphor

*Timing:* Scorpio (October
24–November 22)

CAVALLO DI COPPE    KNIGHT OF CHALICES
CHEVALIER DE COUPES    CABALLO DE COPAS

RITTER DER KELCHE    BEKERS RIDDER

### Quick Connections

*Affirmation:* Moving
gently, I hold true to
my heart.

*Meditation:* "Quick to
anger, quick to love, quick
to leave when the going
gets tough."

## The Lesson of the Knight of Cups
### *Getting to Know the Court a Little More*

We find ourselves today with the Knight of Cups. When this signifies a person, it will be someone on a quest to fulfill his or her emotional desires. Though they are passionate, they can sometimes be self-absorbed. When this refers to a situation (see guidance in previous lessons), it can indicate that we have got lost in the emotional content of the event and may not be seeing it clearly.

So, idealistic dreamer or narcissistic seducer?

Crowley certainly captures the negative qualities of this character; I agree with Lon Milo DuQuette that Crowley must have had a bad experience with someone similar, although I also think that he may have been projecting his own qualities… "the moral characteristics of the person pictured in this card are subtlety, secret violence, and craft. He is intensely secret, an artist in all his ways. He is thus completely without conscience in the ordinary sense of the word, and is therefore usually distrusted by his neighbours. They feel they do not, and can never, understand him …Thus he inspires unreasonable fear. He is in fact perfectly ruthless. He cares intensely for power, wisdom, and his own aims. He feels no responsibility to others, and although his abilities are so immense, he cannot be relied upon to work in harness." (Crowley, *The Book of Thoth*. Weiser, 1985.)

That actually sounds a lot like Crowley himself, to me! It may be interesting to go through your favourite tarot book and work out if there is a particular court card the author does not like themselves!

On another level, it is interesting this card in the WST really shows the Knight with the Grail, because authors such as Mary K. Greer suggest that A. E. Waite put a lot of the "Grail Myth" into this tarot deck. What other cards might suggest elements from the romances and tales of Arthur?

## The Card in Your Life/Reading

*Careerwise & Financially* this card indicates a proposition that whilst attractive will also require careful thought and a realistic attitude before acceptance. It can indicate progress in the arts and other creative fields. Though this card is not entirely positive for finances, it does indicate you can find contentment in your present situation.

*Healthwise* this card might be taken to symbolise dependency on influences outside your own body. As the search you might interpret this card as telling you that you have the power of healing within as well as without.

In *Relationships* this card indicates seduction and romance—an entirely heady blend. The Knight of Cups brings a welcome tide of emotion into your life and opens up deep feelings. You should advance positively in the fulfilling of your desires at this time.

In *Travel & Lifestyle* this card indicates a search for new experience that is emotionally gratifying. It is also an openness to new suggestions and opportunities no matter how fanciful they may at first appear. However, one is cautioned to avoid complete self-satisfaction at the expense of others.

In *Education* this card indicates refinement, art, and idealism. It might also symbolise the need for you to present your work with more depth and feeling. The Knight of Cups also symbolises an emotional connection to your studies that might be presently lacking. When this card appears, you should consider what first attracted you to your present course of study.

In *Spiritual Awareness & Self-Development* this card shows how we must take our inner feelings as a calling and a quest. It is the card of the Grail Knight who has embarked on a journey. This will lead to adventure and new experiences, as is the case when we follow our true vision.

*You are blocking this card today by:*

1. Being sensible and not letting your heart rule your head
2. Showing your affections for your loved one by shopping, cleaning, and making dinner
3. Looking beyond the superficial
4. Spending some time working in the garden

## Connect to Your Card

Do something unusual for you. Write a love letter. Go the extra mile to make someone smile.

## The Knight of Cups Says

"Do not hold back with your emotions. If you feel strongly about someone or something in your life, do something about it—express your love, hate, and frustrations. 'Get outside what is inside of you.'"

## Keywords

Extravagant, passionate, spontaneous, flighty, exhibition, romantic dreamer, dancer, proposal, seduction, new experience, narcissism, idealistic, idealisation, temperamental, romantic, fanciful, refined, dreams, art, love, approach, lover, rival, seducer, message, offering, proposition, advance, vision, occultism, desire, short, intoxicants.

# —Day 43: Knight of Wands—

*Proving your Passion • Demonstrating Vision*

## Resonances

*Numerology:* 25/7

*Astrology:*
Leo/Sagittarius

*Kabbalah:*
Tiphareth (Beauty)

*Elemental:* Air of Fire

*Perfume:* Lign Aloes

*Timing:* Leo
(July 23–August 23)

CAVALLO DI BASTONI    KNIGHT OF WANDS
CHEVALIER DE BATONS    CABALLO DE BASTOS

RITTER DER STÄBE    STAVEN RIDDER

## Quick Connections

*Affirmation:* Moving
energetically, I draw the
powers of the whole world
to my cause.

*Meditation:* "Great flair
comes from the flames of
enthusiasm, and without
it, you may be the first to
be fired!"

## The Lesson of the Knight of Wands
### Using the Correspondences

We'd like to introduce here the elemental correspondences as well as correspondences in general. When something corresponds to something else, that thing becomes illuminated between the two systems. Thus, if you know the human body—that you have to eat, that some foods are better than others, and that regular eating is essential—you can learn about a vehicle.

In a correspondence between a body and a vehicle, the stomach is the fuel tank. The food is the fuel, and then we can ask, well, what does the exhaust pipe on the vehicle correspond to in the human body…? No answers necessary—this is an imagination exercise only! This is the idea of correspondence. We can make correspondence (how we learn, for example, that the word "dog" corresponds to some things and not others) on an arbitrary system, such as language, or a "likeness" system such as corresponding sunflowers to the sun, because they look like the sun.

In our systems, the Knight of Swords corresponds to the Airy part of Fire. He is the Air of Fire. Crowley also makes a correspondence between this card and the I-Ching, where the Hexagram of the Air of Fire is *Yi*, Hexagram 42. This signifies in that system "with sincere heart seeking to benefit all below" (from Legge's translation). Can we see how the Knight of Swords is someone or symbolic of the energy of "benefitting all below"?

## The Card in Your Life/Reading

*Careerwise & Financially* this card indicates the fiery pursuit of our own ambitions and sudden advancement. It is a card showing rapid breakthrough of any current situation. However, the choice is still yours and you must release the energy to make this progress. Do not hold on to anything that is not serving your purpose.

*Healthwise* this card indicates an energetic fight to secure your health. The burning passion of the Knight of wands is a positive symbol of the struggle to gain the ideal health situation. Sometimes it may indicate the need to take matters into your own hands for a time. It may also be the other people need prompting and reminding of your needs.

In *Relationships* this card indicates passion and adventure. It is always an indicator of new excitement in your life which will fulfill your vision. However, you must be careful that this passion does not burn out too soon lest you become entirely consumed by it.

In *Travel & Lifestyle* this card indicates travel, pilgrimage, and adventure. It is a positive and energetic card for all travel-and-lifestyle-related questions. The only caution is that you do not burn yourself out too quickly.

In *Education* this card indicates the passion for the subject which must be present, particularly at the beginning of any course of study. If you are applying for a course, then it symbolises the energy which you must show and enthusiasm required in order to gain entry. In education questions this card also shows that you must stand your ground and in fact make a proactive attack if you are opposed by others.

In *Spiritual Awareness & Self-Development* this card is the card of the pilgrim who follows their ambition and drive in a creative manner. It symbolises the need to bring your enthusiasm to mundane matters powered by a spiritual sensibility. It also shows the power and energy of those who live their life according to their own values and steer their course by following their passion.

*You are blocking this card today by:*

1. Being slow to anger
2. Being laid back
3. Being tolerant
4. Not taking any risks

## Connect to Your Card

Get a move on. Speed the process up. Don't hold back.

## The Knight of Wands Says

"You need me to get things started; I am the one who as all the good ideas and enthusiasm. However, I have to be in charge and everyone has to know it! I have a tendency to get carried away with myself and lose interest towards the end. I am not much of a team player; I tend to be self-employed."

## Keywords

Fiery, brash, argumentative, hot-headed, advancement, sudden, impetuous, hasty, journey, coming and going, departure from custom, challenge, enthusiasm, vigour, impetuous, daring, impatient, passionate, impulsiveness, pride, traveller, fighter, protection, pilgrim, charming, adventurous, hot-tempered, cocky, daring.

### WAYSIDE LESSON: THE DECANS

We will later see how we can use astrology and tarot correspondences to deepen our readings and also work with the enigmatic and powerful Sabian Symbols, an astrological oracle which was clairvoyantly received by Elsie Wheeler for Marc Edmund Jones in 1925. In our brief wayside lesson here, we will provide a list of the decans, tarot cards, and another set of esoteric Keywords (in the form of card titles) for the minor cards, twos through tens.

The Decans are the thirty-six divisions of ten-degree increments of the 360 degrees of the zodiacal circle. The twelve signs of the zodiac are then placed over these divisions, resulting in each sign spanning three decans. Thus, Aries covers decans 1,

2, and 3 (called Aries I, II, and III); Taurus follows with decans 4, 5, 6 (called Taurus I, II, and III); and so on.

The thirty-six decans are then corresponded to the thirty-six tarot cards of each suit, two to ten. The aces, court cards, and major cards are not included (as this would mean more than thirty-six cards for one thing), as they have separate elemental, planetary, and zodiacal correspondences elsewhere in the system.

Devised by the Golden Dawn and used by its students (including Crowley), this system is an established method of making correspondence between astrology and tarot. In the table below you will see a list of the decans, the corresponding minor card, and its title given by the Golden Dawn.

*Spring Equinox* **Planet**
**MARS**

| Decan | Minor Card | Golden Dawn Title |
|---|---|---|
| Aries I | 2 of Wands | Dominion |
| Aries II | 3 of Wands | Established Strength |
| Aries III | 4 of Wands | Perfected Work |
| Taurus I | 5 of Pentacles | Material Trouble |
| Taurus II | 6 of Pentacles | Material Success |
| Taurus III | 7 of Pentacles | Success Unfulfilled |
| Gemini I | 8 of Swords | Shortened Force |
| Gemini II | 9 of Swords | Despair and Cruelty |
| Gemini III | 10 of Swords | Ruin |
| Cancer I | 2 of Cups | Love |
| Cancer II | 3 of Cups | Abundance |
| Cancer III | 4 of Cups | Blended Pleasure |
| Leo I | 5 of Wands | Strife |
| Leo II | 6 of Wands | Victory |
| Leo III | 7 of Wands | Valour |
| Virgo I | 8 of Pentacles | Prudence |
| Virgo II | 9 of Pentacles | Material Gain |
| Virgo III | 10 of Pentacles | Wealth |
| Libra I | 2 of Swords | Peace Restored |
| Libra II | 3 of Swords | Sorrow |

*Toth Deck*

| Libra III | 4 of Swords | Rest from Strife |
| Scorpio I | 5 of Cups | Loss in Pleasure |
| Scorpio II | 6 of Cups | Pleasure |
| Scorpio III | 7 of Cups | Illusionary Success |
| Sagittarius I | 8 of Wands | Swiftness |
| Sagittarius II | 9 of Wands | Great Strength |
| Sagittarius III | 10 of Wands | Oppression |
| Capricorn I | 2 of Pentacles | Harmonious Change |
| Capricorn II | 3 of Pentacles | Material Works |
| Capricorn III | 4 of Pentacles | Earthly Power |
| Aquarius I | 5 of Swords | Defeat |
| Aquarius II | 6 of Swords | Earned Success |
| Aquarius III | 7 of Swords | Unstable Effort |
| Pisces I | 8 of Cups | Abandoned Success |
| Pisces II | 9 of Cups | Material Happiness |
| Pisces III | 10 of Cups | Perfected Success |

—Gate Seven—

# The Chasm
# of Night

# Abyss Spread—For Letting Go

*The Knights of the Tarot Realm have brought you beyond the Coliseum; you have successfully faced your fear. They have judged you worthy and led you to the fabled Chasm of Night, a dark passage into the unknown. Only you can venture into its shadowy realm, and what you will discover there no one can know. It is time to test your faith as never before.*

Knight of Swords

## Soundtrack for the Journey
### *"Mercy Street" (Peter Gabriel)*

Take your significator card and write in your journal all you have learnt in your journey as the page. Consider progress you have made in engaging tarot in your life, and perhaps you can consider how it may assist your readings in future.

Now decide on one thing that you can let go of in your life. It could be a bad habit, a way of looking at things, or something personal or purchased.

Remove the knight card of the same suit as your significator page card. For example, if you have been the Page of Pentacles so far, you should now remove the Knight of Pentacles. Place these two cards next to each other. In the coming week, make an action that releases something as a result of all you have learnt. When you have done so, you may replace the page in the deck and claim the knight as your significator from this moment onwards.

Whilst this gate may seem easier in comparison to those before, do not be lulled by its simplicity. There may be powerful currents at work attached to whatever you choose to release, and the passage between the page and the knight is a true chasm that requires much energy to cross. Whilst the pages are *channelers*, the knights are *responders*—they take responsibilities on board.

This is the final test, the big leap across the abyss.

# —Day 44: Five of Pentacles—

*Finding Yourself Outside • A Place of Loss*

## Resonances

*Numerology:* 73/1

*Astrology:*
Mercury in Taurus

*Kabbalah:*
Geburah (Strength)

*Sabian Symbol:*
Taurus I—A Clear
Mountain Stream
(Natural Inclination)

## Quick Connections

*Affirmation:* When I look beyond my own needs, I am empowered to make the world richer.

*Meditation:* "Poverty consciousness breeds more poverty; if you do not believe you are worth something and invest in yourself, you will always be lacking."

## The Lesson of the Five of Pentacles

*The Big Bad Boss Spread, for Matters of Career and Promotion*

This spread to practice today is for questions such as "Will I get that promotion?" and "How do I progress my career?"

The Big Bad Boss Spread works in a totally fixed and hierarchical fashion to replicate the conditions found in most workplaces and career paths. It should be used in conjunction with career guidance books such as the *What Color is Your Parachute?* series.

This spread is an example of the innovative "split spreads" found in *Tarosophy* requiring you in this case to split out the deck into court cards, majors, and minors—three stacks.

Remove the court cards from the deck and select three cards: one for you, one for your current boss (or supervisor, or other person who has influence over you), and one for your desired position.

These are cards one, two, and three below:

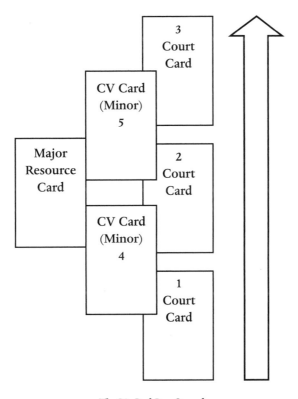

*The Big Bad Boss Spread*

Take the minor cards out of the deck, shuffle them, and lay two cards between the three court cards. These are your "CV (résumé) Cards"; they indicate how you might progress from one position to the next. You can also add a major arcana card to the spread to divine what resources you can draw upon to make that step.

## The Card in Your Life/Reading

*Careerwise & Financially* this card indicates a loss of income and a halt or postponement of your plans. Sometimes this card can show that you have deferred income in pursuit of education or other projects such as charity. This card also symbolises a feeling of disassociation from others in your immediate environment. You might also consider asking for assistance from those who have the resources to grant it.

*Healthwise* this card indicates a sense of worry and hardship with regard to your present condition. You should not avoid seeking assistance or additional resources even if you feel this would not be helpful. In more simplistic terms this card can show that you need to come in from the cold and ensure your comfort is your primary concern.

In *Relationships* this card indicates a difficult situation which may make or break the relationship. In times of hardship, you have a choice to work together or separate. Whilst this can prove a difficult card, it can also bring people closer together.

In *Travel & Lifestyle* this card indicates a lack of resources in order to ensure comfort during this time. You may also miss out on opportunities due to financial issues or lacking the required invitation to attend important events. This is not a positive card to receive in questions of travel and lifestyle, although because it is a five card (that is, halfway to ten) the situation will eventually be overcome.

In *Education* this card indicates the need to put immediate reward to one side whilst pursuing your course of studies. You may have to accept temporary hardship in order to accomplish the task you have set yourself. You will learn far more than you think whilst being outside the usual comfort zone others may appear to be in. If you are engaged in research, this card symbolises the need to be out in the field.

In *Spiritual Awareness & Self-Development* this card shows the insecurity that can come from rejecting mainstream concerns. Whilst you may feel disassociated from the bulk of society, it may be that your contribution is far more valuable than you realise at the present time. Your reward will not be the same as others, and yet it will come.

*You are blocking this card today by:*

1. Speculating to accumulate
2. Volunteering for charity work
3. Being positive
4. Accepting your situation and doing something about it

## Connect to Your Card

Do something outside your comfort zone today. Embrace the uncomfortable. Decline reward.

## The Five of Pentacles Says

"I speak for the displaced, those trying to find a new life, and security. You are halfway there. We have to venture forth into a world that at times seems unwelcoming; we look around and we see so many people that have what we do not. The bright lights of success beckon us, and we feel dissatisfied with where we are at the moment. We have to experience this to strive for a better life, to set off on that hard road of ambition."

## Keywords

Outsiders, adrift, loss, deferred income, destitution, loneliness, improvising, unemployment, lack of hardship, material trouble, loss, ruin, adaption, worry, loss of profession, redundancy, monetary anxiety, insecurity, lack, rejection, hardship.

# —Day 45: Five of Swords—
*Expecting Argument • An Examination of Defeat*

### Resonances

*Numerology:* 59/5

*Astrology:*
Venus in Aquarius

*Kabbalah:*
Geburah (Strength)

*Sabian Symbol:*
Aquarius I—An Old
Adobe Mission (The
Persistence of Faith)

### Quick Connections

*Affirmation:* I am capable
of holding my own speech
when others attempt to
provoke me.

*Meditation:* "If we tasted
our words, we would say
less and eat more."

## The Lesson of the Five of Swords
### *The Discover Your Demon Spread, for Matters of Affliction*

This spread and method works with such questions such as "Why do I always do that?," "Why are things so negative?," and so forth. Here, we will repurpose the nature of an exorcism to draw a demon out from hiding within a situation. In this case, the demon is an attachment, an old pattern, a self-destructive streak, or some other negative recurrent event. Whilst tarot reading does not substitute for counselling or psychotherapy per se, it is a means of examining a personal situation or behaviour with intent resulting in insight.

Consider the nature of the affliction, and lay out the first four cards precisely in order in the shape of a cross as follows. These first four cards indicate:

1. The fear that is at work in this situation. The nature of what you are trying to avoid by playing out your pattern or what this pattern of events means in your life.

2. The advice that can resolve (or even absolve) this situation, which you are perhaps not yet ready to hear or act upon because you do not have the resources.

3. The resources or approach you can take to change this situation.

4. The actual first step of exorcising this behaviour or pattern of events from your life.

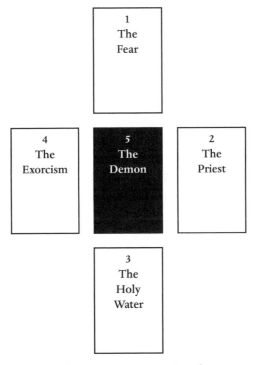

*The Discover Your Demon Spread*

When you have considered these first four cards, take the rest of the deck and begin to shuffle them as violently as possible, contemplating the cross of cards below you. When you feel ready, say in a loud voice, "DEMON BE GONE!" Turn the cards face-down in the centre of the cross.

Pause for a moment and then turn the deck face-up and look into the eyes of your old demon, now ready to be driven out.

# The Card in Your Life/Reading

*Careerwise & Financially* this card indicates trouble and deceit. Whilst it appears to be one of the most negative cards to receive for a financial or career question, it at least signifies the putting away of old battles. You may take this card as a symbol to rest and gracefully accept defeat in order to recoup for later battles.

*Healthwise* this card indicates the need to accept your situation and to put away any dispute which may be harming you far more than you realise. You may have to walk away from a troublesome situation in order to preserve your own health.

In *Relationships* this card indicates the need to lay down one's arms and put to rest the quarrels of the past. There is no profit at this time in repeating old arguments. You might also consider that other people's opinions (even those of the past such as your parents) may still be influencing current conversations. There is more going on in these words than meets the eye.

In *Travel & Lifestyle* this card indicates the likely sabotage of your plans by people or situations outside of your current control. It is best to have a plan B on hand in order to elegantly meet these inevitable problems. If you are currently experiencing difficulties, you should disengage from the situation as fast as possible in order to cut your losses.

In *Education* this card indicates the need to move away from futile argument which will only lead to your humiliation or defeat. It may be that others are already turning away from your position or laying a trap, so you must avoid walking into it.

In *Spiritual Awareness & Self-Development* this card symbolises the need to remain uninvolved in the arguments of others. No matter the attraction, we become what we surround ourselves with; if we stoop to other people's levels, we lower ourselves. There is no benefit to engaging with the others at this time, regardless of how much they may try to provoke us.

*You are blocking this card today by:*

1. Not opening channels of communication
2. Not brokering a peaceful outcome if you have had a falling out with someone
3. Not apologizing
4. Not watching what you say to others

## Connect to Your Card

Let bygones be bygones. Immediately forgive anyone today. See the best in everyone.

## The Five of Swords Says

"Victory is a short-lived state. We may win and we may lose, but always there is another battle to fight. There is never a resolution to conflict as long as we put too much emphasis on being defensive. Take care not to become paranoid and see treachery where it is not."

## Keywords

Uncertainty, debriefing, rebellion, defeat, failure, degradation, cowardliness, malice, humiliation, gloating, dispute, sabotage, overthrow, loss, failure, slander, treachery, malice, affliction, mourning, trouble, enemy triumphs at the moment one fancies victory is secured, infamy, conquest, accepting defeat, surrender.

# —Day 46: Five of Cups—
## Imagining What Might Have Been • The Creation of Guilt

### Resonances

*Numerology:* 45/9

*Astrology:*
Mars in Scorpio

*Kabbalah:*
Geburah (Strength)

*Sabian Symbol:* Scorpio I
—A Sightseeing Bus
(Look and See)

### Quick Connections

*Affirmation:* Drawing myself together, I will take courage for the journey ahead.

*Meditation:* "A need to take time to reassemble thoughts/ambitions after failing to achieve success in a battle; maybe there was no belief in the cause."

## The Lesson of the Five of Cups
### More Kabbalistic Correspondences

Well, we have today a card of loss, the Five of Cups. In the WST this shows a figure robed in black looking down at three spilt cups, whilst behind them are two upright cups.

The fives of tarot are difficult, as they correspond in Kabbalah to the fifth Sephirah of Geburah, constraint and structure. In fact, Geburah is sometimes called *Pachad* ("fear"). If you think about it, whilst numerically the fives are halfway between one and ten, it seems they should be wonderful cards of balance and equilibrium. Actually, they are quite difficult. This is partly because when the ten Sephiroth are drawn on the Tree of Life diagram, it is the sixth Sephirah, Tiphareth ("beauty"), which is in the middle. As Waite and Colman Smith were immersed in that system of correspondences, it is no surprise that the sixes are more beneficial than the fives.

The question for today with this card is that whilst this card signfies loss, despair, sadness, etc., it might also be taken to be more specifically representing the emotion of shame or guilt.

Now, if guilt is a feeling of remorse about something you have done, experienced, or thought from your own perspective (often instilled from parental values, even if it is your own feeling), and shame is a feeling of remorse but from our introjection of other people's perspectives ("How could I, What would my family/colleagues/friends/society think?") ... is this card a card of guilt or shame?

And if both, how would we know from other cards which one specifically this card was showing?

Hopefully this is an interesting line of enquiry on this card, and then tomorrow we are going to draw our last days together on this course with a nice spread to start practising our learning.

## The Card in Your Life/Reading

*Careerwise & Financially* this card indicates partial loss and regret. Some readings of this card show it entirely negatively with regard to domestic and financial situations. However, it is only our own bitterness or disillusionment that brings negativity into our circumstances. It is how we respond to circumstances that makes us and in this card we can see that there are still options available if we can learn to turn our back on past mistakes.

*Healthwise* this card indicates sorrow over our present state. There appears to be much waste in our life and many missed opportunities in the past. This story is not yet over, however, and many other opportunities still exist. This card shows the importance of making continual forward movement and looking to the future no matter how difficult that may feel.

In *Relationships* this card indicates a crisis that comes from the mistakes of the past polluting the moments of the present. You should ensure that you are seeing the present moment for what it is rather than basing it on your previous experiences.

In *Travel & Lifestyle* this card indicates wasted opportunities to fully experience your life or your journeys. There are still options available to you even if they appear to be less rewarding than those you have squandered. It is still your choice to take up what is left to you—or become trapped in the regrets of the past.

In *Education* this card indicates a feeling of discontentment and disillusionment that your studies are not as fulfilling as you imagined. It can also show that you have wasted time and now have limited options available to you. Of course it is up to you to take these options and continue your journey.

In *Spiritual Awareness & Self-Development* this card shows how we may easily be caught up in creating our own future from our obsession with our past mistakes. The river under the bridge passes quickly and is never the same water—our future can still be what we wish it to be.

*You are blocking this card today by:*

1. Being accepting
2. Being happy with what you have now, rather than what may have been
3. Not dwelling on misfortune
4. Taking action to change your life for the better

## Connect to Your Card

Allow any unhappiness to pass by quickly. Don't hold on to anything today. Let the day pass.

## The Five of Cups Says

"It is an inevitable part of attachment, that if it is taken away we will feel a strong sense of loss. We may feel that we have made the wrong decisions in life and we have now found ourselves somewhere we never intended. This conjures up a sense of regret and frustration."

## Keywords

Desolation, over-consideration, fretting, emotional loss, denial, guilt, break-up, bitterness, disillusionment, regret, brooding, crisis, punishment, divorce, miscarriage, loss, disappointment, sorrow, melancholy, union, surprise, patrimony.

# —Day 47: Five of Wands—
*Working Towards Connection • The Expression of Society*

## Resonances

*Numerology:* 31/4

*Astrology:*
Saturn in Leo

*Kabbalah:*
Geburah (Strength)

*Sabian Symbol:* Leo I—
A Case of Apoplexy
(Being Fit to Burst)

## Quick Connections

*Affirmation:* In every confusion there will be a moment for me to bring order.

*Meditation:* "Frantic behaviour without self-control and patience only leads to chaos and delay; rule yourself or be ruled over."

## The Lesson of the Five of Wands
### Listening to the Cards

Today's card is the Five of Wands. As a five, it is another "in-between" card. It should be noted today also that although five is in the middle of one and ten, when drawn as the Tree of Life (on which the WST and other decks are based), the six is the middle (Tiphareth); the five is actually the stage before that balance or middle is attained. Hence the number's rather push/shove nature.

The five in the world of wands is the conflict of interests (five = conflict, wands = values), lack of a plan, competition in vision, etc. It is a card of struggle, confusion, and disruption, and generally not one you want in any situation! On the plus side, this card denotes the possibility of coming together if there were a concerted effort—at least everyone in the Five of Wands is active and involved!

For today's exercise, we'll introduce "talking cards." Find the Five of Wands and imagine a speech bubble above every character's head (in the WST, for different decks, this should work too, even if you have speech bubbles above some inanimate objects—they all have something to say) and fill them in. What are they saying to each other?

Here's mine, reading from the characters left to right in the card, giving them names:

- Jon: Look! This is the one we need! It's the special one!
- Tim: Now I reckon if I took another five centimetres off this, it'd do just right.
- Fred: I am sick and tired of holding this on my shoulder. Someone make your mind up.
- Phil (at front): If anyone's interested, this one might work.
- Dave (at back): Everyone else's looks far better.

Hmmm … no wonder this is such a card in conflict!

## The Card in Your Life/Reading

*Careerwise & Financially* this card indicates a lack of careful planning so that all your resources are fighting against each other. There is nothing being built at this time, and there may even be competition and disagreement. At worst this card is a sign of litigation or wasteful argument between everybody involved. This card advises everyone to stop all activity before agreeing clearly on the way forward.

*Healthwise* this card indicates the need to have everybody agree on the realistic potential in the current situation. There are many things that can support your health if you align them towards a long-term objective. You must ensure that other people realise the importance of what it is you intend to achieve.

In *Relationships* this card indicates a confusion of values amongst yourself and your partner—and maybe friends and family. Whilst everybody is confused about the relative priority and importance of your time, nothing good will come of this. The card can also show a struggle or play-fighting for its own sake—this may be very good practice that does not ultimately create anything.

In *Travel & Lifestyle* this card indicates challenging circumstances in which many people are involved yet without a clear way forwards. This card warns you to not waste energy before having a clear vision in mind and having communicated it clearly to those around you.

In *Education* this card indicates disagreement as to what is trying to be achieved and what is most important. There is confusion because everybody is fighting for their own opinion and there is no single person to make a decision. You should either make the decision yourself or bring in someone who is capable of seeing the big picture to make it.

In *Spiritual Awareness & Self-Development* this card shows what happens when we do not align our own values and remain disconnected from the different parts of ourselves. There can be an internal conflict or struggle which does not make for constructive progress. We must become a single self, a single individual, whole and connected, so that we can build our vision.

*You are blocking this card today by:*

1. Planning what you do before you act
2. Working with others to create a positive outcome
3. Recognising that everybody has their unique talents that can be utilised
4. Learning by doing

## Connect to Your Card

Don't do anything with a plan. Work with a team. Shake something up a bit.

## The Five of Wands Says

"Competition is the name of the game, and you should make sure that you win no matter what. Do not believe what they say about winning not being the most important thing, I will do anything to be seen as the successful one."

## Keywords

Chaos, disconnection, obstacles, competition, courage, fight for rights, challenge, proving, conflict, struggle, sparring (practicing) unrest, disagreement, competition, hassles, struggles, strife, quarrelling, opulence, gain, fortune, tribunal, litigation.

# —Day 48: The Chariot—

*Momentum • Getting Out of Your Own Way*

## Resonances

*Numerology:* 7

*Astrology:* Cancer

*Kabbalah:*
Binah and Geburah

IL CARRO
LE CHAR — VII — THE CHARIOT
EL CARRO

DER WAGEN — DE ZEGEWAGEN

## Quick Connections

*Affirmation:* When I get out of my own way today, I will allow the will of the world to drive things beyond my expectations.

*Meditation:* "You are well on your way, you are driven by your own powerful needs—the needs of survival and security that draw you ever forward to your destination."

## The Lesson of the Chariot
### Mystical Meanings of the Tarot

Today we have the Chariot. Certainly a card of motion, but of what kind?

This card's astrological correspondence is to Cancer, the Crab, a creature renowned for making a cautious sideways movement. So whilst the Chariot may signify a movement forwards, it also suggests we take "the road less travelled." There is another deeper meaning to this card we would like to discuss today, that of the spiritual dimension.

This card was called by Aleister Crowley "the great work accomplished," and his version in the Thoth Tarot shows a heavily armoured figure. In the text accompanying the card, Crowley refers to the Holy Grail and other symbols, which leads one to the conclusion that the armour is empty (well, it does me).

It represents the mystical state of "non-self," a high attainment of the esoteric system or yoga meditation or any other path of enlightenment. On the Tree of Life, this card crosses the "Abyss" which separates all "human" awareness and "divine" awareness. We recommend you take a look at the Frieda Harris/Aleister Crowley Thoth Tarot version of this card.

The armour is empty because the "self" is no longer present in this card. The universe and the divine are merged (the sphinxes, the horses, the male/female symbol on the front of the WST Chariot), and the heavens are open. One has removed oneself from the equation and there is nothing but the pure flow of the Universe arising in perpetual motion.

So when this card comes up, it shows that the person can get out of their own way and things will start to move, even in surprising ways. In this respect, the card shares some similarities with the Wheel card.

The other cards which cross the Abyss are the High Priestess, in the centre of the Tree of Life, and the Hierophant on the other side of the Tree. The Lovers and the Emperor cross the Abyss too.

In what way would you say the Chariot, High Priestess, Hierophant, Lovers, and Emperor symbolise high levels of spiritual attainment in each a different manner?

## The Card in Your Life/Reading

*Careerwise & Financially* this card indicates success, victory, and triumph. It is a powerful new momentum in your career and indicates a rapid change of circumstances should you wish to drive yourself forwards at this time. The Chariot also indicates the need to rein in your spending, whether this be time or money. Everything should be directed to the task at hand.

*Healthwise* this card indicates energy and force bringing a new vitality to you. If you can harness your own inner energies you can make rapid progress forwards. This is also a card that signifies accepting the journey ahead because it is now inevitable.

In *Relationships* this card indicates that you are truly aligned to the energy of the other person or people involved. You will find yourself taken on an incredible journey which may at times feel out of your control. However, you can learn to surrender to the trip and experience a whole new way of life.

In *Travel & Lifestyle* this card indicates rapid progress and success in all those things for which you take full responsibility. You can fully master your situation when this card appears in a reading and become lord (or lady) of all you survey. It is an entirely positive card with regard to lifestyle. If you are travelling, the card shows that you must drive things forwards at a rapid pace.

In *Education* this card indicates the need to consider both sides of the argument, as well as the lessons you are learning in order to find your own place in the scheme of things. You can master the subject that you are learning if you keep your eye on the road ahead. Do not allow yourself to be driven to distraction at this time.

In *Spiritual Awareness & Self-Development* this card is a mystical symbol of allowing the world to work through us in perfect union. This card signifies our position as a channel for the creation of the universe. When it appears in response to a spiritual question, it indicates we must empty ourselves and get out of our own way for things to move forwards. Interference at this time will result in moving us far off our true course.

*You are blocking this card today by:*
1. Taking it easy and not pushing yourself to achieve
2. Just letting life happen to you
3. Letting someone else make all the decisions
4. Being all-loving like Venus and not forceful like Mars

## Connect to Your Card

Go for a drive. Push something through. Don't take no for an answer today. Keep going.

## The Chariot Says

"Just do it, and then go, go, go! Once you know your life direction, do not stop. You must move swiftly if you want to achieve success in life. There is no going back once you are on your way. My momentum will carry you to victory."

## Keywords

Momentum, conquest, success, victory, triumph, responsibility, ( focus) purpose, progress, mastery, energy, centeredness, strength, regeneration, courage, action, fortitude, focus, driven, manic, force, steadfast, stubbornness, might, vitality, Mars, will, assertiveness, progress, journey, quest, movement, swiftness, goal, diligence, willpower, perseverance, determined, vengeance, struggle, aggression, forcefulness, power.

# —Day 49: Strength—
*Appropriate Response • Waking the Lion, Stilling the Beast*

### Resonances

*Numerology:* 8

*Astrology:* Leo

*Kabbalah:*
Chesed and Geburah

### Quick Connections

*Affirmation:* Like a rope
is made up of small
threads, the delicate can
be strong when bound to
one purpose.

*Meditation:* "Humility
is strength naked and
exposed."

## The Lesson of Strength
### *A Self-Reading Spread for Working Towards Fulfillment*

This spread and method for today is particularly appropriate for questions such as "How
can I improve my life?" and "Where do I discover the joy of life?"

In this method for self-reading you first select and remove one card from the deck
which best embodies how you see a fulfilled, happy life. You may wish to choose a deck—
if you have several—which has the most joyous images upon it. You can also play this
method with a querent by asking him or her to select such a card.

Then place that card on your table at four or five cards' distance away from you.

Shuffle the rest of the deck whilst considering that card. When ready, draw out the
first card from the deck. Place that one in front of you.

Say, "This is how it will go if I try and find joy."

If the card appears to be a negative one or one that does not indicate working towards your goal, say "okay, so I will go that way less" and put that card to one side and draw another.

If the card appears to fulfill a step towards your goal, say "okay, so I will go that way more." Leave the card on the table.

With each further card drawn, repeat the process until you have four to five cards which indicate how you may fulfill the steps towards pleasure and joy in your life.

## The Card in Your Life/Reading

*Careerwise & Financially* this card indicates the need for constant assertiveness and applied pressure in a considered manner. This is not the time to overreact or be too passive; the trick is to find exactly the right position where no effort is required. This is a situation that requires some give and take.

*Healthwise* this card indicates a patient tolerance and steadfast resolve in accomplishing your health aims. You must not struggle or waste energy fighting your current condition, but respond to it in a measured and calm way. There is a perfect balance which can be obtained at this time which you have the capacity to discover.

In *Relationships* this card indicates compassionate attention to the needs of another. It could be that you need to apply firm control on the actions of another person. Or you may feel yourself held back by the attention of somebody else. The appearance of this card calls us to recognise the push and pull of all active relationships and find the perfect balance.

In *Travel & Lifestyle* this card indicates faith in your own abilities to succeed and manage the situation. You have the strength and determination to keep a firm grip in response to all situations that arise. This is a good card to have for travel questions because it means you will meet every circumstance with the appropriate response. As related to lifestyle questions, it encourages you to find your own inner strength to meet others' demands.

In *Education* this card indicates constant application to your chosen subject. You must measure out the resources that you have available in order to maintain your energy over a long period of time. This card can also indicate the dynamics of teaching and learning—sometimes it may feel as if you are in control and other times that you have no control at all. This is all part and parcel of the learning process.

In *Spiritual Awareness & Self-Development* this card signifies the perfect balance of mercy and control. It shows that love can be directed to accomplish impossible things.

This card shows the perfection of inner and outer relationship which is reflected in your ability to maintain self-control under all circumstances.

*You are blocking this card today by:*
1. Not caring too much about the outcome
2. Giving into your fears and failings
3. Not believing
4. Being intolerant

## Connect to Your Card
Watch a nature documentary. Learn something from nature. Smile at everyone today no matter if they are friendly in return.

## Strength Says
"Look to the willow and see how it bends and flexes against the might of the wind—it is truly strong. I advocate staying calm in the face of adversity and maintaining composure."

## Keywords
Resolve, stoicism, dignity, perseverance, action, releasing fears, harmony, inner strength, assertiveness, heroism, faith, courage, constancy, self-awareness, compassion, will, steadfastness, patience, tolerance, persuasion, action, self-control, firmness.

—Gate Eight—

The Pyramid Plaza

# Pyramid Spread—For Entering The Mysteries

*The transition of the previous gate has been accomplished and the shadows faced. You have let go of what held you back and emerge into the Pyramid Plaza, glimpsed only by the most esoteric of souls. Small piles of dust lie silently in the voiceless expanse. Your trials are over and you step forwards to enter the great pyramid and the heart of the mysteries of Tarot and your soul.*

## Soundtrack for the Journey
*"Isis and Nephthys" (Nik Turner's Sphynx)*

The fives are often seen as the most challenging of tarot's minor cards. They are indeed a set of **transition** cards, and change always requires energy to accomplish. In the Pyramid Spread, you will set up a new matrix to continue a positive current of change in your life through the tarot. This embodies the cards you have recently encountered, the Chariot and Strength, both of which show a perfect relationship to the Universe. In many decks you will notice the sphinxes on the Chariot indicating your entry to the Pyramid Plaza.

Take the twenty-four minor cards from the tens to the fives.

Take the four pages and knights.

Take the seventeen majors you have encountered as landmarks so far in your journey: the World, Last Judgement, Moon, Sun, Star, Temperance, Hanged Man, Devil, Blasted Tower, Death, Wheel, Justice, Lovers, Emperor, Hermit, Chariot, and Strength.

Place these cards together in a mini-deck of forty-nine cards.

Shuffle and lay out ten cards in a small pyramid as follows whilst considering the question, "**How can I partake of the mysteries in my life?**"

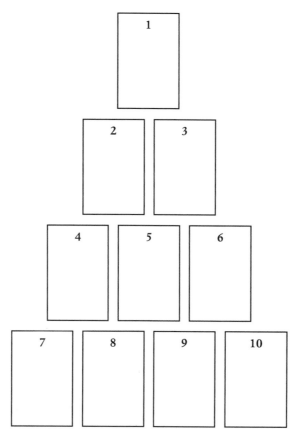

*The Pyramid Spread*

- What is my spiritual core? (card in position 1)
- How can I act to support my spiritual life? (the cards in positions 2 and 3)
- What lesson does the tarot have to teach? (the cards in positions 4, 5, and 6)
- What can I offer the Mysteries? (the cards in positions 7, 8, 9, and 10)

At this point we also see the power of the gated spread method. You may notice cards that have turned up previously during earlier gated spreads for your fears, blocks, and temptations; for your clarity of vision; for your light, path, and place. Your significator may appear also.

Using the lessons you have learnt and all the experiences you have associated with the tarot cards during this journey, this spread will now be elevated into a truly profound reading. Take time over the coming week to consider its implications and refer back to your workbook journal to gain insight.

# —Day 50: Four of Pentacles—

*Finding Yourself Secure • A Place of Attachment*

### Resonances

*Numerology:* 72/9

*Astrology:*
Sun in Capricorn

*Kabbalah:*
Chesed (Mercy)

*Sabian Symbol:* Capricorn
III—A Hidden Choir
Singing (Noumenon)

### Quick Connections

*Affirmation:* I preserve
and save what is good
and reject all that is not.

*Meditation:* "What
started out as a good
living has turned into
a bind that cannot
be undone."

## The Lesson of the Four of Pentacles
### Celtic Cross (Day 1)

Today we start to pull together what we have covered thus far and build up confidence readings with our deck. We will be using the Celtic Cross spread which has been in use since about 1898 and was first printed by A. E. Waite in his *Key to the Tarot*.

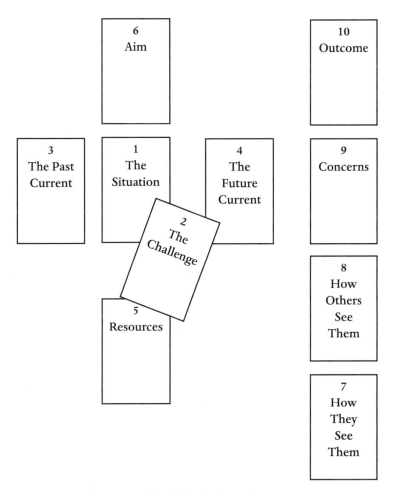

*The Celtic Cross Spread*

We will use the Queen of Pentacles as a significator for this example reading. The Queen of Pentacles, as you discover in this workbook, is a level of energy often manifesting through a particular person, in this case enduring and earthy. The real "salt of the earth," this character is realistic and wise. She can see what's what and what's not.

So in our first part of the Celtic Cross, we will use this Queen as our significator.

We will then lay out two cards in the following positions:

1. On top of the Queen—the Situation

2. Across the Queen—the Challenge (stuckness, opposition, etc., "crossing" the situation)

Say we have the Ace of Swords in the first position, describing the situation, and the Four of Wands in the second (Challenge) position.

Place the Ace upright on top of the Queen, and then lay the Four of Wands on its side across the two cards, forming a small cross shape. This is the centre axis of the "Celtic Cross," although I see it more as a wheel.

The Queen of Pentacles is in a situation depicted by the Ace of Swords, but crossed by the Four of Wands...how do we interpret this? First, take a look at the pictures—notice how (in the WST) the lines appear. The Ace of Swords is straight up and the Four of Wands—usually so open, celebratory, and inviting—now appears pinned on the Ace, like a barred gate. What might this immediately suggest?

Now look at the two suits—how does a wand card (of ambitions and values) impact against a sword card (of thoughts and decisions)? Have a look at the numbers—the Ace is being challenged by the Four, usually a creative and constructive card number...so what might that signify?

Next, look at the meanings we have previously given these two cards over the last two days and see how they stack up when one is placed against the other—what is the seed of the Ace not being allowed to do, and how, by the Four of Wands?

These things usually flash through unconsciously in the mind of an experienced tarot reader; the good news is that we can learn to do these in little steps until they become second nature.

## The Card in Your Life/Reading

*Careerwise & Financially* this card indicates acquisition and possession. It is a constraining card on career and finances and tells us we must save for a rainy day. We must keep control on those things we already possess rather than make new purchases or projects. When this card refers to other people, it indicates they will not release the resources you require.

*Healthwise* this card indicates a steadfast concentration on your own security. You must ensure that all aspects of your health are covered and this coverage is thorough. In terms of health, this card shows us that sometimes we must look out for number one. It is also a warning not to overextend yourself in any way at this time.

In *Relationships* this card indicates selfishness and the inability to open to others. If this card refers to somebody else, it means that they are holding on to their own security and it may be difficult to break through their defences. However the card signifies that there is an important reason for them acting in their current fashion.

In *Travel & Lifestyle* this card indicates a status quo where there can be no changes at the present time. You must use the present time to consolidate your gains and make yourself secure.

In *Education* this card indicates the grasping of material facts and practical applications. Whatever you are learning should be applied to real-world situations. It also indicates the need to revise all that you have currently experienced before extending yourself further.

In *Spiritual Awareness & Self-Development* this card is a card of earthly attachment and signals the danger it presents to our growth and possessiveness. Whilst there is some benefit in material security, we must realise that life is transient and all things change. This card tells us to let go.

*You are blocking this card today by:*

1. Getting up and walking away from all that is keeping you restrained
2. Giving
3. Stopping hoarding, downsizing
4. Stopping wanting to have it all

## Connect to Your Card

Save something up. Refuse to spend time or money on anything. Don't go out today.

## The Four of Pentacles Says

"Consolidation is advisable if you are to maintain the security you have built up so far. Draw upon all your resources to create a steady and safe income. Do not take any uncalculated risks and certainly do not make investments in the stocks and shares."

## Keywords

Maintenance, order, repression, selfishness, love of power, miserly, status quo, possession, security, earthly, influence, steadfast, acquisitiveness, miser, hindrances, desire, legacy, suspense, mean, possessiveness, stubbornness, stagnant.

# —Day 51: Four of Swords—

*Expecting Rest • An Examination of Retreat*

### Resonances

*Numerology:* 58/4

*Astrology:*
Jupiter in Libra

*Kabbalah:*
Chesed (Mercy)

*Sabian Symbol:* Libra
III—A Jewish Rabbi
(Being True to Tradition)

### Quick Connections

*Affirmation:* I find repose in silence and recovery in the moments between speech.

*Meditation:* "Cessation of the babble of thinking and time to rest will allow space for a new cycle of growth and learning; a new day and a new life await."

## The Lesson of the Four of Swords

### Celtic Cross (Day 2)

We now pull the card for the "past" position of the Celtic Cross. We have chosen the Star card for this example, which is often seen as a card of hope and more particularly "vision," having a star in sight to lead us. Consider too that the Star is the light in the Hermit's lantern.

The card corresponds with Aquarius, so you get from this the idea that it is full of whimsy, optimism, and inventiveness without actually being "grounded" or having the resources to carry our schemes to completion. The card is best aspected when surrounded by cards indicating clarity and resources, support and willpower. Otherwise it is merely wishful thinking.

Try this bit of Tarot Yoga … using the WST deck version, try crouching in the position of the figure of the Star card. What do you notice?

In today's lesson, we have drawn the Star card for the "past" position of the Celtic Cross. So let's place the Star card to the left of the small cross we have made already (with the Queen of Pentacles, the Ace of Swords on top, and the Four of Wands crossing).

The left position of the extended cross is the past of the situation. We sometimes refer to it as the "outgoing current" which carries a bit of a wash into the present moment.

So the Star card in the past might indicate our Queen of Pentacles had a bright idea but is now facing a situation described by those central cards. This is useful to divine because it tells us why the situation is as it is—at a standstill. It is not because the person lacks the resources, but in the response to his or her star (the vision or idea). We'll discover more about this with the other cards.

So what else can happen in life where we start off with the Star but soon find ourselves with the Four of Wands crossing us as we try to be all "Ace of Swords" about it?

## The Card in Your Life/Reading

*Careerwise & Financially* this card indicates a complete withdrawing from all activity in order to recharge your batteries. At this time you should take advantage of any constraints in your circumstance to make the most of small things and to recover from the battles of the past and any likely battles of the future. It is not a time to engage the enemy.

*Healthwise* this card indicates convalescence and recuperation. In readings for health this card always indicates the need for rest and to take yourself away from your current situation. This is a spa day card!

In *Relationships* this card indicates the need for solitude and to get away from the complexities of any relationship. The card says "I need time by myself." Whilst this may be difficult for another person to understand, it is essential at this time so that you can come back feeling refreshed.

In *Travel & Lifestyle* this card indicates rest in far-off places. Even if you cannot physically travel at this time, you must take a break from current habits and activities. This card suggests that you can prepare for future activity by resting for now.

In *Education* this card indicates the need to contemplate and reflect upon the deeper aspects of your learning. It is not a time to take on new courses or education but rather a time to silently consider the lessons of the past. Ensure that you are fully rested before making any decisions at this time.

In *Spiritual Awareness & Self-Development* this card is a card of exile and prayer. It shows the point in our journey where we consider our true inner state and perhaps transform ourselves before moving onwards.

*You are blocking this card today by:*

1. Getting out and about
2. Talking a lot
3. Socialising
4. Not giving yourself time to relax

## Connect to Your Card

Take a spa day. Visit a church or religious building. Practice yoga or meditation. Listen to chilled music and take a relaxing bath.

## The Four of Swords Says

"Now is not the time to act on any ideas or make decisions, as you could live to regret them. So withdraw to a safe place, where you can be off your guard and mull over any issues that may be troubling you. If there is something you feel you need to have out with somebody, take time to choose your words carefully."

## Keywords

Memorial, patience, inactivity, inert, rumination, hiding, retreat, exile, convalescence, recharging, recuperation, prayer, respite, quiet, rest, truce, banishment, depression, solitude, retreat, meditation, deep thought, pensive, recovery, hermit, repose, hermitage, circumspect, precaution, contemplation.

## Resonances

*Numerology:* 44/8

*Astrology:*
Moon in Cancer

*Kabbalah*:
Chesed (Mercy)

*Sabian Symbol:*
Cancer III—Gondoliers
in a Serenade
(Living the Myth)

## Quick Connections

*Affirmation:* I turn my head to find hidden opportunities when I least expect.

*Meditation:* "Stubbornly refusing to accept good-hearted offers of support and prevaricating as not to appear emotionally weak is in itself a weakness."

## The Lesson of the Four of Cups
### Celtic Cross (Day 3)

In the original version of the Celtic Cross, there was a way to tell which of the two sides of the significator card was the past position and which was the future. It was based on the direction the significator card was facing. That is to say, because the Golden Dawn court cards were drawn in a specific way, facing one way or the other, it was always possible to tell which card to the side was the "past" (from which the court card faced away) and which card was the "future" (to which the court card faced towards). This was lost entirely when A. E. Waite published the method with the cards he had designed with Pamela Colman Smith, who didn't use this feature in her artwork.

The first publication of the Celtic Cross didn't entirely work with the cards that accompanied the book. As a result, people have argued ever since about which is the "correct" side to put the future card and past card—when no such correct side ever existed! We tend to use the directions most other people use; the position to the left is the past and the right is the future.

Today we have picked the King of Cups for our future card. This is one of two positions in the Celtic Cross that can be considered a "fortune-telling" position. It talks about something about to happen. The other of course is the outcome card which will be discussed last in this sequence of lessons.

So, we have the Star as the outgoing current (past) and the King of Cups as the incoming current (future) in a situation which is very Ace of Swords, crossed by the Four of Wands. The first thing we always consider before going into detail is "What is the water like?" That is to say, do these currents in and out, and the shape of the pool in the middle, make for calm waters, strong tides, or choppy or turbulent waters? What does it feel like? Once I have established the feeling, I can dive into the reading proper.

What do you think? The Ace of Swords in between the Star (outgoing) and the King of Cups (incoming)—calm, choppy, chaotic, deep, shallow, reflective, tidal... what does it feel like?

Now let's look at interpreting the King of Cups for a future position. Our first question is "Is this a person?" A simple rule is if there is only one court card in the spread, it is likely an actual person (this is gone into in more detail in *Tarosophy*) so let's assume—without seeing the other cards yet—this is a person. Someone like the King of Cups is coming into our Queen or Pentacles's life.

What sort of person is the King of Cups? According to us, he (and it is not necessarily a "he" exclusively) is strong, has a firm base, and owns his own emotions. The fish chained around his neck (in the WST) shows that the fish leaping out freely in the Page of Cups is now fixed. This can stand for someone who, whilst in touch with his or her emotions, is bound by them too—the person can be too rigid in this stage of life.

Will this help or hinder the Queen of Pentacles?

## The Card in Your Life/Reading

*Careerwise & Financially* this card indicates a refusal to accept assistance from others when all your own resources have been exhausted. It can also show that you are missing or even ignoring a golden opportunity that is being passed to you. All you need to do is look around and take what is being given to you.

*Healthwise* this card indicates apathy and boredom leading to physical discontent. It is time to shake yourself up and accept others' gifts of assistance. You may have to move out of your comfort zone, which will lead to greater rewards in the end.

In *Relationships* this card indicates a certain sort of boredom in this situation thus far even whilst more is being offered. You may be refusing to take on new emotional responsibilities. Be sure you are not missing a golden opportunity.

In *Travel & Lifestyle* this card indicates world weariness and a sense that nothing can excite you. However, whilst in this state, you are missing opportunities and invitations that would lead to completely new experiences. Take a chance to look around…you may surprise yourself.

In *Education* this card indicates distraction and an inward turning that is not healthy. You should take a fresh look at your studies and find some new way of revitalising them. It is important you connect to a new sense of enjoyment in your course.

In *Spiritual Awareness & Self-Development* this card shows that we have exhausted all the possibilities of the everyday world and yet still have not realised that divine assistance is being offered to us at every moment. Just by opening your eyes a little more you will see that spiritual assistance is at hand.

*You are blocking this card today by:*

1. Expressing more enthusiasm
2. Sharing your feelings more
3. Having faith that you will make the right choices
4. Being contented

## Connect to Your Card

Sit under a tree. Take any opportunity. Try saying yes to everything today.

## The Four of Cups Says

"There is a wonderful opportunity I could put your way if only you could make up your mind and see the potential in my proposal. There is a danger that you will spend so long deliberating over things that you will miss out. You are becoming a little self-obsessed and really need to get out more and stop wallowing in this state of self-pity."

# Keywords

Broody, deferential, defensive, distraction, reevaluation, world weariness, kindness from others, boredom, discontent, apathy, resentment, depression, doubt, hesitation, introspection, self-absorption, dissatisfaction, contemplation, satiety, displeasure, conjecture, sign.

# —Day 53: Four of Wands—
## Working Towards Celebration • The Expression of Welcome

### Resonances

*Numerology:* 30/3

*Astrology:*
Venus in Aries

*Kabbalah:*
Chesed (Mercy)

*Sabian Symbol:*
Aries III—A Young Girl
Feeding Birds in Winter
(Nurture of the Needful)

### Quick Connections

*Affirmation:* I can accept all invitations as a chance to discover myself in the company of others.

*Meditation:* "Celebrate and be thankful for all that is good in your life; be thankful for health, any wealth, and the support of friendship and good friends. Do as Robert Herrick entreated: "Gather ye rosebuds while ye may, old Time is still a-flying: and this same old flower that smiles today, tomorrow may be dying.""

## The Lesson of the Four of Wands
### Celtic Cross (Day 4)

We take for today the bottom position in the Celtic Cross, the resources position. We have chosen the Nine of Swords in this position to illustrate this reading.

This is one of those cards that every querent looks at and sighs. There are other "sigh" cards, such as the Three of Swords, the Blasted Tower, and of course the "gasp" card—Death. Reactions aside, we know there's no such thing as a straightforward card.

Let's look at this position in the Celtic Cross first and the card second. I always read this position as "resources." Imagine an arrow being drawn back in a bow. The Aim card at the top of the spread is where we should…well, aim. The resource card at the bottom is what we can draw upon to get us energy and impetus to reach that aim. The two cards in the past and future positions are what we need to keep in balance to have a steady aim and reach the target.

As the Nine of Swords is usually associated with conscience (according to Mathers) and often indicates a grieving process, this is quite a strong card to receive in a position of resources. I always think in the WST that there's something very deliberate about Colman-Smith not showing the ends of the swords, as if they didn't fit the frame! It perhaps symbolises that the person cannot see an "end" or "point" to the issue. We can also see how the swords form ladder rungs, perhaps indicating nine steps of grieving.

So in the position of resources, this card may indicate that steps must be taken. The fact this card is a nine means the end result is quite near (to the ten), but the quilt on the WST shows signs of the zodiac, meaning time must be taken. It is quite a conflict—so near and yet so far. In our ongoing drama for the Queen of Pentacles, perhaps it indicates the person can make a decision based on the mistakes and regrets of the past, his or her dashed hopes (the Star card in the past). The person will have to really face up to what has gone wrong in the past, (something perhaps already put to bed), and draw strength from that discovery. Perhaps our cards in the "column" part of this spread in the next few days will reveal some skeletons in our Queen's closet…things are getting interesting, aren't they?

What do you think might be the case for someone with the Star in the past and the Nine of Swords beneath him or her as something that can now be drawn upon?

We hope you see now how easily it can come to life when you approach the cards in a narrative fashion, as we have been teaching over these last fifty days. The narrative method doesn't exclude any particular way of reading cards—you can use intuition, deep systems of correspondence, some, or all. The important things remains simple—read the cards and engage them with life.

## The Card in Your Life/Reading

*Careerwise & Financially* this card indicates the benefits of working with others in union. You should find like-minded people and approach them for mutual benefit. If you are being invited for interviews or assessments, they will likely prove successful. If you are looking to invest money, this card indicates investment with like-minded people. Please note, however, that a tarot card reading cannot offer investment advice!

*Healthwise* this card indicates celebration and good friends. It indicates a new phase of life that is welcoming you with open arms. You are almost at your destination, and there is a great deal of care and attention being given to you.

In *Relationships* this card indicates friendship and invitation. It shows that your social life will be shared by another and indeed that this side of your life will expand accordingly. If you are presently looking for a partner, you may be encouraged to accept invitations to parties or other social events.

In *Travel & Lifestyle* this card indicates the welcoming arms of people you meet along the way. This card signifies excellent social connections which will benefit you in many ways. You should accept all opportunities that come your way. Who knows what lies around the next corner?

In *Education* this card indicates the potential to share with others in celebration of your subject. It is time to join new clubs or societies and attend conferences or other social events. You must extend your learning outwards in association with other people.

In *Spiritual Awareness & Self-Development* this card symbolises the importance of being open to community and bringing your uniqueness to society. It is a time when you should become yourself and express yourself to others. You may be surprised by how welcoming people can be to new ideas and experiences.

*You are blocking this card today by:*
1. Being reclusive, avoiding socialising
2. Being introverted
3. Tightening the purse strings
4. Working too hard

## Connect to Your Card
Go out to a gathering, celebration, party, or place where people meet.

## The Four of Wands Says

"You have reached a time where you need to reap the benefits of all your hard work. You need to treat yourself to a well-deserved holiday in the sun! Spend time with close friends and family…and chill out."

## Keywords

Welcoming, jubilant, prosperity, celebration, happy holidays, commemoration, buying a house, gathering, excitement, freedom, settlement, standstill, refuge, society, union, association, concord, harmony, clan, fantasy, cosiness.

# —Day 54: The Hierophant—
## Divine Teaching • *Your Life is a Glass, Clearly*

### Resonances

*Numerology:* 5

*Astrology:* Taurus

*Kabbalah:*
Chockmah and Chesed

### Quick Connections

*Affirmation:* I am part of the tradition of the whole of the world, and I can contribute in each and every moment.

*Meditation:* "Thoughts are mystery—they are hidden until revealed; they are our sacred inner expression. Therefore think deeply and kindly, for your thoughts may be your making or your undoing."

## The Lesson of the Hierophant
### Using the Card Title

Taking a break in our Celtic Cross lesson today, let's look at the Hierophant, today's card. Another Major card. It's sometimes interesting to look at the derivation of the titles for the cards. In this case, the origins of the word "hierophant" comes from the Greek *hiero* and *phantos*, meaning "revealer of the sacred."

So the Hierophant reveals the sacred. It is often taken in readings to indicate the presence of an expert or authority figure, in contrast with the "female pope" (now usually called the High Priestess, who conceals the mysteries or somehow secretly reveals them). When this card comes up, we are counselled to seek wisdom from someone with knowledge, experience, and connection to the issue beyond us. The Hierophant stands in between our known world and the unknown world, whether it's a job interview or a sacred mystery.

Rather than us reading the card today, let's use it as a prompt to explore our own expertise: what do *you* do uniquely that connects you to the world? The questioning is a sacred act in itself. For me, it's when I am writing, teaching, or looking for a book for somebody else—I feel totally lost in the act and there is no division. Like the Hierophant, I am both sacred and revealing.

I *wish* I could feel the same with playing a musical instrument! What about you? Where are *you* the Hierophant?

## The Card in Your Life/Reading

*Careerwise & Financially* this card indicates consultancy. It signifies that you must seek external authority or advice with regard to your current situation. If this card appears in a future position, it can indicate a revelation is ahead. In terms of finances this card shows that you must conserve your resources or hold to traditional methods of income and saving.

*Healthwise* this card indicates expert advice and the intervention of people outside of your family situation. It can sometimes indicate a run-in with authority or disagreement with professionals. Depending on surrounding cards (such as those indicating self-responsibility), it can advise to follow or seek a second opinion.

In *Relationships* this card indicates tradition and marriage. It can show a marriage of minds, a union of two people bound by common ambition, or an actual marriage. The card also suggests in some cases there are external expectations or authority being applied to the relationship which is unwelcome—this is usually parental.

In *Travel & Lifestyle* this card indicates keeping to standard methods and normality in all your dealings. It shows that you must adhere to the rules and work within the boundaries of expectation at this time. It is a card of conformity and tradition—it also signifies religious belief, so it can suggest its lacking or presence in your surroundings.

In *Education* this card indicates a strict moral code and high expectations of your conduct. In a mundane sense it can show all conferences which should be attended. This is not a time to make your own case but to agree to the conventions of your subject matter.

In *Spiritual Awareness & Self-Development* this card is the revealer of the sacred. The Hierophant is our mystical teacher and can be manifest as the world itself. The Hierophant is the opportunity to learn the sacred mysteries from our day-to-day experiences.

*You are blocking this card today by:*

1. Reading celebrity gossip
2. Going on a protest march
3. Being rebellious
4. Speaking your mind regardless of what people may think or feel

## Connect to Your Card

Attend a class. Learn something traditional. Go visit your parents. Visit a religious location.

## The Hierophant Says

"You need to add a good dose of structure to your life. You need a bit of order and discipline to be able to function well in the world. You need to adopt a practice such as yoga that will become a part of your everyday routine."

## Keywords

Teaching, loyalty, dispensation, allegiance, convention, conforming, morality, bridge, celibacy, interface conservation, external authority, expert, conscience, doctrine, marriage, alliance, mercy, beneficence, union, bond, conforming, traditional/tradition, respect, ceremony, goodness, servitude, captivity.

# —Day 55: Three of Pentacles—
## *Finding Yourself Working to the Plan • A Place of Apprenticeship*

### Resonances

*Numerology:* 71/8

*Astrology:*
Mars in Capricorn

*Kabbalah:*
Binah (Understanding)

*Sabian Symbol:*
Capricorn II—
An Albatross Feeding
From the Hand
(Connection to
the Spirits)

### Quick Connections

*Affirmation:* I will realise my aspirations to make small but definite steps towards the fulfillment of my ambition.

*Meditation:* "Aspiring to reach new heights has to be grounded in lowly foundations and worked upwards from there; all creation needs purpose, and we must plan and build and continue to innovate until we reach the pinnacle of perfection!"

## The Lesson of the Three of Pentacles
### *Celtic Cross (Day 5) & Astrological Correspondences*

Today's card chosen in our continuation of the Celtic Cross lesson is the Three of Pentacles. We have put this card above the previously drawn cards in the position called by Waite, "What Crowns Him." This card goes above the central cross, and I read this as the "aim" of the querent. This card to me shows what the person is best advised to aim towards—the card we will look at tomorrow, placed below the cross, I take as the "resources" on which the person can draw to accomplish that aim.

In our ongoing complete Celtic Cross spread we have the aim of the querent being the Lovers. This card does not always mean a relationship of love and romance—in earlier versions, this card signified choice. In the Golden Dawn version of the card, it shows Perseus rescuing Andromeda from the kraken, depicting divine inspiration. This is because the card connects Binah (understanding) on the Kabbalistic Tree of Life to Tiphareth, (beauty). It shows the connection between the great mother of all form and structure in the cosmos (Binah) to our own awareness and sense of self (Tiphareth). Pretty cosmic, this card!

In the case of our Queen of Pentacles, it looks like her aim should definitely be to choose the King of Cups, whether it represents a person or a way of life (patient, caring, not rushing ahead). Would we agree? The Lovers seems to indicate that a relationship is to be worked towards.

We have already covered the Eight of Pentacles, and we spoke about the three cards in the pentacles that embodied different levels of craft mastery—do you recall? We were mainly looking at the Eight of Pentacles, the Journeyman.

Today we look at the Three, the "apprentice" card. Here we see (particularly in the WST) the apprentice at work, with the figures of authority (with the plan) seemingly assessing his work. One figure looks rich, the other priestly, perhaps indicating our mundane work should conform to the social worlds of religion and finance.

In a reading, this card often indicates the need for recognition, support, and approval. It's a "pat on the back" before you really get to work. It requires one to be open to feedback and criticism. In a relationship question, this card indicates a new beginning and steady progress which has the potential to be solid and healthy in a general sense.

Three is a number of positive support (the triangle) and the pentacles correspond to Earth, so this is a sturdy foundation card in any position. It is well aspected in support or past positions, providing a good basis for future trends.

Crowley gives this card as representing work ("material works" in the Golden Dawn), and it corresponds to Mars in Capricorn. Have a look at what astrologers say about people with Mars in Capricorn, and you'll get a better idea of this card too: "Mars in Capricorn natives are working toward realistic and attainable goals. They are productive people who get excited when they see tangible results from their efforts."

What would this card indicate in a one-card reading in answer to the question "My wife and I are thinking about buying a pet. What do the cards say?"

# The Card in Your Life/Reading

*Careerwise & Financially* this card indicates apprenticeship. It signifies a time when you must learn new skills and demonstrate your ability to others. This card shows you will be recognised for your loyalty and given the status as befits your competence. It is important to understand the plans of others at this time in order that you can positively contribute to the overall vision.

*Healthwise* this card indicates the need to make repair on all that has gone before. You should have a good health plan to which you can contribute in order to reconstruct yourself. This card also indicates in health questions the need to have clear goals set by other people who work with you, and regular checkups.

In *Relationships* this card indicates cooperation and teamwork in meeting the expectations of the relationship. The Three of Pentacles shows that we must work together in mundane tasks to build a firm foundation for the emotional level of the relationship. It is also a card (in a future position) that can suggest setting agreed structure to the relationship.

In *Travel & Lifestyle* this card indicates constructive cooperation with others, although you may be given most of the load. You should be prepared to work hard to meet the approval of others in order to achieve long-term and lasting success. In the most literal sense of travel, this card shows visiting sites under construction or demolition—or perhaps religious buildings!

In *Education* this card indicates the need to gain recognition in your craft to be elevated in status. Whilst this may appear to be unnecessary, it is a part of the political nature of the educational establishment.

In *Spiritual Awareness & Self-Development* this card is our apprenticeship to a divine plan. It shows that we are being recognised in our work on a higher level that will elevate our creation in some way beyond the obvious.

*You are blocking this card today by:*

1. Not reading the instruction manual for a new appliance
2. Behaving like an airhead
3. Just not giving a damn
4. Relying on intuition to work out a problem

## Connect to Your Card

Pick up a new skill. Make a new plan. Ask someone for advice. Learn about architecture.

## The Three of Pentacles Says

"We all need a vision to make wishes reality. However, doing so requires dedication and a long-term plan with which to work from and towards. We often cannot do this on our own, and we have to share our vision with other people who can bring their skills to it. Cooperation is the foremost concern."

## Keywords

Loyalty, ambition, consolidation, capability, approval, recognition, employment, competence, status, standing, synergy, construction, material increase, growth, work, business, status, honour, craftsmanship, elevation, rank, commencement, skill, metier, employment, profession, bounty, restoration, reparation, trade, renown, glory, cooperation, teamwork, planning.

# —Day 56: Three of Swords—
## Expecting Separation • An Examination of Exhaustion

### Resonances

*Numerology:* 57/3

*Astrology:*
Saturn in Libra

*Kabbalah:*
Binah (Understanding)

*Sabian Symbol:* Libra II—
A Canoe Approaching
Safety Through
Dangerous Waters
(Cliff-Hanger)

### Quick Connections

*Affirmation:* In every decision I will let go of what is not to be.

*Meditation:* "To have one's heart struck asunder and be forced to examine over again and again the heart's breakage."

## The Lesson of the Three of Swords
### Celtic Cross (Day 6)

We've reached the stage now in our lessons that we must take a leap and start looking at pairing cards together, and there is no better time than with these next two positions of the Celtic Cross.

We now lay out the cards in the "column" to the right of the Celtic Cross. In the original first drawings of this spread within the Order of the Golden Dawn, the column was to the left, which was then changed by Waite in his published version and has remained the standard ever since!

As we want to look at two cards/positions together, we have laid out:

- How the person sees him-/herself: IX (the Hermit)
- How the person is seen by others: Ten of Pentacles

These are the meanings of those two positions that I use most regularly, as it provides striking insight into all aspects of the situation. Some people do not like the Celtic Cross, as they say it is "useless" (I read this on a popular site only recently), but I find with a few tweaks from experience it is amongst the most incisive and deep spreads! I read these two cards often together, and they always provide an a-ha! moment for querents, telling them why people aren't reacting the way they expect, what's being miscommunicated, and much more.

In simple terms, our querent, the Queen of Pentacles, sees herself as the Hermit. She sees herself as holding that star of vision in her lantern, and being true to living with hope. However, as others see her, she presents a Ten of Pentacles face (see how we are now using tarot as a language)—what could that mean?

How does others seeing her as a Ten of Pentacles (good home, domestic, stability, family) contrast or compare with the inner feeling she has as the Hermit? In comparing these two cards we can obtain precise divination of the person's psychological and social situation which the "cross" of the reading has already begun to reveal.

## The Card in Your Life/Reading

*Careerwise & Financially* this card indicates potential arbitration and a splitting of income. The only positive aspect of this card in career or financial situations is that it is always a clean break. This card can also indicate in a literal sense a separation from your career or finances such as a redundancy. Where the situation is entirely positive or shown to be such in the future by other cards in a spread, this card indicates the need to keep your affairs in order by maintaining separate bank accounts as an example. Again, remember the tarot in itself is not a financial adviser!

*Healthwise* this card indicates the need to avoid confusion and anxiety. It suggests we make a clean break in order to quickly resolve the situation and move on, no matter the initial pain this may bring. The card often shows heartbreak and must be taken into consideration most seriously with regard to health questions.

In *Relationships* this card indicates quarrel and disharmony. Most significantly it shows separation and a lack of regard between the two parties. This can lead to arguments and wounding. This is usually the most negative card to receive in a relationship reading, although it does depend on other cards in the spread. Where the relationship is viewed as positive, this card can warn of a slight conflict of interests moving into the relationship.

In *Travel & Lifestyle* this card indicates the need to go through some pain for some gain. There are short-term issues that need radical resolution in order to free yourself up for later expansion. If you are travelling, this card signifies that you must move on or you will experience disappointments.

In *Education* this card indicates the need to clearly define your terms and conditions. It is a card that shows most clearly that some studies require different boxes or allotments of time in order to avoid confusion. If you are engaged in studies, you must ensure they are kept separate from your home or work life.

In *Spiritual Awareness & Self-Development* this card is the sorrow of separation from the divine. It shows the awareness that we are not whole in ourselves and our distance from that unity. However, when this feeling hits, it drives us forwards to an ultimate state of unity.

*You are blocking this card today by:*

1. Walking away from a verbal disagreement
2. Not allowing yourself to being drawn into gossiping about a third party
3. Consulting a therapist and talking over mental anguish with a professional
4. Refusing to listen to your inner turmoil

## Connect to Your Card

Separate yourself from a tricky situation. Say what you mean all day. Be clear.

## The Three of Swords Says

"There is a conflict of emotions that are not being resolved due to petty grievances. Somebody needs to stand back and act as a mediator so the situation can be resolved. There are grudges being maintained that need to be dropped. The situation will only get worse if left alone."

## Keywords

Disappointment, separation, quarrel, upheaval, civil war, woe, loss, turbulence, disharmony, rift, worries, small talk, break-down, overloading, distraction, division, reason, disorder, confusion, alienation, burdened, triangle, verbal joust, necessary strife and conflict, arbitration, destruction of obsolescence, wounding, fraught.

# —Day 57: Three of Cups—
## Imagining Harmony • The Creation of Connection

### Resonances

*Numerology:* 43/7

*Astrology:*
Mercury in Cancer

*Kabbalah:*
Binah (Understanding)

*Sabian Symbol:*
Cancer II—A Large
Diamond Not Completely
Cut (Almost There)

### Quick Connections

*Affirmation:* I am able to connect to others and find the open spirit of all people.

*Meditation:* "Conspire with friends to create joy and happiness."

## The Lesson of the Three of Cups
### Celtic Cross (Day 7)

Let's look at our final two positions in the Celtic Cross today— "concerns" and "outcome". The first is sometimes given as "hopes and fears"; however, I see that a positive concern is a hope and a negative concern is a fear—calling it "concerns" is easier. This position tells me whatever the person is thinking of is not actually real, whether for better or worse, and thus is often a relief or reality-check. We have chosen for today the Seven of Swords. Take a look at the picture, and suggest in a sentence what the card means as a "concern." What would concern you when you look at this card? Is the card one of "hopes" or "fears"? As a clue, we call this card in Tarot Flip "trespass."

*Legacy of the Divine
Tarot Seven of Swords*

In the "Outcome" position, which can be paired with the "concerns" position, let's imagine is today's card, the Three of Cups. How might this determine the most likely outcome for the Querent? How does it compare with their worry seen in the Seven of Swords? Do we think that the worry might be real given this outcome card? It is usually the case that these two positions are as revealing paired together as the previous two positions.

In this Celtic Cross lesson, we see in this card what concerns our Queen of Pentacles, and perhaps explains a few of those earlier cards, such as the Nine of Swords.

## The Card in Your Life/Reading

*Careerwise & Financially* this card indicates the importance of social networks and friends to support material ambition. It can indicate that resources can be found with female colleagues or through social engagements. In the most mundane sense it is a card that signifies cause for celebration out of the blue.

*Healthwise* this card indicates a necessity to have good contacts with other people and ensure that you have their support. It is important for our own well-being that we make connection with those with whom we are at most ease. You should ensure that you can truly be yourself with those around you at this time.

In *Relationships* this card indicates a wonderful situation where there is cause for celebration. It shows parties and the joy of sharing friends within a relationship. In all relationship questions the three of cups indicates that you should take other people into account for good or worse within the bounds of the relationship itself.

In *Travel & Lifestyle* this card indicates meetings and extended social opportunities to enjoy with other people. It is a card that reminds us that our life is built of relationships and these relationships should be given the time to celebrate and be recognised. If you are planning travel whilst thinking about your own future, ensure you throw a few parties!

In *Education* this card indicates teamwork and success. It shows the joy of uniting with others in delightful celebration of shared interests. When this card appears in an education question, it often means that you will be rewarded as part of a group.

In *Spiritual Awareness & Self-Development* this card demonstrates the need to celebrate life and all that it brings to us. It is a card of reward when the heart is most open, particularly in regard to how our life is shared with others. When this card appears in a self-development spread, it means that we must take time to enjoy the company of those around us.

*You are blocking this card today by:*

1. Being boring, boring, boring!
2. Shunning your best friends.
3. Behaving in a jealous, possessive manner.
4. Picking an argument.

## Connect to Your Card

Go out with your friends. Find something to celebrate. Make up for missed connections.

## The Three of Cups Says

"Cheers all around! A perfect triangulation of good will! Good friends should be appreciated, so make the effort to let them know how much they mean to you. Have a get-together, celebrate your friendship."

## Keywords

Harmony, good fortune, artistic talent, hospitality, party, sensitivity, empathy, Facebook, social networks, friends reunited, merge, joy, hobbies, uniting, delight, friendship, celebration, team spirit, exuberance, community, reward, pleasure, fulfilment, abundance, plenty, merriment, success, victory, recuperation, consolation.

# —Day 58: Three of Wands—

*Working Towards Building the Future • The Expression of Ambition*

## Resonances

*Numerology:* 29/11

*Astrology:*
Sun in Aries

*Kabbalah:*
Binah (Understanding)

*Sabian Symbol:* Aries II—
A Man Teaching New
Forms for Old Symbols
(Upgrade and
Re-presentation)

## Quick Connections

*Affirmation:* I allow my spirit to sail wherever it wishes and needs to fulfil its seeking.

*Meditation:* "Set out on a journey of self-discovery; there lies within us un-charted territories and parts of ourselves we are frightened of visiting; these therefore are parts we must plot our course to and discover are our allies after all."

## The Lesson of the Three of Wands
### Recording Your Readings

This method of recording cards is very good for journaling and recording even the most complex of readings for later reference and reflection. It was used by Aleister Crowley and within the Golden Dawn.

Here's an example, a full Celtic Cross: XVI, 4C, 3S, 9W, PC, KnS, X, VI, AP, 5S
The method is quite straightforward:

1. For any minor card, simply write the number and the abbreviated first letter of the suit. So we have 3S for the Three of Swords, 9W for the Nine of Wands, and AP for the Ace of Pentacles.

2. For major cards, write down the roman numeral: XVI (the Tower), X (the Wheel), VI (the Lovers), and so forth.

3. For court cards, simply abbreviate to P(age), Kn(ight), Q(ueen), and K(ing) all followed by the suit. So we have PC and KnS in the Celtic Cross above, the Page of Cups and the Knight of Swords respectively.

We then record them in either the order we lay the spread, or sketch them out quickly in their relative positions. It takes only a moment to record a full reading and it can be looked at again later. You may also choose to take a digital picture of your reading for later reference.

## The Card in Your Life/Reading

*Careerwise & Financially* this card indicates investment and often the appearance of practical help and a mentor. It shows the beginning phases of our projects with no sense yet of how they will fare. This is a positive card showing a takeoff in business or career which is likely to bring appropriate rewards. However, it does warn that there is not much we can do now to change what we have set in motion.

*Healthwise* this card indicates the need to explore further and extend the boundaries of what you currently know or experience. It shows that events have been set in motion which will have a bearing on your health at a future time.

In *Relationships* this card indicates a desire to work with somebody else to achieve a long-term goal. It shows that you will make further progress with another person than you can do by yourself. To some extent you must let events develop naturally at this time.

In *Travel & Lifestyle* this card indicates good fortune with projects that are already set in place. However, you must allow things to take their own course because there is nothing left for you to do at this time. You must now exercise patience and allow others to return with your rewards.

In *Education* this card indicates new experiences are ahead of you which will build from your initial vision. You have yet to see any direct response to your work; however, it is early yet ; so long as you have been true to yourself, a fitting reward will be returned.

In *Spiritual Awareness & Self-Development* this card signals we have made a mission and an investment in our life based on our true vision. We cannot know where this will lead us, but we can be secure in the knowledge we have done our work to the best of our ability.

*You are blocking this card today by:*

1. Not sharing your experience and knowledge with anyone else
2. Refusing to see the situation as it really is
3. Not surveying a potential opportunity properly
4. Not grasping a promising new opportunity

## Connect to Your Card

Go to a harbour or airport and watch the travellers. Read a history book on migrations.

## The Three of Wands Says

"The future holds promise if only you could get out there and explore new horizons. All ventures need preparation and planning to fit any eventuality, so look at what you want out of life, look at your prospects, assess your strengths and weaknesses, check out any opposition or threats that might be out there, and take action!"

## Keywords

Building, cooperation, good partnership, practical help, mentoring, investor, teamwork, work–related travel, assessment, surveying, voyeurism, alert, brisk business, assimilation, exploration, leadership, foresight, intuition, pride, departure, research, enterprise, desire, attempt, trade.

# —Day 59: The Empress—

*Cultivation • You Reap What You Sow*

## Resonances

*Numerology:* 3

*Astrology:* Venus

*Kabbalah:*
Chockmah and Binah

## Quick Connections

*Affirmation:* Abundance creates abundance.

*Meditation:* "Be as creative as possible in every way to avoid a life that is bereft of new life; we were born to create more."

## The Lesson of the Empress

### Opening of the Key Method (Day 1)

Today we take a new turn from our Celtic Cross lessons of the last week and look again at extending our narrative reading, which is reading without position. We're going to also learn a little bit of the "counting method" of the Golden Dawn occult order, which was founded in 1888 and flourished for a good twenty years at the turn of the last century.

We'll need to learn a few correspondences for this, but we'll start off simply, as always. We are not giving the full method yet, just a training version, so don't worry about the question or spread. We're just practising our counting for the next few days!

We are going to end up with a line of cards (which we'll illustrate over the coming days) and count through them from one card to another in a particular way such that we alight on particular cards which are read as a narrative story. We might end up reading all the cards, or only a few. When we reach a card we have already read, we conclude the reading.

In this teaching example, we'll have a spread (so to speak) of ten cards total, so we have pulled these in advance.

They are:

- Seven of Cups
- Queen of Swords
- Four of Swords
- I – the Magician
- Eight of Wands
- Queen of Cups
- Six of Pentacles
- Nine of Pentacles
- Ten of Wands
- Six of Cups

*The Ten Cards for Counting Spread*

Looking at the first card, we are going to create a predictive reading, so we read it as what's going to happen. The first card is the Seven of Cups… perhaps we choose to read this as "You are going to be presented with a range of confusing emotions in the upcoming situation and will not know what is best."

We then count depending on the nature of the card (and there are rules coming up tomorrow) but for now, we have a numbered minor card, so we simply count the same number as the card, i.e., seven, for the Seven of Cups.

We count along the line of cards, going back round to the beginning if we overshoot, seven cards—counting our first card as card one. Count one on the Seven of Cups, two on the Queen of Swords, and so on until the seventh card, which if you'd like to check is… the Six of Pentacles.

*Counting Rule One:* We start counting with the card we are on, and for minor cards we count onwards the same number as on the card itself.

*Counting Rule Two:* When we get to the end of our line of cards we return to the beginning whilst keeping the count, as if they are in a loop.

So if we had started with the Nine of Pentacles, which card would come next? (Clue: don't forget when you get to the end of the row, you come around to the beginning.) Practice today counting to the next card to be read from each of the seven minor cards in that spread. We will see later how we know which card is our starting card—this is a test track!

## The Card in Your Life/Reading

*Careerwise & Financially* this card indicates a certain growth and abundance. Whilst it may take some time to harvest your gains, these gains are assured when this card appears in a reading. In fact, this card often indicates that you will reap far more than you have sown. It is a card that also suggests you should cultivate and tend to your projects, not letting them wither through inattention.

*Healthwise* this card indicates healing and time needed for it. It is time to be whole and well, enjoying the outdoors or a relaxing environment. This card also shows the inevitable healing of the body given time. This is very much a card of the mother and of the body. It speaks of nurturing and nature's wisdom.

In *Relationships* this card indicates the importance of motherhood and the feminine in any relationship. The archetypal mother is nurturing and caring so the appearance of this card suggests we must nurture and care for our relationship.

In *Travel & Lifestyle* this card indicates gradual development over a long period of time where all that you put in will be rewarded. In a purely literal sense it symbolises travel outdoors and the landscape itself. In terms of lifestyle it shows that we become what we surround ourselves with, so we must choose well. In a general sense, the card symbolises accumulation.

In *Education* this card indicates a slow multiplication of knowledge that is gradually forming a structure, gaining you benefit. Whilst this process may appear slow and sometimes constricting, there is care in your teaching; you will gain in the long term. The Empress appearing in an education spread suggests sticking with it for eventual success.

In *Spiritual Awareness & Self-Development* this card is nature herself. All that lives, lives. Our place in nature is as one with it, not separate—the Empress reminds us to take that place.

*You are blocking this card today by:*

1. Not being very nurturing
2. Not being very sympathetic about a friend's problems
3. Not caring about the plight of others in the world
4. Being entirely motivated by selfish desires

## Connect to Your Card

Start gardening. Buy fruit. Look after children. Buy a plant and look after it. Volunteer.

## The Empress Says

"Settle down and create a safe, comforting home life you'll want to come home to. You need to focus on being creative and productive through the expression of creating, whether though your work or home. Now would be a wonderful time to concentrate on self-development—produce artwork or craftwork. Write that long-delayed novel. More creates more—that is the nature of creation!"

## Keywords

Cultivation, marriage, fertility, wealth, contentment, fruitful harvest, healing, love, pregnancy, multiplication, compassion, authentic, natural, embracing, warmth, abundance, fruitfulness, action, clandestine, plan, initiative, veil, development, creativity, nurturing, protection, comfort, mothering, nature.

# —Day 60: Queen of Pentacles—
## Caring for Others • Being the Hearth and Home

### Resonances

*Numerology:* 66/3

*Astrology:* Virgo

*Kabbalah:*
Binah (Understanding)

*Elemental*: Water of Earth

*Perfume:* Clover

*Timing:* Virgo
(August 24–
September 22)

### Quick Connections

*Affirmation:* Persevering in my own care, I can discover my own capability and resources.

*Meditation:* "To care, share, and be there for the good of the whole is what makes the feminine divine."

## The Lesson of the Queen of Pentacles
### Opening the Key Method (Day 2)

Today we continue our card-counting class with the same sequence of cards:

- Seven of Cups
- Queen of Swords
- Four of Swords
- I – the Magician
- Eight of Wands
- Queen of Cups
- Six of Pentacles
- Nine of Pentacles

- Ten of Wands
- Six of Cups

We counted from our starting card, the Seven of Cups, a count of seven to the Six of Pentacles—another minor card. The Six of Pentacles is about charity and measuring your resources, a far more realistic card than our first. It looks like this reading tells of a reality check in the near future.

We now read that card as part of our fortune-telling story, carrying on from the Seven of Cups yesterday. You can practice reading like this by using lots of linking words: and, or, whilst, when, so, because, then. We have also provided many narrative-building exercises in previous days in our journey if you would like to review your skills.

"You will find yourself confused by many possibilities (Seven of Cups) ... **and** will have to weigh out what is most realistic to you financially. Others will gain from this choice also" (Six of Pentacles)."

We now continue counting—and as we said yesterday, we do this until we meet a card we have already met, which signifies the end of the reading. Now luckily we have already learnt the first rule for minor cards, we just count the number on the card, so in this case we are next going to be counting from the Six of Pentacles. What card comes next for tomorrow's reading?

A bonus question—if it isn't a minor card, how do you think we should count from it? What about if it is a court or a major card? Have a think on this question before our lesson tomorrow.

## The Card in Your Life/Reading

*Careerwise & Financially* this card indicates the business sense that comes from experience and patience. In general readings this card indicates security and long-term well-being. In a practical sense this card is good fortune. If you are applying for jobs, the card shows that you are better favoured with practical work and hands-on experience.

*Healthwise* this card indicates nurturing and care. You are advised by this card to allow time for a full recovery or to plan for long-term work on your health situation. It is a card of slow and creative patience leading to the accomplishment of your goals. Take no sudden movement at this time.

In *Relationships* this card indicates dependability and the domestic. Whilst it may not be the most exciting card to have in a relationship reading, it shows a strong foundation upon which you can build. The Queen of Pentacles also symbolises the importance of the feminine principle in the relationship.

In *Travel & Lifestyle* this card indicates slow and steady progress in a practical manner. Events will generally build in your favour until such time that you can reap your rewards. In terms of travel, this card shows very "down and dirty" experiences and a full immersion in your journey.

In *Education* this card indicates the need to be creative and practical with your skills. You must apply them to everyday situations to consolidate all you have learnt. In terms of teaching, this card indicates the need to offer practical guidance for long-term success.

In *Spiritual Awareness & Self-Development* this card shows the nurturing force of the divine feminine when applied to our everyday life. In tending to the smallest things we reflect the care of the whole universe. It can also symbolise the presence of divine forces in our lives—be aware of strange coincidences and synchronicity in your life.

*You are blocking this card today by:*
1. Being irresponsible with regard to money matters
2. Turning away those close to you who need your support
3. Not being nice
4. Letting your heart hold sway over common sense

## Connect to Your Card

Be there for people. Put others first today. Be realistic. Do something homely. It's all about domestic duties today.

## The Queen of Pentacles Says

"Get grounded and connect with the earthy side of life. Learn to be resourceful and practical. Share your resources with others and vice versa. Attend to your financial affairs; think of ways of decreasing your outgoings and bringing more money in. You are capable of turning your hand to most things."

## Keywords

Nurturing, dependable, confident, self-assured, effective, creative, thoughtful, melancholy, practical, abundance, business sense, domesticity, generous, intelligent, charming, kind, timid, prosperity, liberality, assistance, security, magnificence, dependable.

# —Day 61: Queen of Swords—
## Caring for a Fair Deal • Being the Mediator and Diplomat

### Resonances

*Numerology:* 52/7

*Astrology:* Libra

*Kabbalah:*
Binah (Understanding)

*Elemental:* Water of Air

*Perfume:* Mastick

*Timing:* Gemini
(May 22–June 21)

### Quick Connections

*Affirmation:* Persevering
in my own decisions,
I can discover my
true talents.

*Meditation:* "Those who
have the most influence
to change the beliefs and
actions of others do so
by letting the other party
adopt their way and claim
it as their own."

## The Lesson of the Queen of Swords
### Opening the Key Method (Day 3)

We are tomorrow going to add an important building block—elemental dignities—in our narrative reading of the "Opening of the Key" which whilst optional provides even more depth to this powerful method. We'll look at the rules for dignities tomorrow, so let's first read today's card, which we counted to yesterday, arriving at the Queen of Swords:

- Seven of Cups
- Queen of Swords
- Four of Swords
- I – The Magician
- Eight of Wands
- Queen of Cups

- Six of Pentacles
- Nine of Pentacles
- Ten of Wands
- Six of Cups

We have so far read "You will find yourself confused by many possibilities (7 of Cups)…**and** will have to weigh out what is most realistic to you financially. Others will gain also from this choice" (6 of Pentacles).

And indeed our next card is the Queen of Swords, counting six from the Six of Pentacles. Let's add the Queen of Swords to our reading:

"…however you will gain help from a woman who is very direct, ambitious, and speaks sharply."

Now we will have to count onwards from a non-minor card, so we should learn the counting rules in full for the court cards and major cards. These rules are based on the correspondences of the cards to astrology and the elements, but for now we will simply present them as a table.

- For pages: seven
- For kings, queens, and knights: four
- For aces: five (or eleven)

For aces, the Golden Dawn used five and later variations have eleven. We usually use eleven—either works so long as you choose beforehand. If you are using a deck such as Aleister Crowley and Frieda Harris's Thoth deck, don't forget that the princesses are that deck's equivalent to pages, princes are as knights above, and knights are equivalent to kings in this table.

As we have already seen, count according to the number for the minor cards. Majors we count three for the elemental majors, nine for the planetary majors, and twelve for the zodiacal majors. Here below is a table for the major cards showing their elemental, astrological, and planetary correspondences and counting numbers.

| Tarot Card (Major) | Correspondence | Counting Number |
|---|---|---|
| 0: Fool | Air | 3 |
| I: Magician | Mercury | 9 |
| II: Priestess | Moon | 9 |
| III: Empress | Venus | 9 |
| IV: Emperor | Aries | 12 |
| V: Hierophant | Taurus | 12 |
| VI: Lovers | Gemini | 12 |
| VII: Chariot | Cancer | 12 |
| VIII: Strength | Leo | 12 |
| IX: Hermit | Virgo | 12 |
| X: Wheel | Jupiter | 9 |
| XI: Justice | Libra | 12 |
| XII: Hanged Man | Water | 3 |
| XIII: Death | Scorpio | 12 |
| XIV: Temperance | Sagittarius | 12 |
| XV: Devil | Capricorn | 12 |
| XVI: Tower | Mars | 9 |
| XVII: Star | Aquarius | 12 |
| XVIII: Moon | Pisces | 12 |
| XIX: Sun | Sun | 9 |
| XX: Last Judgement | Fire | 3 |
| XXI: Universe | Saturn (Earth) | 9 |

We see that we must count on four for a queen, so we will count four and reach the Eight of Wands. We can read this simply and almost literally for the eight wands flying through the air: "…who will bring you exciting news and move the project forwards…"

Because the next count from this card is eight, which brings us back to a card we have already touched upon, the Queen of Swords, this is the last card in this reading.

So our complete reading for this practice spread of ten cards using the counting method and starting at the Seven of Cups is:

"You will find yourself confused by many possibilities (Seven of Cups) and will have to weigh out what is most realistic to you financially. Others will gain also from this choice,

(Six of Pentacles) however you will get help from a woman who is very direct, ambitious, and speaks sharply (Queen of Swords). She will bring you exciting news and move the project forwards."

As an optional exercise for today, you may try reading through this test-track spread by starting at any of the other cards and seeing what happens. You will soon see how many potential variations of reading are hidden within the ten cards. Don't forget to loop around if you reach the end of the track. Again, stop reading when you land on a card you have already landed upon and read.

## The Card in Your Life/Reading

*Careerwise & Financially* this card indicates quick and sharp decision making in order to gain clarity. This is a card of immediacy, where you must make snap judgements and apply intense thought to your decisions. It is a card of meeting deadlines and being independent. It can also show in an adverse position in a reading that others are speaking against you.

*Healthwise* this card indicates an acknowledgement of what has been decided. It requires versatility to assess the situation and now make future plans based on what you have been told or learnt. In a predictive sense it indicates that information will be available sooner than you think.

In *Relationships* this card indicates sharp wit and strong will. It can indicate disagreement or differing ideas about the relationship. You should make it absolutely clear what you think in order to clear the air. If someone is being confusing, you should call that person on it for immediate effect. This is not a time for the relationship to be uncertain.

In *Travel & Lifestyle* this card indicates direct and confident movement forwards towards your ambition. It shows that you can be strong willed and get the job done. Be confident in your decisions and stick to the plan.

In *Education* this card indicates the ability to quickly see the point of what is being taught or the subject matter. It can indicate the clarity of teaching or swift decisions about your education. It is a card which indicates fast resolution of the matter at hand, and when it is in a spread, you should consider other cards for the nature of this speedy decision.

In *Spiritual Awareness & Self-Development* this card indicates the power of the will and the mind to guidance in the world of thought. The keen eye of the Queen of Swords takes experience and observation into account before making decisions. This is the part of others that observes our life and makes unemotional decisions. If this card has appeared, it shows that you must first detach yourself from your concern in order to make a clear decision.

*You are blocking this card today by:*

1. Being touchy-feely
2. Taking the line of least resistance when someone confronts you verbally
3. Being forgiving and broad-minded
4. Showing a lot of humility

## Connect to Your Card

Really pay attention to the news today. Always have an opinion and offer it. Strike up discussions.

## The Queen of Swords Says

"Be your own person and maintain your strong convictions, no matter what opposition you come up against. Do not be afraid to stand alone from the rest and say exactly what you think—as long as you express it with full confidence and stick to being straightforward, you will receive the acknowledgement you rightly deserve."

## Keywords

Acknowledgement, intense perception, quick, confident, strong, strong will, sharp wit, autonomy, keenness, discernment, perceptive, ordered, precision, astute, knowledge, individualistic, just, intelligence, alertness, independent, versatile, slanderous, quick, sly, bigoted, gossip, malice, prudery, astute, unpretentious, straightforward.

# —Day 62: Queen of Cups—
## Caring for the Heart • Being One Who Listens and Understands

### Resonances

*Numerology:* 38/11

*Astrology:* Scorpio

*Kabbalah:*
Binah (Understanding)

*Elemental:* Water of Water

*Perfume:* Benzoin

*Timing:* Pisces
(February 19–March 20)

REGINA DI COPPE    QUEEN OF CHALICES
REINE DE COUPES    REINA DE COPAS

KÖNIGIN DER KELCHE    BEKERS KONINGIN

### Quick Connections

*Affirmation:* Persevering
in my own depths, I can
discover my true heart.

*Meditation:* "Feeling
your way through relating
and therefore seeing
beyond what is there on
the surface."

## The Lesson of the Queen of Cups
### *Opening of the Key Method (Day 4)*

Today we are going to look at one more skill to practice before we return to our ongoing narrative and gestalt readings tomorrow—the skill of "dignities." We're not yet going to explore that fully; for today, we're going to see how two cards can affect a card between them in a spread or a linear spread.

We're going to play Tarot Friend or Foe!

What we do is take a card out of our deck, and then lay two further cards either side of it. We then decide if the two outer cards are friends or foes to each other and how this affects the central card's reading.

As an example, let's take the Five of Swords as our central card. Take a look at the reading of this card in a relationship question:

In **Relationships** this card indicates the need to lay down one's arms and put away the quarrels of the past. There is no profit at this time in repeating old arguments. You might also consider that other people's opinions (even those of the past such as your parents) may still be influencing current conversations. There is more going on in these words than meets the eye.

We now select for practice the Blasted Tower and the Knight of Wands either side of the Five of Swords. You can see this is also a simple way to produce a powerful and deeper three-card reading, taking this approach of dignities even on this straightforward level.

*The Three Cards for Dignities Spread*

So what do we think about the Blasted Tower and the Knight of Wands—friend or foe with each other? There's no middle ground in this exercise—you must decide if they are friendly or antagonistic. You might try to visualise them both going into a bar together... do they get along?

Once you have decided friend or foe, now interpret the middle card, Five of Swords, but this time in the context of the friendly or antagonistic noise coming from the Blasted Tower and the Knight of Wands. How does that affect the Five of Swords? Does it hamper the meaning, amplify, or assist one aspect of its meaning?

Practice today with a few more sets of three cards and we will look tomorrow at the rules for using dignities in readings.

## The Card in Your Life/Reading

*Careerwise & Financially* this card indicates good faith and consideration of others. One has to be more careful at this time not to upset the apple cart. Whilst you may feel at a disadvantage, it is important not to get emotionally drawn into the situation. In terms of finances this card advises prudence and saving rather than investment or risk.

*Healthwise* this card indicates care and tenderness. It is not a time to overextend yourself but rather to take a rest and recuperate. It is a card of vacation and a new environment. In a mundane sense this card can indicate the return to childhood enjoyment and pastimes.

In *Relationships* this card indicates that attention is needed on an emotional issue that has not yet been opened. Whilst it may be difficult to share this feeling it is important that you meet halfway in order to uncover it. If the resistance is from the other person, then you must take care to allow him or her space to open up their feelings safely.

In *Travel & Lifestyle* this card indicates comfort and luxury. This card shows you should take the best of the best and not settle for half measures. If you need to save for an upgrade, this card shows you should have the patience and not compromise. Your care for yourself at this time is paramount.

In *Education* this card indicates intuitive awareness is rising about your course or subject and your relationship to it is profoundly changing. You have the feeling there is still more to discover you have not yet unlocked or to which access has not been granted. The Queen of Cups asks you to make a deep connection to the heart of the matter.

In *Spiritual Awareness & Self-Development* this card is the card of divination and prophecy. It shows the ability to tap into the deep well of the emotional realm in order to gain wisdom. This is the card of intuition, poetry, and the psychic. Its appearance suggests you must reconnect to this part of yourself to gain insight at this time. You cannot just think things through.

*You are blocking this card today by:*

1. Closing down your psychic radar
2. Being closed down emotionally
3. Being aloof
4. Expressing little empathy

## Connect to Your Card

Spend the day with your cards. Record your dreams. Only follow your instincts today.

## The Queen of Cups Says

"Follow your heart and intuition—you cannot go wrong! Tune in to the feelings of others and respond accordingly. Show compassion where it is needed, and do not turn your back on those who need your support. Be introspective, look within, and see where you can become more loving and caring towards others."

## Keywords

Affection, poetic, dreamy, gentle, good natured, otherworldliness, remembrance, divination, prophecy, heart, melodramatic, spontaneous, generous, empathy, compassionate, loving, psychic, intuitive, tender, beloved, adored, introspection, dreaminess, illusion, tranquility, imaginative, coquettish, prudence, happiness, virtue.

# —Day 63: Queen of Wands—
## Caring for Recognition • Being Activating and Inspiring

### Resonances

*Numerology:* 24/6

*Astrology:* Leo

*Kabbalah:*
Binah (Understanding)

*Elemental:* Water of Fire

*Perfume:* Red Sandalwood

*Timing:*
Sagittarius (November
23–December 21)

### Quick Connections

*Affirmation:* Persevering
in my own enthusiasm,
I can discover my
true spirit.

*Meditation:* "At the heart
of creation is will-power,
then action, followed by
form and reason to be."

## The Lesson of the Queen of Wands
### Opening of the Key (Day 5)

We saw yesterday that we can look at how cards affect a card between them in a simple three-card spread. When we read cards in the "opening of the key" method, we look at the two cards either side of the card we are reading to determine how that card is "dignified" in the whole reading: whether it is a strong, weak, or neutral force. The "opening of the key" method provides a context for the whole reading, as certain cards become more "important" than others. For example we may see that a card is constrained by the two cards either side of it, and take more notice.

The rules are based on the cards' elemental correspondences, and whilst there are more complex rules based on the planetary correspondences, for this seventy-eight-day trip into tarot we will stick with elemental basics. So let's look at how we read a card using full elemental dignities—this is the last thing we need to learn by rote for this method, honest!

As an example, we will take the Eight of Wands, with the Magician card one side and the Queen of Cups, the other. We take the card we are reading, the Eight of Wands, and look at the cards either side of it.

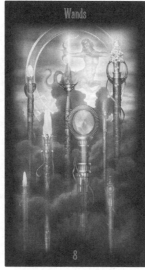

*The Magician, Eight of Wands, and the Queen of Cups*

We then reduce the cards to their elemental correspondences (in this particular version of the method) using the following table:

- Pentacles: Earth
- Swords: Air
- Wands: Fire
- Cups: Water

For the major cards, we have to learn a few more correspondences to reduce them from their planetary or zodiacal correspondences to their elemental correspondences:

- Fool: Air/Uranus
- Magician: Air/Mercury
- High Priestess: Water/Moon
- Empress: Earth/Venus

- Emperor: Fire/Aries
- Hierophant: Earth/Taurus
- Lovers: Air/Gemini
- Chariot: Water/Cancer
- Strength: Fire/Leo
- Hermit: Earth/Virgo
- Wheel of Fortune: Air/Jupiter
- Justice: Air/Libra
- Hanged Man: Water/Neptune
- Death: Water/Scorpio
- Temperance: Fire/Sagittarius
- Devil: Earth/Capricorn
- Tower: Fire/Mars
- Star: Air/Aquarius
- Moon: Water/Pisces
- Sun: Fire/Sun
- Judgement: Fire/Pluto
- Universe/World: Earth/Saturn

So for our example, we have:
- Magician: Air
- Eight of Wands: Fire
- Queen of Cups: Water

That's a Fire card between Air and Water cards. We then take the rules for dignities (from the Golden Dawn system):

- A card is strong or weak, well dignified or ill dignified according to the cards next to it on either side.
- Cards of the same suit on either side strengthen it greatly, for good or evil according to their nature.

Cards of opposite natures on either side weaken it greatly, for either good or evil.

These pairs do not get on with each other:
• Swords (Air) are inimical to Pentacles (Earth).
• Wands (Fire) are inimical to Cups (Water).

These combinations *do* get on with each other:
• Swords (Air) are friendly with Cups (Water) and Wands (Fire).
• Wands (Fire) are friendly with Swords (Air) and Pentacles (Earth).

If a card falls between two other which are mutually contrary, it is not much affected by either.

So we use these rules to compare our two outside cards, air and water; these are friendly. They therefore support the Eight of Wands in the middle. That means we can read the Eight of Wands as positive movement, news, acceleration of a project, etc.

For an even more advanced reading, we can also look at the meaning of the two cards either side of the Eight of Wands—the Magician/air and the Queen of Cups/water—and see that the news will be emotionally satisfying (exactly what the person wants), very direct, and to do with resources and skills. Again, the reading is very positive!

By learning to use these elemental dignities, we can get under the hood of the reading and see the basic elements at work supporting, detracting, tensing, and releasing the reading. They can provide very profound insight into the likelihood of events, and the obstacles in the way of their manifestation.

This is the most "advanced" we will get in our seventy-eight-day course; tomorrow we will return to more lessons. However if you would like to explore the full "Opening of the Key" method—which contains five different spreads, all read with the counting and dignities you have now learnt—please see the videos and handouts for free on our Tarot Professionals site.[15]

### WAYSIDE LESSON: FURTHER CONSIDERATIONS ON THE DIGNITIES

If you take a look at an original Golden Dawn member actually performing this reading, you'll see some variant approaches, such as Annie Horniman's reading reproduced in Mary K. Greer's *Women of the Golden Dawn*, pp. 285–90. Here, when Annie did the counting, she read the counted card **and** the two outer cards around it as a **triad**, coming up with a blended interpretation, which accounts more for the meaning of the cards and little for their elemental dignities. She counted to the Queen of Swords, which had the Three of Cups and the Chariot on either side, reading it as "I am in a happy, friendly, successful current."

She only considered the elemental dignities when she paired the cards, something we haven't covered in this seventy-eight-day class (covered in the full instructions on the Tarot Professionals site). She here marked the pairs as Weak, Moderate, Moderately Strong, and Very Strong according to their dignity with each other, another way of simplifying it.

It's difficult to read according to a fixed set of rules. Mathers provides these and examples (see pp. 132–33 of *The Golden Dawn Tarot* by Robert Wang) such as: "10C 2W 6C Weak, evil. Victory which is perverted by debauchery and evil living. But other cards may mitigate the judgement."

Then there are off-the-cuff examples such as: "9W 9S High Priestess. Recovery from sickness."

Similarly, Mathers gives an example in which he says to ignore a particular dignity because the whole question is one "of Wands." We rapidly return to what you may call a fluid approach—one I take too! We think it is important to learn the dignities and then apply them in practice. However, intuition is the most important in conjunction with the actual card meanings and their overall context. In an inspired moment; however, all bets can be off anyway.

## The Card in Your Life/Reading

*Careerwise & Financially* this card indicates independence. It shows a strong person capable of making good judgements and commanding respect. This is a strong card in career questions, symbolising that your own power must be drawn into the circumstances. It is time to take the lead and stamp your authority on the situation. With regard to finance questions, this card suggests taking the advice of independent consultants.

*Healthwise* this card indicates optimism and a positive outlook in your situation. No matter what occurs, you can take matters into your own hands and live life according to your own values and dignity. There may be a need to fight for your opinion to be heard, but this card bodes well in such circumstances.

In *Relationships* this card can often mean that you must take a firmer role in directing the relationship and be more dynamic. It is your time to be attractive and bask in the limelight for a change. If this suits the other partner more, it is possible he or she is doing likewise, which is not benefiting the relationship at this time.

In *Travel & Lifestyle* this card indicates a powerful current set in motion that will lead you to all that you desire. The fiery energy of the Queen of Wands will ignite your passion to explore new horizons in your life journey. It shows that you can take control and will be respected for doing so.

In *Education* this card indicates being true to your own ambition and not being swayed by others' opinions. You can draw upon your own experience to see things clearly. As a teacher, the Queen of Wands demonstrates that we can be secure in our own authority without being aggressive.

In *Spiritual Awareness & Self-Development* this card embodies being true to your own vision and living life according to your own standards. It is a card of honour and faith as well as being aligned to your true will. When this card appears, it is a reminder to do what feels most real in the whole of your being and soul.

*You are blocking this card today by:*

1. Being shy and retiring
2. Being slow to anger
3. Being in a despicable manner
4. Being complacent

## Connect to Your Card

Show someone you mean business. Do something dramatic. Be the centre of attention.

## The Queen of Wands Says

"Do not withdraw from intimidating situations. Believe in your power and focus on arriving at your destination—yourself. You were born for great things. Be imperious, walk and talk like a queen. Who cares what people think? You need to adopt old-fashioned witchy glamour and ooze charm and magic from every pore, beguiling everyone you meet!"

## Keywords

Independence, power of attraction and command, honourable, sound judgement, ambition, demonstration, limelight, career, versatility, faith, magnetic, attractive, fertility, optimism, assured, obstinate, domineering, flamboyant, dynamic, hyperactivity, honesty, loyalty, steadfastness, attractive, cheerful, energetic.

# —Gate Nine—

# The Temple
# of the King

# Devotion Spread—For Returning Home

*It has been a long journey and you have realised your spiritual vision. As you begin to understand the wisdom of tarot, you also begin to wonder how you may use the experiences of this journey in your life. How will you bring back some of the knowledge of tarot into your world? The Temple of the King awaits your presence for this final illumination to be given. You will learn tarot to engage life, not escape it.*

## Soundtrack for the Journey
### *"Temple of the King" (Rainbow)*

Remove the Empress and the Hierophant card from your deck and place them side by side. Take the thirty-two minor cards from tens to threes. Next, remove the court cards. After that, find the seventeen majors you have encountered as landmarks so far in your journey: World, Last Judgement, Moon, Sun, Star, Temperance, Hanged Man, Devil, Blasted Tower, Death, Wheel, Justice, Lovers, Emperor, Hermit, Chariot, and Strength. Place all these cards together in a mini-deck of sixty-three cards. Shuffle the mini-deck, and consider your whole journey so far. Now ask **"What can I learn and teach the world through my life?"** or more simply, **"What is my spiritual path?"** Gaze upon the Empress (understanding) and the Hierophant (wisdom). Lay out four pairs of cards below the Empress and the Hierophant.

Each pair shows a different level of your spiritual path as what you can learn (the card below the Empress) and teach (the card below the Hierophant).

1. The spiritual level, which is the highest divine inspiration of your personal path.

2. The social level at which you work with others.

3. The inner level of your creativity, dreams, and vision.

4. The daily level at which you live in all your actions.

Make a note of these in your journal and see also how the levels interact with each other, like a tuning fork. Notice where there are strong patterns (similar suits, numbers) or major cards indicating a powerful current in that area of your life. Notice lower-numbered cards which might indicate potential you have not yet realised, or higher-numbered cards which show that this area of your life is coming to an end.

The Temple of the King is a place of devotion and homecoming through the two pillars of understanding and wisdom. It is a place where we create our home through our daily life, divined.

# —Day 64: Two of Pentacles—

*Finding Yourself With What You Have • A Place of Organisation*

### Resonances

*Numerology:* 70/7

*Astrology:*
Jupiter in Capricorn

*Kabbalah:*
Chockmah (Wisdom)

*Sabian Symbol:* Capricorn
I—A Native American
Chief Demanding
Recognition (A Question
of Authority)

### Quick Connections

*Affirmation:* In times of change I am able to find the required strength to keep things moving.

*Meditation:* "To create something practical we have to use our abilities of discernment, and we have to weigh what will work and what will not. All creation comes with accountability, a reckoning of the consequences."

## The Lesson of the Two of Pentacles
### Using Scales of Energy

Today we turn our attention to the Two of Pentacles. We will soon cover the other twos, so it is timely we look at them as a set. In the Golden Dawn system, we see the four elements as four worlds on a Tree of Life, in this order: Fire, Water, Air, and Earth.

Today's study card, the Two of Pentacles, is on the bottom rung of the twos like so:

- Two of Wands
- Two of Cups
- Two of Swords
- Two of Pentacles

If we see these cards as a scale of "twoness" in four elemental worlds starting with the fiery creation of the wands, and ending in the earthy juggling of the pentacles, perhaps we can see how "twoness" manifests at each level. It is certainly happier at the top rung, with the whole world before the Two of Wands. Then contentment at the next rung down, with the Two of Cups. Then it begins to get confused and conflicted at the next rung, in the Two of Swords, and finally with the Two of Pentacles it finishes in quite a restless and dynamic state.

The Two of Pentacles is a picture of something powerful at a difficult level. It requires work, management, balance, and constant agility. The juggler and spinner of plates is hard at work on this card! There is a requirement for dedication in this card and—perhaps at a more spiritual level—a Zen-like blending into the moment to work effortlessly.

If this card came up in a one-card reading for a simple question, but not an obvious one for this card (i.e., "Will I have to work hard on my new sailing and juggling business?"), what would you give as a reply?

"I find it hard to relate emotionally to people, and this seems to be in the way of my new relationship. What does the tarot say?"

You pull the Two of Pentacles. What do you say?

## The Card in Your Life/Reading

*Careerwise & Financially* this card indicates the need to work within constraining circumstances; for example, juggling your finances. In a career decision, this card signifies the need to weigh up the pros and cons of the situation before committing yourself. Whilst it may appear as if there are many changes occurring in your environment, this card tells you that you have the ability to manage them.

*Healthwise* this card suggests that you accept the constraints of your present circumstances and work within them no matter how difficult it may appear. Amidst all the changes taking place, you will not be able to rest, and as a result, you must ensure the situation is constantly managed.

In *Relationships* this card indicates the give and take of time required to build a successful relationship. You must ensure you achieve harmony and balance between time to yourself and time with your partner. This card can also indicate that there is an imbalance in a relationship's material matters that requires addressing.

In *Travel & Lifestyle* this card indicates a need for flexibility under tight and changing circumstances. You will need to keep on your toes throughout this time in order to keep the situation under your control. The Two of Pentacles tells you that it is up to you to hold things together.

In *Education* this card indicates learning a skill by experience and practice. It may be that you need playful practice in a safe environment before you take your education into the real world. At this time you should experiment and learn from your mistakes.

In *Spiritual Awareness & Self-Development* this card speaks to you of the transitory nature of time and space. All things change, and nothing is forever—how we respond to it is the most essential nature of our soul.

### *You are blocking this card today by:*

1. Being awkward
2. Being totally disorganised with finance
3. Totally indulging yourself with no regard to the consequences
4. Giving up on your responsibilities for the day, letting someone else take the flak

## Connect to Your Card

For everything you do, ensure someone else does something. Keep a balance. Learn to juggle. Look after anything mechanical. Move money around.

## The Two of Pentacles Says

"Be in control of your finances. It is important for you to be aware of balancing your incomings and outgoings. Take responsibility, and don't let your spending get out of control. You need to look at how you can make use of the resources you already possess. If finances are tight, look at ways you can save money, say by recycling or reusing. Do not buy into today's throw-away society; instead follow the motto: reduce, re-use, recycle."

## Keywords

Organisation, harmony, flexibility, juggling finances, coping, embracing harmony, balance, monetary obstacles, difficulties, good work, gaiety, recreation, techniques, mastery, agitation, composition, balancing, dexterity, speculating, procrastination, hedging your bets.

# —Day 65: Two of Swords—
### *Expecting Decisions • An Examination of Choice*

### Resonances

*Numerology:* 56/11

*Astrology:*
Moon in Libra

*Kabbalah:*
Chockmah (Wisdom)

*Sabian Symbol:* Libra I—
A Butterfly Perfectly
Displays Its Beauty,
Impaled by a Pin
(Therapeutic Pain)

### Quick Connections

*Affirmation:* In times
of indecision I am
able to call upon my
inner knowledge.

*Meditation:* "Maintaining
a state of non-action
due to internal conflict
will ultimately transform
to brute force in
the long term."

## The Lesson of the Two of Swords
### *The Soul Boat, for Matters of the House of the Self*

This spread is useful for questions such as "Where is my life going?," "Who am I?," and "What should I do?" It is based on the ancient Egyptian concept of the soul boat, or the barque of the Sun. The Sun was seen as traversing the sky in a vast boat, and the nature of the Sun changed as day and night progressed. As the central glyph of the self or soul, the Sun is here used as the significator. The remaining cards are shuffled and dealt as depicted. The ancient Egyptians also believed in a serpent adversary to the Sun, Apep, who is also reflected in the reading.

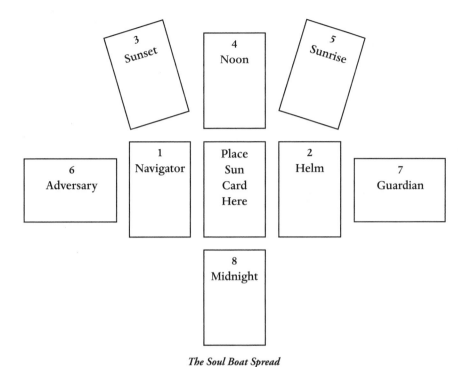

**The Soul Boat Spread**

1. Navigator: This card indicates what steers you in your life, journey, or vision. It is a signpost or beacon.

2. Helm: This illustrates your resources, things which can be drawn upon, avenues which can be explored, and assistance that can be given.

3. Sunset: This is a part of your life that must be allowed to fade.

4. Noon: This is a part of your life that must be recognised and enjoyed.

5. Sunrise: This is a part of your life that must be developed and nurtured.

6. Adversary: This is what blocks you.

7. Guardian: This is what defeats the blocks.

8. Midnight: This is the secret core of your life which must be brought into the light.

As with any other reading, do not mistake the positions and numbering as anything other than a convenient description. You can read the cards in any order and recognise patterns as you read. In this spread, you may wish to read the Helm and Guardian cards together and then the Adversary, for example, comparing to the Midnight card.

## The Card in Your Life/Reading

*Careerwise & Financially* this card indicates a settlement which may be in nobody's favour. It can show a stalemate or indecision on your part leading to a blocked situation. When the Two of Swords appears in a finance reading there can be no progress until a decision is made. You may lack the necessary information to make a decision, but the tide will soon turn and a decision will be forced upon you.

*Healthwise* this card indicates denial leading to blocked feelings. Whilst the situation may appear clearly, it is likely you are avoiding committing yourself to the obvious implications of your circumstances. Once you do so, the situation can begin to resolve itself.

In *Relationships* this card indicates a lack of communication between two parties leading to a stalemate. It can also show a truce; however, this may be because both parties are not providing all the relevant information or avoiding discussion.

In *Travel & Lifestyle* this card indicates a plateau and inactivity. There can be no progress made at this time until the environment changes. You must wait your turn until another settlement is made.

In *Education* this card indicates analysis and the separation of a subject into its component pieces. You must take this card as advice to make clear distinctions in your education, to avoid confusion, and to prevent becoming overwhelmed by too much information.

In *Spiritual Awareness & Self-Development* this card more profoundly represents peace. It shows a peace of mind reached when all opposites are cancelled out and balance is found in the middle of thought. It is the perfect point where thought mirrors reality.

*You are blocking this card today by:*

1. Taking control of your life
2. Making a decision that you have been putting off
3. Facing up to your inner demons, releasing yourself from conflicted thoughts
4. Putting your mental guard down

## Connect to Your Card

Be decisive. Do something, anything. Walk away from trouble. If something you are doing isn't working, do something else. Speak your mind.

## The Two of Swords Says

"Mentally, you feel like you are stuck in a situation over which you have no control, alone in the barren landscape of mental turmoil. You are holding on to distressing thoughts that are immobilising you and depressing you. At the moment, you are your own worst enemy because you refuse to see that only you can release yourself from this prison of your own construct."

## Keywords

Confusion, stalemate, indecision, truce, balance, uncertainty, paradox, suppression, settlement, friendship, protection, valour, refusal of responsibility, magnetism, affinity, equipoise, denial, blocked feelings, repression, dismissive, reticence.

# —Day 66: Two of Cups—
### *Imagining Companionship • The Creation of Unity*

### Resonances

*Numerology:* 42/6

*Astrology:*
Venus in Cancer

*Kabbalah:*
Chockmah (Wisdom)

*Sabian Symbol:*
Cancer I—A Furled
and an Unfurled Flag
Displayed From a Vessel
(A Turning Point)

### Quick Connections

*Affirmation:* In times of
connection I am able to
find more than myself.

*Meditation:* "Like
attracts like; it is wise to
maintain good loving
thoughts to ensure a
harmonious unity."

## The Lesson of the Two of Cups
### *The He Said, I Said, She Said Spread, For Relationship Matters*

This spread is very useful for questions such as "What's going on in this relationship?" and
"Will this relationship work?"

The majority of questions asked of a tarot reader are about relationships. We can work
to divine the nature of the communication between two people in a relationship at all
levels. Doing so will lead to an interpretation of how the relationship may progress.

In this eight-card spread we use the four worlds of Kabbalah to see the relationship
on all levels.

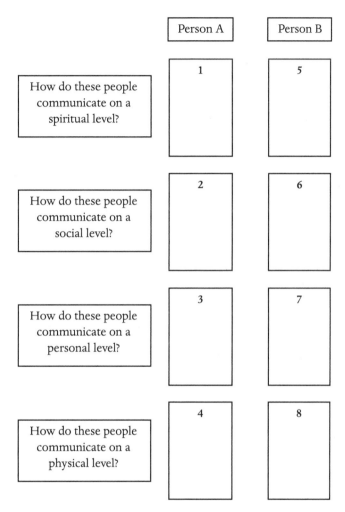

*He Said, She Said, I Said Spread*

## The Card in Your Life/Reading

*Careerwise & Financially* this card indicates creation through cooperation. It is a card symbolising that working with another can produce more than either of you by yourselves. It symbolises a trusting partnership and sharing although one partner may be more proactive than another. In predictions this card signifies that your advances will be favourably met.

*Healthwise* this card indicates emotional balance and gentle healing. The Two of Cups shows that healing comes through our connection to others. In trusting to the care and attention of others we can begin our own healing process. It is time to let others care for us.

In *Relationships* this card indicates a new romance or friendship. Sometimes this indicates the transition of a friendship into something more. Whatever the situation, something is blossoming out of the time you spend with another.

In *Travel & Lifestyle* this card indicates that approaching people with your open feelings will be beneficial. When you open yourself to others, they will trust you and work with you to achieve and explore more than you could possibly imagine at the present.

In *Education* this card indicates that by partnering with someone who shares your passion for a subject, you will gain insights otherwise unavailable to you alone. Indeed there are many breakthroughs that can be made by bouncing ideas off others.

In *Spiritual Awareness & Self-Development* this card shows that we must understand our attraction to the world is the attraction of our soul to itself. From our own reflection in the world, the divine is both created and channelled.

*You are blocking this card today by:*

1. Turning away a good opportunity of happiness
2. Turning your back on a good friend
3. Being repulsed by what attracts you
4. Not wanting to share with another

## Connect to Your Card

Work with someone close. Generate new ideas by bouncing them off someone else. Share a moment with a good friend.

## The Two of Cups Says

"Stop kidding yourself that you are better on your own without anyone else to think about but yourself. You need to share your life with another, someone who shares your motivations and interests. Two is better than one, especially when you are compatible. If you've had a disagreement with somebody, you need to come together, find a compromise, and heal the rift!"

## Keywords

Trust, new romance, friendship, partnership, cooperation, well balanced personality, sharing, reciprocity, reconciliation, common ground, diplomacy, attraction, relationships, connections, truce, cooperation, compromise, reciprocity, reflection, understanding, marriage, attachment, sincerity, passion, compatibility, mutuality, companionship.

# —Day 67: Two of Wands—

## Working Towards the Completion of the Map • The Expression of Vision

### Resonances

*Numerology:* 28/1

*Astrology:*
Mars in Aries

*Kabbalah:*
Chockmah (Wisdom)

*Sabian Symbol:* Aries I—
A Woman Rises Out of
the Sea, a Seal Rises to
Embrace Her
(Emerging Potential)

### Quick Connections

*Affirmation:* In times of opportunity I am able to see my own vision.

*Meditation:* "The call of ambition is strong and we must try to act upon it, lest we spend a lifetime regretting what we didn't do. As a wise man once said, 'People cannot discover new oceans unless they have the courage to lose sight of the shore.'"

## The Lesson of the Two of Wands

### The Wish You Were Here Spread for New Projects

The spread for today's lesson considers how we might answer questions such as "Will this outlandish project come to anything?"

When there is little history to determine whether a project, relationship, or other creative act will be successful, a tarot reading can divine the likely outcome based on a future-past perspective. In this spread, we look at the "Hopes and Wishes" that lead to them being fulfilled. This house is particularly accorded to friendship, so we also look to see who can assist us in the fulfillment of these hopes.

Take the Star card out of the deck, for use as a *future significator.*

Place the Star card in the centre of your table or reading space.

Place a circle of four cards (1–4) around the Star card to divine the project's constraints.

Place four "ray" cards (5–8) to show what can shine through those constraints.

Place four "halo" cards (9–12) to show where help might be found in others.

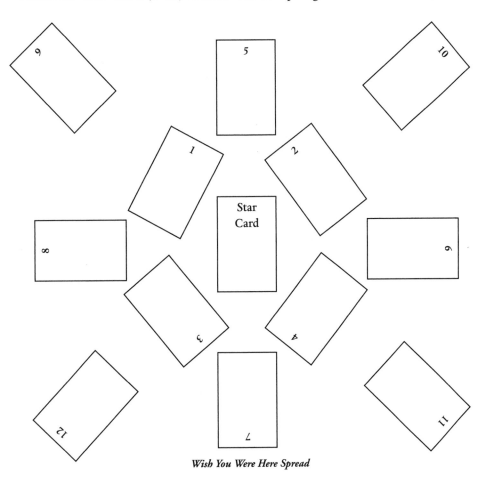

*Wish You Were Here Spread*

# The Card in Your Life/Reading

*Careerwise & Financially* this card indicates planning and aspiration. It is important to have a full model of the real situation in order to set your goals. It is not yet a time to reach out but rather assess the situation and conduct research. It is early yet, and any fortune is a long way away from your present desire.

*Healthwise* this card indicates the need to gain a clearer picture of a situation in order to assess your priorities. You must have faith in your own knowledge and ability to see what is in front of you. Most importantly, you should make judgement based on your own values before considering others' opinions.

In *Relationships* this card shows that you have a larger vision in mind than your partner or those around you. It may be time to share your big picture with those closest to you so that they can help it become a reality. Do not be afraid of connecting to your desires or ambition and expressing these in full.

In *Travel & Lifestyle* this card indicates the initiative for big plans. The card indicates that you are in a position to have a vision of what can be. There is a time of planning required before you can make any commitments, however. Do not waste this opportunity to gain as full a picture of the situation as possible.

In *Education* this card symbolises formulation and modelling. It is important to make an entire scheme of your studies or produce a framework in which your studies can be made. Whilst there is little outside activity or demands on you, you should use the opportunity to revise or prepare.

In *Spiritual Awareness & Self-Development* this card features as that model of the world as based on our values, beliefs, actions, self-identity, and sense of time and space. The more comprehensive, consistent, and congruent our model, the more we can define and divine our life.

*You are blocking this card today by:*

1. Taking action before thinking about the consequences
2. Being closed to new opportunities
3. Doing something the same old way because it's how you have always done it
4. Going along with what someone else wants to do

## Connect to Your Card

Use the Internet to discover someplace new to visit. Plan a day out. Order something online.

## The Two of Wands Says

"You have ambitions and you need to fire yourself up and get out there. However, you also need to plan ahead and be strategic: where do you want to get to? Think about what you have got to give, think innovation, new fresh ideas. You are in an excellent position to join forces with another who shares your vision."

## Keywords

Planning, creative ability, waiting, opportunity, collaboration, faith, ambition, initiative, aspiration, riches, fortune, magnificence, sadness, mortification, achievement, courage, worldly desires, autonomy, planning, form, possibilities, dominion, doubt, promise, formulation, boldness, originality, innovation, daring, vision, perspective, positioning.

### Resonances

*Numerology:* 65/11

*Astrology:* Taurus

*Kabbalah:*
Chockmah (Wisdom)

*Elemental:* Fire of Earth

*Perfume:* Benzoin

*Timing:*
Capricorn (December 22–
January 20)

### Quick Connections

*Affirmation:* Ruling my
own inner kingdom, I
am able to draw upon a
wealth of experience.

*Meditation:* "A small sum
of money used wisely
by a pauper is far more
enriching than a large
amount squandered
by a king."

## The Lesson of the King of Pentacles
### Using Numerology in Tarot

We have presented each card throughout these seventy-eight days with a numerological correspondence, which follow the correspondences of the cards through Astrology to Numerology. Where the number is larger than nine, it is also given as its reduced number 1–9. For example, 24 resolves to 6 (2 + 4) and 48 reduces to 3 (4 + 8 = 12, then reduced again 1 + 2 = 3). We would recommend *Numerology and the Divine Triangle* given in the reading list for further considerations of the tarot and numerology.

In today's lesson we will cover a simple method of using numerology in small readings of three to five cards, where it is possible to quickly resolve the spread into a numerological result.

Perform a simple three-to-five-card spread, non-positional (i.e., a spread read as a narrative rather than having fixed meanings for each location) and read/interpret as usual. At the conclusion of the reading you can then consult the numerological correspondences of the cards, in their reduced value (i.e., 1–9) and add them together.

Reduce this number until you resolve it to a value between one and nine. You can then consult the simplified chart below to provide an overall summary of the reading.

As an example, if you pulled the Knight of Wands, the Six of Cups, and the Hermit, this would correspond to the numbers seven, one, and nine. These total 17 (1+7+9) which reduces to 8 (1+7). We then consult the value for eight in the table below to include in our summary of the reading.

1. The situation is full of potential yet to be manifest and realised.
2. Circumstances are not fixed and there is still flexibility to change.
3. There is an expansive environment which can be built upon.
4. The situation is stable, somewhat fixed and rigid.
5. There is a lot of dynamic change and action at work.
6. The situation is interconnected with many other events and people.
7. The reading suggests a lot of reflection and consideration rather than action.
8. The reading suggests action is taken at this time rather than planning.
9. The situation is coming to a head and will soon be resolved.

Your further studies of numerology will suggest deeper interpretations of these numbers and many other ways of applying numerology to your spreads and tarot work.

## The Card in Your Life/Reading

*Careerwise & Financially* this card indicates being up front in all your dealings and taking firm control over all you survey. The King of Pentacles is reliable and a solid investment and so symbolises all that is gained from perseverance. When this card appears in a financial question it shows long-term success, whilst in career questions it indicates management and mastery through long-term work or planning.

*Healthwise* this card indicates good support and firm recovery. Whilst it is a card of long-term endurance and patience, it is entirely positive with regard to matters of the body. The material nature of this card is so strong it symbolises we must not be overwhelmed by our own physical frame or its failings. It also shows the inherent strength of the body and its ability to repair itself.

In *Relationships* this card indicates a good solid basis on which a relationship can be built. There is a wealth to be found in your emotional investment even if it is only a matter of security. The figure of this card is not usually dynamic and exciting; however, they do bring stability into your life.

In *Travel & Lifestyle* this card indicates the need to stay fixed and firm within your current environment. Others should come to you, and you should not extend your resources or extend yourself in any way. Whilst this may appear indulgent or even lazy, the card shows that you have set the time to enjoy your position.

In *Education* this card indicates a good solid grasp of the facts backed up by experience. When learning this card shows the importance of a regular schedule and firm structure to your work. When teaching, this card shows the importance of applying a comprehensive overview of the subject into real-life examples.

In *Spiritual Awareness & Self-Development* this card expresses the highs and lows of the material plane. Whilst there are many rewards to be gained by our participation in the world, we must not allow ourselves to be overtaken by our attachments. This card shows a right relationship to add experience in the world. Perhaps its appearance in a spread suggests the need to pay attention to this relationship.

*You are blocking this card today by:*

1. Behaving in a reckless manner
2. Going on a spending spree
3. Being overly emotional
4. Not fulfilling an obligation

## Connect to Your Card

Review your finances and take inventory. Do something practical. Make a will.

## The King of Pentacles Says

"There are good opportunities out there to be realised, but be practical about it. There is no room in the world of success for ambition without any real grounding. You need to think about future security and not just about today; try to create long-term plans. Never invest your time and expertise in a project without first investigating the small print. Before you speculate to accumulate, make sure the project/opportunity is viable."

## Keywords

Obviousness, reliable, accomplished, solid, steady, security, reliability, calmness, wealth, perseverance, worldly wisdom, indomitable, practicality, success, influential, speculator, wealth, attainment, enterprising, supportive.

# —Day 69: King of Swords—
## *Doing What is Right • Declaring Judgement*

### Resonances

*Numerology:* 51/6

*Astrology:* Gemini

*Kabbalah:*
Chockmah (Wisdom)

*Elemental:* Fire of Air

*Perfume:* Olibanum

*Timing:* Libra (September
23–October 23)

### Quick Connections

*Affirmation:* Ruling my
own mind, I am able to
draw upon the knowledge
of the ages.

*Meditation:* "Adopting
the discipline of right
thinking and living by
it day by day."

## The Lesson of the King of Swords
### *Timing in Tarot*

Whilst Tarosophy has a number of methods for timing in readings and spreads, here we'll look at an elegantly simple one based on numerology and Kabbalah. If you know the general timescale of a likely event, such as a house move "it'd have to be within the next year or two" or a law case "within the month," etc., you can apply the following method.

We'll use as an example some of the cards we've looked at. Imagine they are in a ten-card spread, such as the Celtic Cross:

- Two of Wands
- Five of Wands
- Four of Cups
- The World

- Ten of Swords
- Seven of Wands
- Queen of Wands
- The Emperor
- The Hierophant
- The Devil

Just take the numbered cards and work out an average for them, so we roughly get how far in the sequence of Ace to Ten the cards are falling in the divination. In this reading we get the numbers 2, 4, 5, 10, and 7. That's 2 + 4 + 5 + 10 + 7 = 28 and divided by the number (of numbered cards) which is five, for a sum of 5.6. Therefore the cards are "five-and-a-half-way" through the sequence of one through ten. So in a situation where the timescale is anything up to a year, it means the "flow" of events is already more than halfway. The outcome is likely six months or so away.

In a reading with lots of low-numbered cards, the event is far away, and with high-numbered cards in the majority, it is closer. This is a simple rule with a good "method" that is numerologically and kabbalistically sound!

You can also refer to any major cards in the reading as providing an indication of timing:

- Tower: Suddenly
- Devil: Not for a long time and after struggle
- Wheel: In the hands of the divine
- Empress: Will happen eventually and naturally (nine months)
- Sun: A year
- Moon: A month

You can also refer to the timing correspondence on the court cards in this book either by performing a reading using only the twelve court cards or by observing these cards in a full-deck spread.

# The Card in Your Life/Reading

*Careerwise & Financially* this card indicates analysis to the point of suspicion. In this sphere, the card is a warning to pay attention to those around you and the situation before committing any action. The card counsels extreme caution in finance and career—you must hold back no matter what the provocation or apparent opportunity.

*Healthwise* this card indicates the need for further analysis and caution when making any decisions. The King of Swords is here to warn you that you must think things through clearly if you want to take advantage of your current situation.

In *Relationships* this card indicates distrust and over-analysis leading to thoughts that will need resolution. The King of Swords may equally indicate a figure who is rational and cool. When appearing in a spread position for yourself, this card means you must take a critical look at the relationship from a detached position.

In *Travel & Lifestyle* this card indicates planning and careful consideration to an extreme degree. Now is not a time of action; it is a time to think everything through in as many ways as possible. Whilst you may want to take sudden and abrupt action, remember that it should be based on clear thinking.

In *Education* this card indicates an ability to be a clear communicator. It also shows the position of the critic. Whilst your work may be judged harshly, you must separate out the learning experience in order to make progress. From your own point of view this card shows you must be absolutely ruthless in your work.

In *Spiritual Awareness & Self-Development* this card is the height of rational thought and its ability to analyse the world in all its complexity. When we reach this card, we know the limits of logic and its expression through language in our life. It is a card of eloquent understanding of the rules of the world gained through clear observation and reflection.

*You are blocking this card today by:*

1. Responding in an impulsive way verbally
2. Being receptive to any request regardless of how insignificant it is
3. Being very trusting
4. Being very intuitive in your dealings

## Connect to Your Card

Volunteer to be the chairperson or leader of an event. Make a speech. Write a letter.

## The King of Swords Says

"Now is not the time to be off your guard; you must deliberate before communicating. You should ask yourself, 'Could this be taken down and used as evidence against me at any time?' I did not get to where I am now without plotting and contriving, without a strong dose of caution. Do as I say and you will not go far wrong; I am a wise old man with success behind my sword."

## Keywords

Deliberation, judge, firm, command, wise, authority, truth, analysis, drive, judiciousness, distrustful, suspicious, brevity, manipulation, declaration, affirming, orator, wariness, paranoia, extreme caution, rational, malicious, plotting, obstinate, supremacy, judge, critic, severe, crafty, ruthless, authority, tyranny, articulate, direct, just, analytical.

# —Day 70: King of Cups—
## Doing What Feels Good • Declaring Satisfaction

### Resonances

*Numerology:* 37/1

*Astrology:* Cancer

*Kabbalah:*
Chockmah (Wisdom)

*Elemental:* Fire of Water

*Perfume:* Opoponax

*Timing:* Cancer
(June 22–July 22)

### Quick Connections

*Affirmation:* Ruling my own heart, I am able to draw upon the depths of all time.

*Meditation:* "Live life like there is no tomorrow, wallow in all the happiness that comes your way, and never look back. Let go of old grudges."

## The Lesson of the King of Cups
### Creating Your Own Tarot Affirmations

To create your own tarot affirmation, it is important to ensure the affirmation meets your own personal inner space. We can use an NLP technique to quickly discover this space and then make a correspondence to tarot that empowers the affirmation.

You can perform this exercise with someone else or by yourself, writing it in your journal or simply making statements out loud.

First, ask yourself "What am I?" and answer with the most obvious answer, such as "a human being." Take a moment to acknowledge that statement and then say to yourself, "I am a [human being] but what else am I?" Make another obvious statement, such as "I am a man/woman." Again, acknowledge your state and make another gentle enquiry, "I am a [man/woman] but what else am I?"

Continue with this simple pattern, and begin to move into metaphors and images. If you were a force of nature, a plant, or a part of a town or house, what would you be? Be as descriptive as your free association can be, such as "I am a solid rock" or "I am a map."

For each answer, acknowledge it for a moment and then make further enquiry to yourself. Make a note of at least three to four of these images, particularly those which hold some emotional charge for you when you say them. Then, go through your tarot deck and find the cards which most closely correspond, either obviously with a similar or identical image, or intuitively by the feeling of the card, to those three to four images from your own inner landscape.

Then create a series of three to four affirmations from what we have provided for those cards, or consider writing your own. You can use this affirmation illustrated by the cards for as long as you require activating those influences in your life.

## The Card in Your Life/Reading

*Careerwise & Financially* this card indicates diplomacy, compassion, and composure. You must trust your instincts and feelings in approaching a delicate situation. It is not a time to be over-analytical or critical; instead, take in the emotional content of the circumstances. This card can indicate that others are not expressing their feelings fully and you may be required to draw them out further before personally committing.

*Healthwise* this card indicates the dignity of maintaining one's composure during a difficult situation. How you hold yourself at this time will have a profound effect on yourself and those around you. This is a card of the hidden depths you are capable of reaching even under restricting circumstances.

In *Relationships* this card indicates a depth of feeling and quiet power beneath a calm exterior. This is a positive card to receive in relationship readings because it denotes that you are drawing upon deep parts of yourself.

In *Travel & Lifestyle* this card indicates a satisfying future. In everyday terms, this is a card of elegance and sophistication; given the choice, you should choose the most engaging solution. The King of Cups is able to open himself to a vast range of experience and you are advised to do likewise.

In *Education* this card indicates connecting to the deeper principles of your study to expand your horizons. It can indicate artistic and creative satisfaction, and is entirely positive in relation to educational endeavours. This card also shows that we can gain recognition for our craft if we find the right audience or marketplace.

In *Spiritual Awareness & Self-Development* this card symbolises the profound depths of our own emotions by which we can connect to the deep structures and patterns of the universal flow. When this card appears in such questions, it foretells a sharing of wisdom from the universe to yourself.

*You are blocking this card today by:*
1. Not suffering fools in any manner at all
2. Not bothering to engage emotional sensibility before speaking
3. Being impatient and not giving away any of your precious time
4. Really lording something over someone

## Connect to Your Card
Do something satisfying. Be generous all day with your time and attention to others.

## The King of Cups Says
"There is more achieved in gaining support for a certain endeavour/project through quiet stealth than badgering people. If you have an emotional issue, remember it is so important to remember the quote 'dignity, always dignity.' On the inside you may be falling apart, but if you can maintain a composure of calm externally, it will put you in a stronger position to fight onwards! Try to set a good example—be the sort of person you would want giving you support if you needed it."

## Keywords
Recognition, considerate, calm exterior, quiet power, elegance, sophistication, dignity, wisdom, compassion, composure, peace-maker, principles, stability, diplomacy, generosity, wise, caring, tolerant, kindness, helpfulness, skill, manipulation, crafty, knowledgeable, benefactor, tutor, liberating, liberality.

*Doing What Is Envisioned • Declaring Inspiration*

### Resonances

*Numerology:* 23/5

*Astrology:* Aries

*Kabbalah:*
Chockmah (Wisdom)

*Elemental:* Fire of Fire

*Perfume:* Olibanum

*Timing:* Aries
(March 21–April 20)

RE DI BASTONI / ROI DE BATONS / KING OF WANDS / REY DE BASTOS / KÖNIG DER STÄBE / STAVEN KONING

### Quick Connections

*Affirmation:* Ruling my own life, I am able to draw upon the heights of the divine.

*Meditation:* "Fireworks only flare up in the night sky; this is their time to display their reason for creation. You too must take action to express your reason to be."

## The Lesson of the King of Wands
### *Using the Sabian Symbols and Tarot*

Throughout these seventy-eight days we have provided for the minor cards, two through ten, a Sabian symbol (description) and its nameplate (key phrase or title). These are channelled symbolic scenes which correspond to the 360 degrees of the entire zodiacal circle. If you would like to use the Sabian symbols more fully, we highly recommend *The Astrological Oracle* by Lyn Birkbeck, which provides a comprehensive oracle using the Sabian symbols. You can also consult the Sabian Fountain in Tarot-Town.[16]

The Sabian symbol given for each of the cards in this workbook is the first degree symbol of each decan. As each decan has ten degrees (see the earlier Wayside Lesson on the decans), we take these to correspond to the ten levels of each card through Kabbalah. Without going into too much detail, the first degree corresponds to the Kether or "point" of the card, and the tenth degree corresponds to its manifestation or action in the world.

In order to use the Sabian symbols in your reading, note the corresponding Sabian images for any of the cards two through ten in your spread, and then write these images on a single sheet of paper. Write down the "nameplate" key phrases also given along the bottom of the paper.

You can also sketch out an illustration of how you think these images might interact with each other or leave the text descriptions alone.

Place the sheet near to your bed and contemplate it before sleep for several days. You may soon discover that the symbols provide powerful dreams from their enigmatic and timeless images. These dreams can provide further information for your divination.

## The Card in Your Life/Reading

*Careerwise & Financially* this card indicates motivation and vitality. The King of Wands knows exactly what to do and how to do it. It may also signify delegation to others to fulfill your vision. The King of Wands is authentic and true; in a financial reading he indicates that the situation is as it is presented.

*Healthwise* this card indicates that you must take command of your own situation and state things firmly from your point of view. You have achieved the right position from which to speak and must do so. It may also indicate that you must follow your burning passion to improve your health.

In *Relationships* this card indicates fiery passion and burning desire. It brings warmth and charm into any relationship, and if you can sustain it, the enthusiasm brings its own rewards. The card shows how a relationship may create its own vision and then manifest that vision in every way. As an outcome card, the King of Wands shows a relationship will be all-consuming.

In *Travel & Lifestyle* this card indicates enterprise and vision. You must be bold enough to make dramatic steps forward in accomplishing your goals. The fire aspect of this card is your enthusiasm which will be rewarded when it is applied. This card says simply, "Go!"

In *Education* this card indicates counselling and discussion. The King of Wands is the ideal mentor and coach—someone who inspires you and draws out inspiration from you. With this card is the advice to seek counsel from someone in whom you have complete confidence.

In *Spiritual Awareness & Self-Development* this card is the burning core of our values and vision. It reminds is that we must manifest and be true to our vision, else we are consumed by it. No matter how idealistic or unrealistic our vision may appear to be, it is to be lived.

*You are blocking this card today by:*

1. Being ineffectual
2. Being apathetic
3. Doing exactly as you have been told to do
4. Not taking the initiative

## Connect to Your Card

Make immediate decisions all day and trust your experience rather than argue.

## The King of Wands Says

"Develop the best of my qualities—I possess the best of both worlds in that I am practical, confident, and orderly as well as the energy of being enterprising, dramatic, viral, and forceful. I am a master of putting a new spin on any situation; I can put new vigour into any occasion I grace with my presence. I can inspire enthusiasm of spirit where there is lethargy."

## Keywords

Authenticity, handsome, passionate, generous, noble, leader, agile, wit, charm, motivation, commanding, enterprise, vision, powerful, bold, inspiring, vitality, dramatic, ardent, nobility, virility, fortitude, generous, provocative, inspirational, influence, persuasion, counsel, deliberation, warmth, enthusiasm, confidence, creative, forceful.

### WAYSIDE LESSON: TAROT LABYRINTH

In the Opening of the Key method of the Golden Dawn (taught in my own intermediate courses and within the works of that order and Aleister Crowley), one lays out cards in long sequences and makes use of a counting method to select which cards are read in the spread. The counting rules are based on correspondences and are reasonably straightforward, if you know your correspondences to the majors! To me, these correspondences are the difference between a "beginner" student and an "intermediate" student—the latter is able to bridge the tarot to other systems.

In the Opening of the Key, one learns the following rules for counting cards. There are variations, and given the minor confusion that often occurs with the Golden Dawn/Thoth deck titles of the court cards, this is my own chosen method:

- Aces count eleven
- Minors two through ten count the number on the card
- Pages/Princesses count seven
- Knights (princes), queens, and kings (knights) count four

For the majors, count according to the type of correspondence present on that card, be it elemental, planetary, or zodiacal:

- Elemental count three
- Planetary count nine
- Zodiacal count twelve

Rather than teach the Opening of the Key, I would like to present a secret of the Golden Dawn based on the major cards. This "secret" is taught within a particular order and is here given for the first time—the Count of Creation.

Assuming that the cards have settled into a reasonably stable archetypal pattern reflecting something like what we call reality, this method suggests that a sequence embodies the pattern and structure of all creation. This pattern is seen within our "universe as hologram" concept examined in section four of the Introduction. Through correspondence, a hermetic analysis of the universe and its connections—the "invisible knots"—we also assume a reflection of a deeper pattern. Having established that position, we can now discern secret patterns in the threads of the tarot tapestry by the method of counting through correspondences. That is to say, every card in the major arcana has its own journey; you may know the Fool's Journey and the Adept's Journey, but there are journeys for *each* card, based on this counting method. There is a hidden High Priestess's Journey, a Hermit's Journey, and a Journey of the Wheel as well. To discover these journeys for yourself, follow this simple method.

Taking the Fool's Journey first, starting with the Fool (and in this method, you count the card from which you commence), count appropriately through the majors based on correspondence. Where the count ends, that is the next stage of the

Fool's journey. You repeat this counting, cycling back through the majors, until you encounter a card which you have already counted.

If we take the Fool, corresponding to Air (an element), we count three, taking us to the High Priestess. From the High Priestess (Moon, planetary) we count nine, taking us to the Wheel (Jupiter, planetary). Counting nine from there, we reach the Moon (Pisces, zodiacal) and count twelve, reaching the Chariot (Cancer, zodiacal). Counting twelve again takes us to the Moon. As we have already selected the Moon, the count stops here.

Thus, the Fool's Secret Journey takes him to the High Priestess, Wheel, Moon, and Chariot. In discussion with some of my advanced tarot students, we saw this as a parable of the spirit discovering that the world was veiled and revealed, that everything was connected, and though the world itself was reflected light, the Master of the Temple—a correspondence of the Chariot—transcended this state. It led to a very profound and somewhat Gnostic discussion of the universe!

You may now choose to discover the hidden journeys of each major card through this previously secret system. One student recently suggested that those discovering through numerology or astrology (or other methods) their "birth card" (one of the majors), "life card," or "year card" could make use of this system to see further the journey of discovery that waits.

It is also a suitable method for developing single-card major-only readings, where the card itself is merely the gateway to the journey that naturally follows—a universal "necessity," as Crowley called the tarot's structure.

Another method of engaging with this exercise is to draw and plot the paths of each journey as paths in a labyrinth or forest, with coloured pens to show the different paths between cards—elemental, zodiacal, or planetary. This will show you an incredible "garden of forking paths" as Borges might call it, with interesting loops, dead ends, major thoroughfares, and intersections—all hidden in plain sight. You will see that the High Priestess is the most connected card in the garden!

The tarot is a fascinating device, and through correspondence and intermediate study it becomes a veritable map of creation itself, of which it is part and reflection.

—Gate Ten—

# The Throne

# Room

# The Crown Spread—For Finding Yourself

*Ahead of you are the majestic figures of the High Priestess and the Magician, sat in the Throne Room of the Most Ancient of Mysteries. You approach them and at the same time realise they are approaching you. All is one, and you are one with the journey itself. You look around for the last remaining card, the seventy-eighth card of the deck, the enigmatic Fool. And at that very moment, you find yourself.*

## Soundtrack for the Journey
### *"Bad" (U2)*

Take all the cards in the deck. You now have found your full deck of possibilities.

Review your journal and the spreads so far.

Consider all that you have changed in your life in so short a time.

Shuffle the deck.

Ask the question, **"Who am I and what is the universe?"**

Find the Fool card in the deck. The two cards either side of the Fool are the answer to your question. Which way around they are is now totally up to you.

# —Day 72: The High Priestess—
## The Mysteries • The Light Is Not the Source

### Resonances

*Numerology:* 2

*Astrology:* Moon

*Kabbalah:*
Kether and Tiphareth

### Quick Connections

*Affirmation:* There
are mysteries beyond
mysteries, and I am
constantly revealed
to myself.

*Meditation:* "The
full moon on a clear
night gives off enough
illumination to show the
way home. Be subtle
like the moon and you
too will see what needs
to be seen to take you
home safely."

## The Lesson of the High Priestess

Have a look at the High Priestess, Empress, Temperance, Star, and World cards. They all show (on most decks) female figures—what are the qualities of the feminine in each of these? How do they differ? We'll ignore the Justice card, as whilst it depicts a female figure it is not exclusively a feminine archetype—something we cover in *Tarosophy* but don't have space to look at here.

## The Card in Your Life/Reading

*Careerwise & Financially* this card indicates that unknown forces are at work behind the scenes. You must not assume that everything has been made clear to you. In financial matters, whilst the High Priestess appears to hold the law, there is much that is not revealed. It is a card that speaks of unwelcome secrecy. On the positive side, this card shows that you can trust your intuition where you have experience in matters in order to make the right decision.

*Healthwise* this card indicates the depths of your inner wisdom and the importance of intuition. It is a card of healing from deep sources. When this card appears in a health reading, it symbolises assistance from one who is powerfully in touch with his or her intuition and emotions. It is not a card of instant or rapid change; you must also allow for time to pass.

In *Relationships* this card indicates a profound connection at a deep level between the people involved. It shows that there are hidden currents drawing from their past into the present and future. This card shows that both parties have lessons to learn whilst they establish their relationship. It is also a card of potential; however, it requires discretion and care in order for fulfillment to be achieved.

In *Travel & Lifestyle* this card indicates how important it is to go with the flow of our own intuition. In life or whilst travelling, sometimes we find a current to which we can surrender and follow. It is time for you to take the path between the extremes—follow your instincts.

In *Education* this card indicates expertise and experience in a deep and profound manner. This is a card of teaching and wisdom. If you are a student, it indicates that you must continue to follow your path even if not all is clear at the present time. For teachers, this card shows how your teaching goes beyond the classroom and into life itself.

In *Spiritual Awareness & Self-Development* this card symbolises the hidden teachings of the world. We encounter the high priestess in moments of revelation and enlightenment and her wisdom is profound and life-changing. When this card appears in self-development or spiritual questions, it indicates the possibility of initiation.

*You are blocking this card today by:*

1. Being extroverted and forceful
2. Gossiping and telling everybody all your innermost secrets
3. Being very loud; being discreet today is not for you
4. Being tactless and compromising others' privacy by doing this

## Connect to Your Card

Act mysteriously all day. Consult your cards. Be enigmatic. Give riddles rather than responses.

## The High Priestess Says

"I am a vessel full of mystery and hidden wisdom. Plunge the depths of my inner space and you will encounter revelation. From this will come a healing of the unconscious. You need to realign with your divine self to uncover your true purpose."

## Keywords

Revelation, mystery, enlightenment, depths, hidden inner space, insight, esotericism, soul, containment, potential, mystery, stillness, wisdom, secrets, intuition, discretion, clairvoyance, inspiration, prophetic, unconscious, healer, silence, tenacity.

# —Day 73: The Magician—
## *The Magick • There Can Be Only One*

### Resonances

*Numerology:* 1

*Astrology:* Mercury

*Kabbalah:*
Kether and Binah

### Quick Connections

*Affirmation:* In the magic of the world and the universe, my self is the most magical machine of all.

*Meditation:* "We never stop learning as long as we live; we are surrounded all our life by what we need to teach us all we need to know."

## The Lesson of the Magician
### *The Tablet of Union (Enochian) Spread, for Matters of Protection*

This magical and advanced spread is for questions such as "How do I best protect my job?" or "How do I conclude a matter?"

In the Enochian magical system developed by John Dee and Edward Kelley in 1582–1587, the angels themselves transmitted teachings and communications of a vast and complex nature. In the centre of this system stood the Watchtowers of the Elements, and an array of thirty *Aethyrs* the angels inhabited and passed through when travelling from one world into another.

To comprehend this vast system, a Tablet of Union was given, where a simple synthesis of the elements could be viewed and from which all followed. Here we take that elemental root to create a 25-card spread that gives the absolute basics of a situation—

ensuring all sides are seen, whether to protect ones assets or to get a comprehensive overview of a tricky situation.[17]

| | Spirit | Air | Water | Earth | Fire |
|---|---|---|---|---|---|
| **Spirit** | **1** **Spirit** **of** **Spirit** | 2 Spirit of Air | 3 Spirit of Water | 4 Spirit of Earth | 5 Spirit of Fire |
| **Air** | 6 Air of Spirit | **7** **Air** **of** **Air** | 8 Air of Water | 9 Air of Earth | 10 Air of Fire |
| **Water** | 11 Water of Spirit | 12 Water of Air | **13** **Water** **of** **Water** | 14 Water of Earth | 15 Water of Fire |
| **Earth** | 16 Earth of Spirit | 17 Earth of Air | 18 Earth of Water | **19** **Earth** **of** **Earth** | 20 Earth of Fire |
| **Fire** | 21 Fire of Spirit | 22 Fire of Air | 23 Fire of Water | 24 Fire of Earth | **25** **Fire** **of** **Fire** |

*Enochian Spread*

1. Where is this situation coming from, ultimately?
2. What is the simple idea that captures the heart of this event?
3. What is this trying to teach me?
4. How can I best bring it to conclusion safely?
5. Where can I best bring down my ambition/passion into this situation?
6. What needs communicating?
7. What is free to move?
8. How can I best maintain my emotional stability?
9. What must I see in order to know the reality of this event?
10. Where can I best spend my time?
11. Where am I safest?
12. Where is clarity and expression to be best discovered?
13. What is free to be felt?
14. Where might I come unstuck?
15. Where is the source of tension and conflict to be fought out?
16. What value needs to be drawn upon to protect those in this situation?
17. What is the simplest way of seeing what is going on?
18. What can I do about where I feel pinned down?
19. What is this situation trying to achieve in reality and manifestation?
20. What fire needs putting out immediately? What needs to be dealt with first?
21. What spark can I rescue from this position?
22. What can I give life by paying attention?
23. How can I bring my own resources and feelings to bear in this situation?
24. What will assure long-term success and protection?
25. What is the ultimate message I must live?

## The Card in Your Life/Reading

*Careerwise & Financially* this card indicates organisational skills and the ability to manage your environment. You must ensure you have all your resources gathered together and understand the direction to which you must take them. This card shows how you can channel grand visions into realistic manifestation. It is a card of the skilled businessperson and indicates your will to succeed in a reading. In a predictive sense this card shows eventual mastery and success.

*Healthwise* this card indicates willpower and a marshalling of your forces towards recovery or better health. This is a card that symbolises commitment to the goal or target in mind. You cannot rely on others—your success lies in your own hands at this time.

In *Relationships* this card indicates a powerful drive within the relationship and a coming together of different aspects to make a single whole. Whilst it may be dramatic, there is a slight warning that communications could be tricky or changeable. This may not be a relationship you can quite pin down.

In *Travel & Lifestyle* this card indicates constant change and the ability to respond to whatever life presents. It is a card of the adept or experienced adventurer who can meet all obstacles with skill and drive. It indicates success and powerful assistance in all questions of travel and lifestyle. You need only ensure that you have the will to carry yourself forward and all will be well.

In *Education* this card indicates teaching by example and experimentation. It shows how we can learn by following the examples and teachings of the others, however we must also forge our own path in our studies. It is a card of the maverick or individual who takes a new path.

In *Spiritual Awareness & Self-Development* this card is the card of magic, pure and simple. It is when we use our will to make changes in our life and our life mirrors our inner self perfectly. This is a card of ambition and divine will aligned so that we become a channel of higher forces. There is no doubting the Magician.

*You are blocking this card today by:*
1. Not wanting to learn
2. Not making the most of the technology that is at your disposal
3. Not focusing on the task at hand
4. Being very nervous and ill at ease

## Connect to Your Card

Practice your skills. Get better at something. Learn. Teach. Demonstrate. Present.

## The Magician Says

"It's all in the know-how! You need to use all the resources around you to attain the success you deserve. The perfect blend of intellect, willpower, concentration, organisational skills, and action alongside that flair of innovation and creative potency will magically materialise what you desire!"

## Keywords

Success, originator, creative, organisational skills, ability, willpower, skill, self-confidence, vision, decision, action, initiative, power, concentration, intellect, tradition, intuition, agility, wit, craft, potency, conduit, focus, adaptability, resourceful, power, channelling, conducting, improvisation, adept.

# —Day 74: Ace of Pentacles—
### Finding Yourself Infinitely Resourceful • A Place of Wealth

## Resonances

*Numerology:* 69/6

*Astrology:*
Earth Signs

*Kabbalah:*
Kether (Crown)

## Quick Connections

*Affirmation:* I am the seed of all that can be created.

*Meditation:* "Great oaks from little acorns grow." Allow yourself to be like the little acorn; know that you will grow forever upwards and fulfill your destiny."

## The Lesson of the Ace of Pentacles
### *The Well of Untapped Reserves, for Matters of the House of Resources*

This new method for today answers such questions such as "What am I missing?", "What can I do?", and "How can I make it happen?"

This unique spread puts to use not only the symbol and image of a house—but your actual house or apartment itself! It is specifically designed as a self-reading, although if performed on behalf of a client, you can do it as written, or map out (with the client) his or her house and use it as a layout. In Jungian terms, the house is a symbol of the self, and the locations in a house often appear in dreams, indicating aspects of the self. Here we also take the physical locations as representing functions.

Take your deck and shuffle whilst standing in whatever place you regard as the "centre" of your house or apartment. Take out the first card and lay it somewhere in the space around you, saying:

1. This is the card that tells me exactly what I have.

Now move to the next room or area of your property, and lay out a card according to the function of that location. I have given some examples below:

2. Kitchen: This is the card that tells me what nourishes me.
3. Study: This is the card that tells me what I can yet learn.
4. Children's room: This is the card that tells me what delights me.
5. Bedroom: This is the card that tells me what will give me rest and relaxation.
6. Basement: This is the card that tells me what is hidden from which I may draw upon.
7. Attic: This is the card that tells me what I can still aim for.
8. Hallway: This is the card that tells me how I will get there.

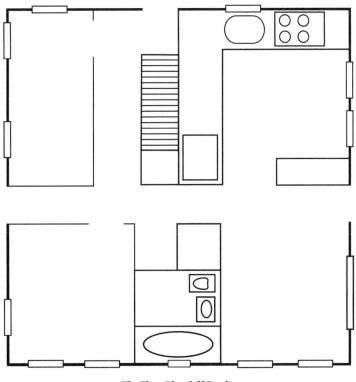

*The Floor Plan Self-Reading*

You can use your own imagination for this reading, and have fun with it. You can lay down more than one card in any particular area and then go back through your property reading the cards. Be careful with this reading not to lose any cards or perform the reading when lots of other people or animals are passing through the place!

Whilst the bathroom card may indicate what you must "flush away," please be careful not to get your cards wet or damp! Similarly, whilst it is fun to be clambering into the attic to receive a card that otherwise would not make itself known, be careful!

## The Card in Your Life/Reading

*Careerwise & Financially* this card indicates good fortune lies ahead and wealth awaits you. Although this is only the seed of a new beginning, it contains great potential for financial reward. The Ace of Pentacles is an excellent card in all questions of career and finance. It may also indicate a helping hand is being offered you which you should accept.

*Healthwise* this card indicates the root of health from which you can build. You must concentrate on the smallest things and work towards a brighter future. Whilst the journey ahead is long, you can make a new beginning at this time.

In *Relationships* this card indicates the beginnings of a stable and realistic relationship. You should consider where you wish to go from this point, as there is a window of opportunity to change course. This card also signifies the financial aspects of relationship and the rewards at that level. The appearance of this card shows that there is still further potential to work towards a positive result.

In *Travel & Lifestyle* this card indicates great new beginnings and the potential to gain reward in your pursuits. Although this is merely the start of a new journey, the seeds of success are already planted in the future. You may not be given immediate rewards, but you should take care of what is presented to you.

In *Education* this card indicates a realistic attitude and the commencement of something which will be financially rewarding. However, it can also indicate the need to choose the most practical and realistic course possible. This is a down-to-earth card that requires you to get real.

In *Spiritual Awareness & Self-Development* this card symbolises the creation of all matter and the wealth of opportunity it presents to our experience. We are the senses of the entire cosmos and we should decide to give it a treat to remember!

*You are blocking this card today by:*

1. Not investing in your future security
2. Turning down that lucrative deal you have been offered
3. Not buying a lottery ticket
4. Refusing the support you have been offered

## Connect to Your Card

Plant a seed—whether literally or one of an idea. Have a fresh start at something new.

## The Ace of Pentacles Says

"There is a material opportunity in the making that is not yet fully formed. You must be open and receptive to material reward; good times could be awaiting you. Now is the time to set the ball rolling on any venture or transaction, or to court prosperity by merely investing in a solitary lottery ticket."

## Keywords

Wealth, inheritance, windfall, a helping hand, prosperity, contentment, avarice, abundance, economy, felicity, profit, realism, dividend, investment, profit, opportunity, business plan.

# —Day 75: Ace of Swords—
*Expecting Endless Energy • An Examination of Change*

## Resonances

*Numerology:* 55/1

*Astrology:* Air Signs

*Kabbalah:*
Kether (Crown)

## Quick Connections

*Affirmation:* I am the seed of infinite ideas.

*Meditation:* "If like attracts like, we should take care to make our thinking as kindly as possible. When you wake in the morning, try to think a kind thought to start the day well."

## The Lesson of the Ace of Swords
### Reading the Aces

Today's card is the unequivocal Ace of Swords. In most decks this is a straightforward image, a single sword, held upright and sharp! As an ace, it is a "seed," a nascent possibility, barely connected to the cards that follow. It is just the potential, but absolutely pure In the world of swords, this is exactly the place they like to be: singular, decisive, cutting, and purposed. The Ace of Swords is pure thought and pure intellect—the thought before the thought even gets clothed in images or actions.

In a reading, we can read this as the germ of an idea, the seed of a thought, the beginning of a new purpose. It requires nurturing—but each of the aces of the suits all require different forms of nurturing.

  • Ace of Swords—requires grounding to grow
  • Ace of Pentacles—requires space to grow

- Ace of Cups—requires channelling to grow
- Ace of Wands—requires … ?

# The Card in Your Life/Reading

*Careerwise & Financially* this card indicates leadership, fresh ideas, and victory. This is a card of the ultimate force being applied and the taking of complete responsibility. It shows that your idea is true and will cut through all obstacles ahead. This is a powerful and simple card that suggests you already know what to do; the timing is right to take action. It can also show a downsizing is required.

*Healthwise* this card indicates swift and decisive action must be taken. In mundane matters it can simply signify the birth and the beginning of a new current of life. However, this card shows generally that we must take our own life in our hands and make decisions in order to move forwards. As with all the aces, this card shows a window of opportunity has opened, requiring immediate action.

In *Relationships* this card indicates the need to communicate clearly and to establish in reality your own thinking about what is required from the relationship. The appearance of this card shows the timing is right to take action, even if it appears somewhat forthright. It is a card that suggests we must take the rose by the stem, even if we will be damaged by its thorns.

In *Travel & Lifestyle* this card indicates direct action and clear determination. You must be forceful and sudden in your actions and followthrough with whatever consequences arise. This card is saying "come hell and high water"; you should heed its call. Now is not the time for passive acceptance—the door is open and it is you who must walk through it. In lifestyle questions this card shows simplification and cutting back on your involvements.

In *Education* this card indicates clarity and a cutting away of all that is muddled. You must achieve simplicity and a clear view ahead. In all other matters of education, this card is entirely positive and signals the potential of great success in your chosen study.

In *Spiritual Awareness & Self-Development* this card is the root of all our thoughts about the universe. It is our mental sphere and shows its use to guide our decisions in a state of clarity. However it can also show the danger and damage that result from misapplication of thought. Logic has its limits, and it is important that we work from all the aces, not just one.

*You are blocking this card today by:*

1. Not making clear your future objectives.
2. Not speaking up for yourself at a crucial moment. Remember, you only get one chance most of the time.
3. Just not thinking full-stop.
4. Not being true to yourself.

## Connect to Your Card

Resolve a situation that is on your mind ensuring you have clarity in all dealings.

## The Ace of Swords Says

"You possess enough verbal incision to cut though any obstacles at the moment, a new blade cuts sharp, and those who cross your path just now should take care that you do not cut straight through them with your acerbic wit. You are prone to not suffering fools gladly so when you decide the time has come to embark on a new initiative, people had better keep out of your way."

## Keywords

Movement, champion, victory, leadership, birth, power, fresh ideas, force, timing, radical change, intellect, conquest, activity, traditional, authority, triumph, initiative, force, affliction, execution, clarity, justice, truth, brain-storming, ideas, pre-meditation, premise, announcement.

# —Day 76: Ace of Cups—
*Imagining Boundless Creativity • The Creation of Dreams*

## Resonances

*Numerology:* 41/5

*Astrology:* Water Signs

*Kabbalah:*
Kether (Crown)

## Quick Connections

*Affirmation:* I am the
seed of compassion
and perfection.

*Meditation:* "Love, there
is nothing more to say."

## The Lesson of the Ace of Cups
### *Learning to Read Fluently*

The more you practice your reading skills—as with any other skill—the more you will see improvements. You can, however, practice and rethink your fluency when delivering a reading by using the following practice. Take a moment to look at today's card, the Ace of Cups. You will see a number of images which also relate to the keywords of this card, for example, creativity.

Begin to speak out loud describing this card, perhaps using the four layers we looked at previously during our seventy-eight days, starting from the literal. As you speak, start to use those linking words we spoke of earlier. The aim is to not let the sentence end. Obviously this is not the way we usually speak, however it can encourage a narrative flow and fluency when speaking in everyday circumstances.

Here is an example:

*"Looking at this card I can see how the water flows and the hand holds the cup whilst there is a bird and a sea of deep water which represents the emotions and the bird is flying down bringing with it a blessing of grace so that the cup can continue to flow new emotions into even the most stagnant situations because there are many times in your life where you will need to know that there is no end to your resources and capability to heal so you can find that there is an infinite depth when considering your own emotions when…"*

Sometimes practising this method whilst gazing on a tarot card can also reveal new insights from your unconscious.

## The Card in Your Life/Reading

*Careerwise & Financially* this card indicates a breakthrough that will come in a most rewarding way. You will achieve satisfaction without effort, and there will be an ease and powerful flow to your projects. It is important at this time to follow the flow where it is strongest and be prepared for a sudden acceleration of events.

*Healthwise* this card indicates all the good things related to health. There is an ease of motion leading to healing. This is the most perfect card to receive in health-related questions because it signifies blessings and abundance.

In *Relationships* this card indicates a powerful depth of feeling involved in the present circumstances. It shows how love can become its own blessing and lead to an opening of intimacy. In mundane terms, this card signifies weddings and celebrations. It can also signify the birth of a child.

In *Travel & Lifestyle* this card indicates peace and compassion. It shows a gentle current is at work on which you can write easily and accomplish your vision with no effort. The Ace of Cups also shows how authentic actions and activities are often blessed beyond your original expectations. Be true to your own feelings in the matter of this question and all will be well.

In *Education* this card indicates a deep connection to your chosen subject and a breakthrough in your understanding. It can also show emotional support from others whilst you are engaged in your research. Whilst this is not a practical or intellectual card, it is an important aspect of learning and teaching—to be emotionally connected and enthusiastic about the subject matter.

In *Spiritual Awareness & Self-Development* this card illustrates divine blessing when the heart is most open to receive grace. The Ace of Cups shows a profound force is at work within your current circumstances. Whilst this can be overwhelming, there is a call to surrender to the flow.

*You are blocking this card today by:*

1. Not letting your emotions flow out/repressing them
2. Not using your emotions for the creative process
3. Not responding emotionally to the sensitivity of those close to you
4. Hanging on to old hurts from the past

## Connect to Your Card

Simply give of yourself all day, whatever anyone wants or whenever you can give a blessing.

## The Ace of Cups Says

"Recall the first heady fever of first love and the emotional force and passion that drove you on. Remember your feelings of first love and how you possessed such hope for the future; you wished it would stay like this forever. Well, that is me, and when I come into your life you will discover the renewal of your capacity to feel."

## Keywords

Motion, breakthrough, love, joy, beauty, health, renewal, imagination, creativity, peace, compassion, blessing, intimacy, emotional force, intuition, marriage, motherhood, fertility, contentment, abundance, unrequited love, feasting, inconstancy, inspiration, enthusiasm, sanction, tear-jerker, feelings, sensitivity.

# —Day 77: Ace of Wands—

*Working Towards Absolute Accomplishment • The Expression of Will*

## Resonances

*Numerology:* 27/9

*Astrology:* Fire Signs

*Kabbalah:*
Kether (Crown)

## Quick Connections

*Affirmation:* I am the seed of all that I can be.

*Meditation:* "If you have an idea, always act upon it. If it is something you truly believe in, you cannot lose, even if it does not lead to success. Never stop striving for what you want."

## The Lesson of the Ace of Wands
### Making Your Point Clearly

There are so many things said during a tarot card reading that it is almost impossible without a recording to remember every aspect of the reading. In fact, most people will only remember seven to nine key points of a reading. Whilst working through your interpretation and delivery, you should be aware of at least five key points you wish to make during your reading. You should then return to these five key points during a five-minute summary of the reading to conclude the session.

It is always helpful to give your querent an image of the reading; for example, a digital photograph which can be sent afterwards via e-mail or a full recording. Be aware that keeping such records may be covered by legislation in your country such as the data protection act, so it is best to check the requirements.

We recommend providing an anchor card for the reading by selecting one particular card and asking the querent to remember some of the features of the card. This will help the person recall more of the overall reading. You can select this card through intuition, one you refer to often during the reading, or one the client finds particularly alluring.

## The Card in Your Life/Reading

*Careerwise & Financially* this card indicates high energy and inspiration. Like most of the aces, this is a perfect card to receive for career and finances. It shows new business, invention, and originality. However, it is also a card which tells us that we need to be our own boss and manage our affairs in our own way. This is a card of independent thinking and vision. If you are applying for jobs, this card suggests you must choose something to which you fully agree or work it out for yourself.

*Healthwise* this card indicates strength and energy with the possibility of new beginnings. It shows that you can make a fresh start and gain enthusiasm for life and new activities. It also suggests that you need to be solely responsible for your own condition at this time.

In *Relationships* this card indicates birth and the possibility of new beginnings. There is a new energy in the situation of which advantage can be taken. If you take matters into your own hands, there will be new surprises ahead and the release of your vision.

In *Travel & Lifestyle* this card indicates adventure and excitement. It is a time to be enterprising and start new projects which excite you. The appearance of the Ace of Wands shows a dynamic drive has appeared in your life, and it is time to make rapid progress. The card also shows concentration is required for the things you find most important.

In *Education* this card indicates a turning point in your studies. You may receive new inspiration or have a creative vision that can be acted upon. This is truly an exciting card to receive in questions of education, for it shows the alignment of your vision to your chosen subject. The result is a dynamic drive igniting a original creation.

In *Spiritual Awareness & Self-Development* this card is the card of true will. This card symbolises our true nature and direction in life. It requires that we make focused decisions based on our highest ideals. When we are most truly ourselves and following our own direction, divine providence comes to our assistance.

*You are blocking this card today by:*

1. Being negative and gloomy
2. Not believing in the magic of potentials
3. Giving in to apathy and weariness
4. Giving up when you have only just begun

## Connect to Your Card

Support others in every way by word and deed. Be encouraging all day.

## The Ace of Wands Says

"You are not happy to stay where you are at the moment; there is an urge to set out and do something new. This could be making that decision to move to a new neighbourhood, start a new career. You are full of a pioneer spirit that drives you on at the moment, you must make the first move to get you moving. Believe in your vision, it may be the making of you!"

## Keywords

Advancement, new business, birth, career, drive, energy, birth, turning point, inspiration, invention, ignition, new beginnings, originality, trigger, spark, spur, incentive, adventure, creative vision, fresh start, creation, invention, enterprise, principle, source, family, origin, strength.

# —Day 78: The Fool—
## Finding the Beginning at the End • Spiritual Freedom

### Resonances

*Numerology:* 22/4 (0)

*Astrology:* Uranus

*Kabbalah:*
Kether and Chockmah

### Quick Connections

*Affirmation:* In laughter and learning I find there is nothing more to do.

*Meditation:* "Men and women who know themselves are no longer fools; they stand on the threshold of the Door of Wisdom." (Havelock Ellis)

## The Lesson of the Fool
### The Immanent Tarot Method, for Matters of Spirit and Vision

This profound method seeks to answer such questions such as "What is the universe about?", "Is there a God/dess?", etc. Although it would be nice to provide a conclusive spread to such grand questions about the universe and our role within it, this method simply gives an exercise to practice experiencing the immanence of the world through tarot.

Take a major arcana card. Place it by your bed and for seven nights, visualise it before sleep, leaving it face-up. Record any dreams. For the seven days following that, take the card and turn it face-down at night. Turn it up in the morning, and see if you can observe the card in your daily environment. As an example, if it were the Blasted Tower card, you might see a demolition of a chimney on television or in real life. Make a note of the event. For the seven days immediately following, imagine that the whole universe is inside that card, including yourself. Sense that the presence of that card is on the outer edge of everything that is occurring for the whole of that time. Make a note of any observations, experiences, and particularly coincidences.

You may find this exercise promotes intuitive awareness, an increase in strange events and experiences, and even synchronicities—visionary-type experiences of meaningful coincidence.

## The Card in Your Life/Reading

*Careerwise & Financially* this card indicates the paradoxical nature of risk taking. Whilst we cannot make progress by playing it safe all the time, sometimes we must be careful not to risk everything in a foolish endeavour. The Fool shows freedom of choice and usually suggests taking the leap. When hunting for a career, this card signifies more options will be available to you than you'd dare hope.

*Healthwise* this card indicates freedom and unexpected possibilities. This card signifies a lightness of step and lack of expectation must be adopted for any significant progress to be made. Although you may feel close to the edge, there are still choices available to you on the road ahead.

In *Relationships* this card indicates trust and faith must be placed in the relationship as it develops. There has to be freedom and optimism for the relationship to be able to grow. You may have to avoid the dog of doubt nipping at your heels; however, this is essential to avoid taking a fall.

In *Travel & Lifestyle* this card indicates a complete freedom in which no decisions can be made at the present time. Whilst this may liberate you, it can also lead to confusion because there is no clear framework in which to make decisions. The appearance of this card shows that you must be able to enjoy the moment until further events transpire.

In *Education* this card indicates optimism and opportunity. You could be presented with new and liberating choices and yet have no means by which to judge your response. This card suggests that you live moment to moment, not committing yourself to any long- or intermediate-term plan.

In *Spiritual Awareness & Self-Development* this card is the absolute symbol of enlightenment. It is both the beginning and end of our journey and indeed the journey itself. The Fool has transcended even total unification to become both all things and no particular thing. This is the true meaning of freedom and illumination.

*You are blocking this card today by:*

1. Being ruthless and calculating
2. Reacting in a suspicious paranoid fashion with no reason
3. Not making a decision because you need to think about it for a while
4. Not allowing yourself to dream the impossible dream

## Connect to Your Card

You know what to do. Just be yourself.

## The Fool Says

"You must follow your path to wherever it may take you and trust that you will be looked after along the way. Do not be held back by people who say you are a 'dreamer' and nothing good will come of your willful lack of responsibility and sense of duty. If you want to do it, well then do it! Remember that some of the most miraculous inventions were created by people who were labelled as fools."

## Keywords

Frivolity, choice, possibility, innocence, freedom, potential, opportunity, oneness, wonder, optimism, child–like purity, lightness, trust, spontaneity, infatuation, risk, impulsive, faith, folly, delirium, mania, dexterity, adventure, guileless, carefree, innocence, oblivious, unburdened, simplicity, cunning, thoughtfulness, chaos, dreamer, originality, unique, fresh, aspiration, optimism, unplanned, unexpected, irrational, willful, foolish, extravagance, gambler, careless, unformed, pure.

# Conclusion:
## *There Is No End*

$\mathcal{I}$t may seem like some time or no time at all since you commenced your journey into tarot with us seventy-eight days ago. It is only two months and two and a half weeks, and yet in "tarot time" that is no time at all—and all time.

From choosing your page, making your tentative way through the tens, to becoming a tarot knight and adept, and arriving to begin again with the Fool, we trust you have found the realm of tarot to be one of absolute application to everyday life as well as the more profound spiritual questions.

We have provided a reading list for your further discoveries and links to our websites which can support and develop your tarot beyond the box.

May a full deck of possibilities be yours!

# Our Website Links

To learn more about the many innovative techniques featured in this book, become a member of Tarot Professionals through your national Tarosophy® Tarot Association—for students, newcomers and experienced tarot readers—at www.tarotprofessionals.com. Membership includes subscription to the world's leading tarot magazine, *Tarosophist International,* now with over 1,000 pages of quality tarot articles, insights, and methods.

Tarot-Town, our thriving social network of tarot students and enthusiasts, can be found at **http://www.tarot-town.com.** You can join thousands of tarot townsfolk in a vast range of activities, projects, discussions, and learning at all levels. We have video classes, gated spreads, free guides, and more, taking tarot education to whole new levels.

For more on Marcus Katz's philosophy and ground-breaking book on tarot, *Tarosophy: Tarot to Engage Life, Not Escape It,* see the official website at **www.tarosophy.com.**

For tarot book lovers, please stop by the Tarot Book Club at **www.tarotbookclub.com** hosted by Nadine Roberts. You can get reviews, recommendations, and author interviews for all the latest in the tarot book world.

Our peer-reviewed and professionally edited tarot deck review site can be located at www.thetarotreview.com for considered and practical reviews of tarot decks.

If you are interested in a comprehensive course of tarot studies, we have a range of courses from beginner to advanced, with our flagship course being the online Hekademia Tarot Course, a two-year "degree-style" program delivered with the latest learning technology. This also features one-on-one supervision by Marcus Katz. You can enquire, register, and enroll at www.tarosophyuniversity.com.

You can meet and make friends in your area through one of our friendly Tarosophy Tarot Houses, where you can gain membership in our national Tarosophy Tarot Association, perform exclusive practice exercises, and have fun with others learning tarot. Our growing register of Tarot Houses is at www.mytarothouse.com.

Tarot Professionals also hosts an annual Tarosophy Conference in the beautiful Lake District of England, attended by such luminaries as Rachel Pollack, Lon Milo DuQuette, and many others each year. Details may be found on the main site at www.tarotprofessionals.com.

As a free service to the tarot community, Tarot Professionals Ltd. also provides a growing database of legislation, laws, and statutes with regard to fortune-telling and tarot worldwide. This can be found at www.fortunetellinglaws.com.

Tarot Professionals also supports Den Elder's World Tarot Day™ (May 25) at www.worldtarotday.com. This day aims to raise awareness of tarot in contemporary society and bring together tarot readers worldwide.

For courses in the Western esoteric initiatory tradition, alchemy, kabbalah, witchcraft, tarot, apprenticeship, inner guide meditation, Thelema, and the Hermetic Order of the Golden Dawn (online and in person in the beautiful Lake District of England), visit the Far Away Centre at www.farawaycentre.com.

# Further Links

For truly innovative and considered tarot at the leading edge and beyond, please visit our honorary members, ACE Members, friends, and partners through the websites in the section before this and/or the following websites:

- Rachel Pollack—http://www.rachelpollack.com
- Mary K. Greer—http://marygreer.wordpress.com
- Dr. Art Rosengarten—http:// www.moonlightcounseling.com
- Lon Milo DuQuette—http://www.lonmiloduquette.com
- James Wells—http://jameswells.wordpress.com
- Enrique Enriquez—http://tarology.wordpress.com
- Magicka School (Wicca Courses, etc.)—http://www.magickaschool.com
- Emily Carding's Transparent Tarot—http://www.childofavalon.com
- Carrie Paris's Talking Tarot—http://www.talkingtarot.com
- Adam McLean's Tarot Art and Decks—http://www.alchemywebsite.com/tarot
- Lyn Birkbeck's Astrology—http://www.lynbirkbeck.com

- Tarot by Phil—http://www.tarotbyphil.com
- Tero Hynynen—http://www.tarotpuu.com
- The House of Life (Naomi Ozaniec)—http://www.thehouseoflife.co.uk
- Mike Hernandez—http://www.justenoughtarot.com
- Stella Luna—http://thetarotreader.com.au
- Beyond Worlds Radio Show—http://www.tarottribe.com
- Theresa Reed, The Tarot Lady—http://www.thetarotlady.com
- Jonathan Kaneko-James—http://www.erasputin.com
- Diana Granger-Taylor—http://www.dianataylortarot.com
- Ginny Hunt's 78 Notes to Self—http://78notes.blogspot.com/

# Reading List

Anonymous. *Meditations on the Tarot*. Rockport, MD: Element, 1991.

Bunning, Joan. *Learning the Tarot*. York Beach, ME: Weiser, 1998.

Crowley, A. *The Book of Thoth*. York Beach, ME: Weiser, 1985.

Decker, R. A., and Dummett, M. *A History of the Occult Tarot 1870–1970*. London: Gerald Duckworth & Co., 2002.

Farley, H. *A Cultural History of Tarot*. I. B. London: Tauris, 2009.

Gearhart, S., and S. Rennie. *A Feminist Tarot*. Watertown, MA: Persephone Press, 1977.

Javane, F., and D. Bunker. *Numerology and the Divine Triangle*. Atglen, PA: Schiffer Books, 1979.

Katz, M. *Tarosophy*. Chiang Mai, Thailand: Salamander and Sons, 2011.

Katz, M., and T. Goodwin. *Tarot Flip*. Keswick, UK: Forge Press, 2010.

———., and T. Goodwin. *Tarot Twist*. Keswick, UK: Forge Press, 2010.

Louis, A. *Tarot: Plain and Simple*. St. Paul, MN: Llewellyn, 2003.

Pollack, R. *The Forest of Souls*. St. Paul, MN: Llewellyn, 2003.

———. *Seventy-Eight Degrees of Wisdom*. New York: Thorsons Publishers, 1997.

Rosengarten, A. *Tarot and Psychology*. St. Paul, MN: Paragon House, 2000.

Steinbrecher, E. C. *The Inner Guide Meditation*. Wellingborough, UK: Aquarian, 1982.

Waite, A. E. *The Key to the Tarot*. London: Rider, 1910.

Zodiastar. *30 Different Ways of Card Fortune-Telling*. London: Universal, 1932.

# Appendix 1:
## *A 78-Day Tarot Tale*

*I*f you would like to try a final exercise in your seventy-eight-day course, why not shuffle your entire deck and see if you can read a tale by using every single card in the deck? Removing the Fool to start, take one card at a time. Create a narrative using all the skills you have learnt during these last few months, testing and consolidating your learning.

We have provided an example which we created in about ten minutes with a shuffled deck.

## The 78-Day Tarot Tale

1. Fool (0): We set off on our journey with no expectations and an open mind

2. Page of Wands: And we find an open road full of possibilities ahead of us

3. Tower (XVI): Although we are going to have to shake old habits and behaviour

4. Hierophant (V): And learn many things in a traditional manner

5. Seven of Cups: Until it seems like our imagination will run riot

6. Two of Swords: And we can't seem to decide which of many meanings to choose

7. King of Pentacles: So we will have to get to grips with what we know

8. Seven of Wands: Even if other people don't think it is important to learn tarot

9. Five of Pentacles: And we feel somewhat excluded from the everyday world

10. Page of Cups: However who knows what surprises we have in store for us

11. Sun (XIX): As we set off with an open heart to the light of new learning

12. Two of Pentacles: And juggle what we are being taught in small pieces

13. King of Wands: Feeling strong in our resolve to accomplish our ambition

14. Seven of Pentacles: Whilst realising that some skills will take time to develop

15. Strength (VIII): And others will need practice and perfecting

16. Ace of Swords: Although we may surprise ourselves with sudden insights

17. Queen of Swords: And be able to gain keen insight into the workings of the world

18. Knight of Pentacles: That will actually have a practical application

19. Three of Wands: Taking us forwards into new areas of life previously unexplored

20. Judgement (XX): Waking us up to new possibilities

21. Ten of Cups: Which in turn bring about a deep sense of understanding and contentment

22. Ace of Cups: Opening up to others this new wisdom

23. Ten of Swords: Whilst laying old ideas to rest

24. Eight of Cups: We continue on with our journey into a whole new way of life

25. Six of Cups: Exploring cherished memories and visions from childhood excitement

26. Four of Swords: And gaining a new alignment to the very deepest parts of ourselves

27. Nine of Cups: And whilst others may be content in their circumstances

28. Queen of Wands: We know that we will continue to strive towards our values

29. Eight of Pentacles: Working hard at perfecting our craft as a tarot reader

30. Eight of Wands: And communicating with others as we make progress

31. Magician (I): Leading to new skills and demonstrations of our art

32. Ace of Pentacles: And even financial rewards from clients

33. Ten of Wands: When we make clear to them how they are carrying too much

34. Four of Cups: Missing new emotional opportunities

35. Two of Wands: Or where we clarify their ambitious plans for the future

36. Page of Pentacles: Giving them a good basis for future growth

37. The Star (XVII): And offering a new vision of life's hopes and dreams

38. Knight of Cups: Where we are true to our own depths

39. Five of Swords: Putting away the hurts and injustice of the past

40. Temperance: (XIV): In order to create a new alchemy of tarot

41. Three of Pentacles: Which begins to build together in community

42. The Chariot (VII): Pulling everyone together in a shared goal

43. Seven of Swords: So that my learning prepares for whatever comes in life

44. Eight of Swords: And I see that I am not trapped in my thinking

45. Queen of Cups: And can access my own emotional depths

46. Five of Wands: Working though the confused values of those around me

47. Six of Wands: Holding my head high so I can lead others too

48. High Priestess (II): By revealing the deeper currents of life

49. Emperor (IV): And not abusing my knowledge and position

50. Six of Pentacles: Because I will share it in charity and fairness

51. King of Cups: Tapping into my own experience and offering my growing wisdom

52. Six of Swords: So that I can take people to new ways of thinking

53. The Moon (XVIII): And guide them in the darkest times of their circumstances

54. Four of Wands: Towards the most beneficial outcome we can imagine

55. Justice (XI): In accord with universal laws and balances

56. Three of Cups: And joyfully respecting and celebrating with others

57. King of Swords: I can learn clearly and sharply as I gain experience

58. Ten of Pentacles: Whilst practising and seeing how tarot works in society

59. The Hermit (IX): With my role as a way-shower and light to other seekers

60. Death (XIII): Now transforming myself through tarot experience

61. Four of Pentacles: No longer holding on to the constraints of the past

62. Two of Cups: Generating from my cards whole new relationships to the world

63. Wheel of Fortune (X): Seeing how luck, fate, fortune, and destiny work

64. Three of Swords: Cutting myself off from powerlessness

65. Knight of Swords: Taking my own life in my hands

66. Ace of Wands: Accepting all responsibilities as my own choices
67. The Hanged Man (XII): And in tarot now understanding the world in a totally different way
68. The Devil (XV): Free of the fear and ignorance I may have experienced in the beginning
69. Nine of Wands: Able to stand my own ground in my learning
70. Page of Swords: And having a clear idea of the way ahead in my studies
71. Knight of Wands: Which I will take with enthusiasm
72. The Empress (III): For there is so much more to reap from this work
73. The Lovers (VI): And new blessings every day
74. Queen of Pentacles: Which will create abundance and pleasure in every way
75. Five of Cups: So that I recognise what is possible for me to overcome
76. The World (XXI): And a whole world of possibilities opens up to me
77. Nine of Swords: Wondering why I had not come this way sooner
78. Nine of Pentacles: To find myself in myself, content.

# Appendix 2:
## *Tarot Scripts for the Major Cards in the Celtic Cross*

When I first learnt to read tarot, for almost two years I read with only the twenty-two major cards in the Celtic Cross. Over the next thirty years I have seen students struggle to interpret the majors in the positions of the spread, so I here provide a sample of scripts for all twenty-two cards in each and every of the ten positions of the spread, some 220 scripts in total. It is hoped you will find this appendix useful for learning how to create your own flexible interpretations for the majors in this and any other spread.[18]

The positions of the Celtic Cross can be seen as:

1. This is you in your current state, symbolised by ...

2. The challenge of your current issue is ...

3. The flow of the next few months is ...

4. The past in relation to this issue is ...

5. You should set your sights on…

6. The resources you can draw upon include…

7. You see yourself in this situation as…

8. Those around you see you as…

9. The concerns you have which are not actual (negative/fears, positive/hopes) are…

10. The overall outcome of this matter is summarised by…

The cards can be interpreted for these positions as follows.

# 0. Fool

- This is you in your current state, symbolized by the ever-wandering Fool. Like this figure, you are free to choose at this time, but every choice is a leap into the unknown. This is the price of freedom—any step you take now will result in a wholly new situation, but you are free to make this choice. Do not be distracted by the barking of the dog of the past—his time has gone, and you must move on.

- The challenge of your current issue is that your choices have been constrained, and there seems nothing you can do to move. The Fool has been tipped on his side and cannot get up whilst the dog of panic barks for attention! Your challenge is to take time to recover yourself and make yourself whole before setting off on any new direction. Take time, rest; do not be in a hurry to jump into the unknown.

- The flow of the next few months is one of increasing freedom, where every step moves a little bit closer to your true path in life. Be ready to take any opportunity to leap into the unknown—if you are unsure about something, be encouraged, like the Fool, to go for it, knowing you are on the right track when the right thing to do seems the most foolish.

- The past in relation to this issue is one of confusion and folly. It seems like everything you did came to no real result. However, in this case, what was going on was far deeper—you have been moved to this current part of your life to see something you weren't able to see before. There is more in the last few months than meets the eye—discover what new opportunity awaits you from here, now. This is why you've been brought by the Fool to this new viewpoint, no matter how ridiculous the past.

- You should set your sights on whatever frees you, whatever gives you time to yourself. Do not aim to appease others or set things right in the eyes of another. It is time to work towards your own plan and accomplishments, and set yourself straight again on your own inner path. Like the Fool, take to the open road, for there awaits a new you!

- The resources you can draw upon include the wisdom of those who see things freely, who are uninvolved, and who appear to have no care in the world. At this time, it is wise to trust the court jester, who says things that cannot be said by others. What is it that cannot be said at this time? It is time to face up to that unspoken truth and free yourself from it. There is no cliff, just the edge of your freedom.

- Your own state in this matter is one of folly and carelessness. This may be a good attitude if it frees you from imaginary concerns, but watch that the dog does not trip you up! You may be feeling reckless, but do you truly wish to step into the void? Are your responsibilities obsolete or do you bring them in your pack? You might want to take a step back inside yourself and get real before moving on.

- Those around you see you as being on the edge of something new. They may wonder if you have considered the consequences of your actions, and you should let them know if you have! You might want to share your viewpoint with others, as they may not see things the way you do just now.

- The concerns you have which are not actual are those that seem most foolish. You are right to let go of those issues that seem ridiculous—they are! A more serious and realistic viewpoint is called for now; it is time to listen to the warnings barked by the dog; what is real, and what is silly? At this time, everything is exactly as it appears to be, and if it feels wrong, it probably is.

- The overall outcome of this matter is summarised by the unnumbered card of the Fool. He is free to wander the entire deck and in this position symbolises that what will happen is already being written. You are already on the path to your destination, no matter how confusing things may appear. Take the time to enjoy the journey, and stop worrying about the destination. You'll be getting there soon enough.

# 1. Magician

- This is you in your current state, symbolized by the powerful card of the Magician. You have all the elements at your disposal and, if everything is arranged in the right order, unlimited energy to attain your ambition. It is time to be firm, directive and active—don't take no for an answer!

- The challenge of your current issue is that you do not have all the resources required to accomplish your desire. Not everything is in place, and you are getting ahead of what is realistic. The Magician crossing you is like a magical binding spell—it seems that everything you do is frustrated. So step back and start again, don't bang your head against this particular break wall—it won't break, you will.

- The flow of the next few months is one of mercurial quicksilver—a fast river of events and decisions that will take you every which way but loose! Like the Magician, you must learn to guide yourself and stay close to your original decisions, ambitions and plans, rather than get swept off course! You may wish to commit yourself in writing now, and keep reviewing your progress against your desires.

- The past in relation to this issue is one where magic seemed to be happening everywhere! However, as this current fades, you may feel yourself missing something now. The past was very controlled; now things may seem chaotic and confusing in comparison. You must reconnect to your inner magician and take control again, make some magic for yourself.

- You should set your sights on connecting to your highest principles and making them real. You should strive to stay true to your values and ensure that every decision you make is connected to the things in which you truly believe. It is time to act and aim with principle and dignity, with ambition and courage. Ban half-measures for a while and don't sell yourself short.

- The resources you can draw upon are well-balanced at this time. It seems you can count on assistance from all sides in this particular issue. So long as you clearly communicate what you wish, others will arrange things accordingly. Indeed, then, a time to act and not waste the opportunity!

- Your own state in this matter is one of control and willpower. You feel very much that this issue is close to everything that is important to you in all aspects of your life. If you don't, it might be timely to consider how much this means to you, and where else it affects. The Magician is your will here—the focus you have inside must be present in your behaviour, so communicate your requirements clearly!

- Those around you see that you are truly living your life in the flow at the moment. Whilst it may appear differently to you from the inside, others don't think you need any help or assistance, and will stay out of your way. It is a good time to arrange for everyone in your life to suit your own needs—be a little selfish; others will appreciate your honesty!

- The concerns you have which are not actual are those of the Magician as Trickster. You may worry that you are being taken for a ride. However, in this position, the Magician tells us everything is as down-to-earth as it gets, and your flights of fancy, hopes, dreams, despairs, and worries, are nothing more than illusions—take everything at face value, be straight-talking, and you'll find things a lot simpler.

- The overall outcome of this matter is summarised by the wonderful card of the Magician. He is truly himself, in charge of his environment, and in the right relationship to those around him. The right person in the right place at the right time—this is truly magic, and how this situation will conclude. You will find yourself magically capable, and the result may also seem magical in exceeding your expectations.

## 2. High Priestess

- This is you in your current state, symbolized by the enigmatic High Priestess. You are in-between, above and beyond, caught in a halfway house. It is exactly at the time things seem borderline that you have access to your own intuitive self—trust in your instinct and the veil will be parted, the future revealed. Your inner voice has much to teach you at this time and is connected to the flowing river of time and change—learn to listen and for once, you may be right!

- The challenge of your current issue is a refusal to see beyond the current concern. What is happening now is part of a bigger change that is going on in your life, and it is not yet over—in fact, it may just be the beginning. So, make like the High Priestess and sit above the situation—rise above it and this challenge will be met—pull back the curtain and face the day!

- The flow of the next few months is mysterious and wonderful; the High Priestess has a robe like a river, which flows as it will, shifting like the light of the moon. In the next twenty-eight days you will see how this pattern will manifest in your life, taking you in unexpected directions. Go with the flow!

- The past in relation to this issue is one of silence and secrecy. There was a lot that was hidden and veiled, and only recently discovered. With this moving now into your past, you have chance to re-tune yourself to all that is now the case—and begin to move on. But this journey will be more inwardly directed for a while; do not expect to make many changes of the outside just yet.

- You should set your sights on discovering all that is hidden from you and connecting to your own intuition. You are being asked to meet your own needs and requirements, and aim to trust your gut-instinct. If you feel off-beam or off-course, then set your sights again with your own internal compass. Keep checking that you are going with the flow and not fighting against it—if it is a struggle, you're not going the right way!

- The resources you can draw upon include the mysterious depths of your very own unconscious mind. Find unexpected help and assistance from strange happenings, weird coincidences, profound synchronicities and dreams, symbols and visions. Look for the High Priestess empowering you to succeed in the most unusual ways. Her message is hidden yet clear—you are being helped in ways you don't yet see.

- Your own state in this matter is one of detachment; as the High Priestess you are able to rise above all passing things and attain a sense of inner peace. You may feel yourself more in tune with the deeper cycles and bigger picture of what is going on, so trust that inner sense and move where it wills. It is a time when what you feel deep down is truly connected to the reality of the situation.

- Those around you see that you have a clearer idea of what is going on than perhaps you yourself think! It may be that others come to you for advice and you have no idea about the whats and the whys! However, others can sense that you are truly in touch with yourself in this matter, and it is important for you to share that intuition.

- The concerns you have which are not actual are those based on your intuition. Sometimes your gut-feeling can be off-centre, and this may be a time when the truth of the matter is not what you feel deep down. It is time to check your facts, make sure you know everything about the situation, before jumping to conclusions.

- The overall outcome of this matter is summarised by the mystery of the High Priestess. It is she who holds the scroll of the Torah—the Law—and her decision is final. The outcome of this situation is as it should be, with all sides balanced and everything taken into account—even those things hidden. It will all come out in the wash!

# 3. Empress

- This is you in your current state, symbolized by the Empress. She is fruitful and bounteous; growing and abundant. It is a time of creativity, when everything flourishes without work or effort. You are blessed by fertile opportunities—time to make hay whilst the sun shines, then!
- The challenge of your current issue is one of growth. It may feel that everything has gone flat and is about to go stagnant, like still water left in the sun. You must look over your garden, your life, and see which shoots need watering and tending, and which shoots are failing to grow. You cannot look after them all, so like a wise mother, choose where you direct your attention.
- The flow of the next few months is one of abundant growth. Everything that you have planted will bear fruit and the rewards will be in equal measure to the work you have put into this situation. You will need to tend to things as they grow, and prune back where things might get out of hand. Too much growth can choke everything; be a wise gardener!
- The past in relation to this issue is one of significant growth. The Empress has allowed things to develop in their own time, without effort or labour. You are now seeing the results of that work, but must be careful that you continue to manage the situation so that it does not grow beyond your ability.
- You should set your sights on a gradual growth now and for the next few months. Allow things to take their natural course, and do not interfere too much. A little pruning, a little planting, but no entire landscape remodelling at this time! Everything is connected, and your aim should be to join the dots and make new connections at all times, bringing everything together.
- The resources you can draw upon include your ability to let things take their course. You can draw upon your mothering instinct or inner-gardener at this

time. Nurture but do not interfere with the flow of things, and it will be easier for everyone.

- Your own state in this matter is one of grace and care. You are loving and nurturing, qualities that are being brought out at this time. You may need to decide if being so is appropriate and relevant to the results you want.

- Those around you see that you are deeply connected to the matters in hand, and have a direct interest in their growth. You may feign a lack of care, but others see you as fully involved. Do you wish to be perceived as a gentle mother or a persistent meddler in this matter? You are not able to be seen as anything other!

- The concerns you have which are not actual are those related to the growth of this matter. You perhaps hope or dream things will come out the way you desire, but in truth, things will grow the way nature has intended for them. You must recognise this and step back from interfering; your concerns may trip you up, and they are not useful at this time!

- The overall outcome of this matter is summarised by the Empress, the Queen of Nature who bears the sign of Venus, of the feminine and love, upon her heart-shaped shield. Here she signifies that everything—and I mean everything—will grow to its fulfillment. A truly wonderful and abundant outcome card is she; all will be well, and all will be abundant joy!

## 4. Emperor

- This is you in your current state, symbolized by power, power, and more power! The Emperor rocks! You feel that you need to lay down the law and enforce it; set things straight and keep control of the power present at this time. Sitting up straight, you are doing as you will in the world—go for it!

- The challenge of your current issue is one of authority. It is unclear who is in charge of this situation and it is an obstacle that must be met head-on. Face up to your own responsibilities or delegate them to another, but it must be done. Whilst you don't make up your mind, someone else will.

- The flow of the next few months is one of increasingly exerting control. A lot of stabbing at the brake of the car or short, sharp bursts on the accelerator pedal are called for, but you must assume control.

- The past in relation to this issue is one of control issues—you may feel like you have lost power over someone else, and indeed the Emperor is a temporal card and one of human power. So this person's time is past; perhaps you need to remember now that it is you who can call the shots.

- You should set your sights on achieving a dominant position, in charge of your life. It is time to step on the gas and get things going—start as much as possible, even if the outcomes seem unlikely. Put energy into your work, and take things up a notch wherever and whenever possible. Keeping this in mind will lead to sudden victories and immediate rewards.

- The resources you can draw upon include your ability to get things going. You must look at where you lead and inspire others and have authority, even in the smallest of things. This is where you must start to come out from, a position where you already have strength. In doing so, you will draw more out of yourself than you knew you possessed!

- Your own state in this matter is one of keeping a tight lid on everything. You need to be in charge and order events. Of course, not everyone else may see it like that—are you being viewed as a leader or a dictator? Maybe it's time to change your management style!

- Those around you see you as being in control. Of course, you may not feel that way inside! Don't be surprised if others look to you for advice—they see the strength of your uncommon experience. Feel free to speak your mind—others expect this!

- The concerns you have which are not actual are those of authority. You may fear that you are not in control, but this is far from the truth. You have more willpower than you think, when you are pointed in the right direction. Try moving in smaller bursts, but always to your aim; that will work. Go when you have the energy, and rest in between—life is sometimes like that.

- The overall outcome of this matter is summarised by the Emperor, who signifies authority. The current time in your life is heading to a situation where you will gain more control and ability to not only make decisions, but see them enacted in the world. Rule on, then, but remember to use your power wisely!

# 5. Hierophant

- This is you in your current state, symbolized by the Hierophant—one who reveals hidden things. You have been made aware of new information that has shed light on the situation, so take time to reflect upon what you have learnt. The card shows that what is revealed is important, so do not dismiss anything out of hand. There are important lessons to be learnt now.

- The challenge of your current issue is to uncover what has been kept from you. This may be intentional or not on the part of others, but it is no time for them to play the authority figure or for you to bend the knee. Find out what you need and demand to know until you do!

- The flow of the next few months is one of approaching others, and seeking advice from the experience of experts. Do not be afraid to ask questions and gain clarity from those who have been here before or are even now in the same situation. But choose your authority figures based on their experience, not just on what they say!

- The past in relation to this issue is one of authority figures and constraints, of teachers and lessons. Even when we leave school, we can sometimes bring the playground with us—have you been allowing others to frame the situation too much? If you have been taking a back seat in the past, look to the future to apply what you know to be good for you.

- You should set your sights on nothing less than complete revelation! The Hierophant is a card of discovery, of revealing what is hidden. Have a complete clean sweep and aim to get everything out in the open. Everyone will feel so much better when you work towards transparency!

- The resources you can draw upon include your ability to guide and teach others. Perhaps you need to apply that skill more to yourself and face up to what you would tell yourself if you were someone else!

- Your own state in this matter is one where you feel as if you possess the facts and others do not. So you have a choice: what do you communicate and what do you keep hidden? When others come to you, be prepared to find the right line between saying what you know and a little discretion.

- Those around you see you as holding some wisdom in their affairs, and may be seeking advice from you. They don't know what you don't know, so be confident!

You can use this situation to your advantage, but don't get caught out if someone calls your bluff.

- The concerns you have which are not actual are whether you have the right advice or not. The Hierophant in this position is uncomfortable, as he is always sure of his knowledge. Perhaps that niggling doubt you have needs testing out; perhaps that information which seems too good to be true actually is? Check your facts and put your mind at ease.
- The overall outcome of this matter is summarised by an appeal to a greater authority. This situation must be reviewed by someone outside of the whole thing for a clearer perspective. Don't be afraid then to prepare your argument and present it to someone for their opinion. You need to get outside advice!

## 6. The Lovers

- This is you in your current state, symbolized by a blessed union. The Lovers is not just a loving relationship but a creative one also. Your current state is one where something is being created by your relationship to another. This union is graced by a unique time and space for your endeavours, so a time of enjoyment and pleasure is assured.
- The challenge of your current issue is to find the right relationship. This is not just a personal relationship, but can be a relationship relevant to your work or a particular issue. At present this is not in balance and is not bearing the results you desire. It is not due to the people and the situation, but rather how they are arranged. Have a look at what communications need to be introduced and the matter will resolve itself more quickly than you expect.
- The flow of the next few months is one of joyous creative relationship. More will come out of your relationships in that time, and you may even be blessed by a presence of love!
- The past in relation to this issue is one where your relationships and choices seemed blessed to be good at all times. That this is now fading into the past may signify that the honeymoon is over and you need to get down to the real work now. You can recall the magic of the past to create more magic in the future, but for now, it's time to get real.
- You should set your sights on achieving the right relationship. Those around you need gentle persuasion to be put in their right place for everybody's good. You

should aim to be the diplomat, the lover, the unseen guide, and ensure that the heart of love rules over all.

- The resources you can draw upon include your loving nature. You are truly aware of the power of love and must work on manifesting that love to others and applying it to situations where you presently feel frustrated. If you do, you will be blessed by surprising results, as if there were invisible forces helping you!

- Your own state in this matter is one of strong relationship and the choices that come with such relationship. Whether in relationship to work or another person, balances have to be struck and lines established. You are being called to make those clear.

- Those around you see you as being faced with a choice. Did you know that? The story of Adam and Eve pictured in the Lovers also featured a decision. Do you see that you are being presented with a choice of knowledge or freedom? Everyone else around you does, so perhaps it is time to take off your blinders!

- The concerns you have which are not actual are those surrounding love and relationship. This card in this position indicates that these worries are not present in the real world, so perhaps they are the result of past scars which have not yet healed? Look at this present situation as if you had newly come to it, with a sense of innocence. Free yourself from past decisions that didn't work out. Always start fresh!

- The overall outcome of this matter is summarised by a blessed union. In this card, we see how when everything is in the right place, the sum is larger than the parts. The result of the present situation is positive and beautiful, a loving time and space where you are free to be yourself. Enjoy!

# 7. The Chariot

- This is you in your current state, symbolized by the Chariot. Here we see someone balanced in their forward motion, with everything reined to pull them ahead. You are in the right place at the right time, being driven by a wave that is not entirely of your own making.

- The challenge of your current issue is one of going against the inevitable flow. You are banging your head against a wall and knocking on a door that will not open. It is time to turn entirely around and do something else. If you always do what you've always done, you'll always get what you've always got.

- The flow of the next few months is incredible! The Chariot will pull you along as fast as you wish to go—new horizons will open; a new you is entirely possible. It is time to bring everything together to serve your own ambitions. Prepare for movement!

- The past in relation to this issue is one of dynamic movement and drive. This may have run its course, and you should look to the rest of this reading for the best advice to move onwards. It will not be as it was in the past, so you may feel some disappointment—but that speed could not have been maintained forever.

- You should set your sights on becoming the driver and not the driven in the future. You have to prepare to take the reins and make your own decisions. The aim is to learn how to avoid getting in the way of others or avoiding them, whilst you drive ahead to your own goal. Be clear and stick to your course! You are Ben-Hur in this chariot race!

- The resources you can draw upon include your own drive and ambition. Where you have clear and easy drive towards something, draw upon it. Avoid those tasks that you feel require too much artificial interest on your part. The Chariot calls us to focus on the flow and ride the wave! Draw from where you feel excitement, not boredom.

- Your own state in this matter is one of drive and focus. You feel as if you have everything together, even if it requires constant checking on your part. Be aware that even driving can be tiring; all that concentration and alertness will take its toll on you. Ensure you take rest breaks along the way!

- Those around you see you as driven and ambitious, even if you do not feel this way. Perhaps they are trying to get you to rest when you see this as interference and obstruction! Do not take it this way; others are trying to look after you and you may not be seeing the inevitable exhaustion your current attitude may cause.

- The concerns you have which are not actual are those which relate to long-term goals and ambitions. It may feel as if these are out of sight at the present, or your drive towards them has faded. It may be that you feel as if you are no longer on the path you once set for yourself. But these are merely concerns, and they aren't real—you are always only a moment away from yourself! Is it time to remember that, perhaps?

- The overall outcome of this matter is summarised by the Chariot, which signifies movement and victory ahead! This is a spectacular card in this position and shows that your current matters will resolve in a good fashion; it's a clear win!

# 8. Strength

- This is you in your current state, symbolized by the Strength card. See the lady holding the jaws of the lion and realise this is a picture of your strength at this time. You are using your resources wisely to maintain peace and avoid being eaten up! You must maintain this deliberate balance, for who knows what might happen if the lion was let loose!

- The challenge of your current issue is one of maintaining the right level and type of relationship to what is going on around you. You must find the line between engaging and being swallowed up by events; between entirely disengaging and letting things get out of control. Perhaps the lady and the lion symbolise that the right persuasion at the right time is all that is required, without making too big a deal.

- The flow of the next few months is one of gentle strength. You are assured that where you place your efforts you will be rewarded, but things may require a constant watchful eye to avoid wildness.

- The past in relation to this issue is one which has really required you to maintain control. It may feel as if you are somewhat redundant, obsolete, or a surplus to requirements. Do not despair! The lessons of the past prepare you for the future—look to the other cards for more advice on this.

- You should set your sights on maintaining a manageable equilibrium. You must aim to have a good work/life balance and set your house in order. Your aim should be to find the point between struggle and submission; the strength that is slow but steady, sure and secure.

- The resources you can draw upon include your own passion, held in check to your ambition. It is time to harness your inner desires and bring them slowly out into the world, come what may! This is a powerful card in this position, and you should not underestimate how much you can accomplish when you tap into your fire.

- Your own state in this matter is one where you feel as if you have struck the right balance. However, be aware that others may perceive you as struggling and feel some concern. Allow people to assist where they wish or gently thank them for their kind offers with assurance they are not required.

- Those around you see that you are holding it together, but you may not be so sure. If you need help with this lion, shout for it—don't expect others to notice your struggle.
- The concerns you have which are not actual are whether you can maintain your hold on things just now. Be assured that you have the resources and inner strength to go through with what you must just now. Keep hanging in there and ultimately, you will see things weren't so bad after all!
- The overall outcome of this matter is summarised by Strength. This might be a picture of the famous phrase "what does not kill me makes me stronger." You should look forward to learning a lesson in the events ahead, one that will become more obvious when it is done, and prepare you for what follows. Your outcome is Strength; it will be up to you to decide how to apply it.

# 9. The Hermit

- This is you in your current state, symbolized by the aloof Hermit. You may feel divorced from the crowd in an exposed and solitary position with little outside light. The Hermit is a card of a chosen retreat, time you need alone. From this time comes an inner light which can lead the way ahead. You also become an example to others when you make your own way in this manner.
- The challenge of your current issue is not to retreat into yourself. It is time to be outgoing and fully engaged with the world, to get out and about and make contacts. The time for deep navel-gazing is over; there is nothing else there to learn! Go and make new connections, the world is waiting for you!
- The flow of the next few months is one of timely solitude, reconnecting with your own way. Let your light shine brightly, and lead your own way. Others will follow, if they choose.
- The past in relation to this issue is one of quietness and a certain loneliness. This time is passing into a busier and more interactive time, where you are required to come out of your shell a little more. Take time to do this only as quickly as you feel comfortable.

- You should set your sights on finding your own guiding light, not following the example of others. Becoming your own teacher, you may need to take time out to reassert your own priorities in the midst of others' demands. But take the time and get it right—you have your own path, go find it!

- The resources you can draw upon include your own inner Hermit. He is the guide and guardian of the heights and holds the star of vision in his lantern. You should take time to listen to that quiet voice inside you and learn from your intuition. It has more to say now than ever before, amidst the distractions of everything else going on around you.

- Your own state in this matter is one of solitude. You just want to be left alone. Don't let others call you back into the fight—they must also be made aware you need some "me time."

- Those around you see you as being aloof and trying to be above it all. This might be your intention, but if it isn't, ensure that others realise you are just trying to see everyone's side of the story, not entirely get out of it!

- The concerns you have which are not actual are of your own ability to find your way. You should not doubt that the immediate way will be made clear to you as soon as you begin to make your own decisions, even if the longer goal ahead cannot be glimpsed. Take small steps up the mountain and don't doubt that you can make it to the top.

- The overall outcome of this matter is summarised by the Hermit. It seems you will find yourself left to your own devices when this present situation is resolved, with your own vision still close to you. It may be that you should prepare for this now by sticking to your principles. You must not be left with regrets when this is all over.

# 10. The Wheel

- This is you in your current state, symbolized by the rapidly spinning Wheel of Fortune. It just doesn't stop for you, does it?! Life seems upside down and back-to-front, inside out, and up and down! And just when you think you're getting on top of it, the Wheel spins down again! The trick, of course, is to find the still centre in the middle of this turning—become the axis around which everything else revolves.

- The challenge of your current issue is that there is no change, no opportunity, no excitement. A period of boredom and dullness has settled in, and life lies stagnating. Your challenge is to grasp the Wheel when it turns, and ride it upwards at the next opportunity. Be impulsive, take a chance—sometimes a little risk and a gamble is part of life!
- The flow of the next few months is one of constant turning, upside and downside. The Wheel does not rest, but for you it will be particularly noticeable in the near future. It is time to learn to save something during the good times for the bad, and to see the light of hope even in the darkest downturn.
- The past in relation to this issue is one of constant change, life's little ups and downs. You feel as if you have been on a merry-go-round or carousel that just hasn't stopped. Now that it has, you should take a moment to find your feet before moving on. Take stock of your resources and plan ahead. If you set off too quickly, you're apt to make dizzy judgements!
- You should set your sights on preparing for inevitable change. The Wheel is going to turn for you, so you better be ready. If you are looking for a job, start training; if a relationship, start making time; if travel, start packing your bags. It is a good time to tidy away the old and be ready for life to turn another corner.
- The resources you can draw upon include your ability to remain fixed in the middle of change. You are able to stay centred when all around you is in chaos. So, be reminded of your own values, take a deep breath, and stay the course whilst confusion abounds. Do not move!
- Your own state in this matter is changeable; you're not sure whether you're coming or going, or able to trust things to stay the same. This uncertainty may be projected outwards even if it is not spoken. Are you sure that others aren't trusting you to make up your mind when you remain unsure? Time to be clear.
- Those around you see that your life is full of ups and downs and considerable change just now. They are unlikely to stay by your side for the time being whilst they wait for things to settle down.
- The concerns you have which are not actual are symbolised by the Wheel. This card is one which shows cyclic change—the sort of change which is inevitable and natural but that we can try to avoid. We must be prepared for things to pass from one state to another and let go when we need to—otherwise we are bound to the Wheel and its feels horrible. At this time, you should learn to let go.

- The overall outcome of this matter is summarised by the Wheel, a difficult card in this position. It shows that the outcome will rapidly shift into a new situation, and one thing will follow another—nothing is fixed. So the best thing you can do is find now the things you truly value and want to take along for the next ride!

# 11. Justice

- This is you in your current state, symbolized by the Justice card. Your sense of fairness and rightness is at play at the moment, and it is important you weigh everything presented to you carefully. It is time to square things off and keep the peace. It is time to ensure that everyone gets their due.
- The challenge of your current issue is that you are finding it difficult to get what you believe is a fair reward for your efforts. What you are getting back is not what you expect. Your values are not being met. It may be challenging, but you need to re-negotiate this deal, whether it be at work, with your partner or family—times have changed and they should too.
- The flow of the next few months is one presided over by Justice. She will weigh everything in her scales. What you reap you will surely sow. It is a time to look forward to getting what you deserve and for everything to be balanced out. Ensure you present your case to others for the best possible results.
- The past in relation to this issue is one of law and order, where everything was brought out into the open and made clear. The scales may or may not have been in your favour, but now is not the time to go on about past decisions. It is time to leave behind what may have been unfair and move forwards—next time you'll be better able to make your case based on your past experiences.
- You should set your sights on achieving a fair result for all concerned. The sword of Justice must be raised to defend everybody's rights in this matter, and you must be the one raising it.
- The resources you can draw upon include your innate sense of fairness. Trust your feelings of getting the best result for as many possible and make decisions based on the benefit of the many, not the individual. All's fair in love and war, so you may have to tread on toes to get what's best for everyone.
- Your own state in this matter is one where you find your own values being questioned. Is everything what you thought it was, or have your scales of fairness

been tipped over? The sword of Justice may feel cutting, but it is usually for the best; perhaps it is time to face up to a new reality.

- Those around you see that you are trying to be diplomatic, patient, and helpful to everyone, but you may be trying too much. They'd prefer it if you let go a little and weren't always the peacemaker! If you're being seen as too uptight, it's time to put down the sword of righteousness and get into a party mood.
- The concerns you have which are not actual are those concerning your sense of fair play. It may seem to you that the present events are somewhat unfair, but this may be a limited impression not taking into account all parties in the situation. This card suggests you take a wider view.
- The overall outcome of this matter is summarised by the Justice card. The sword and scales will ensure that all happens as is fair and the law will prevail. Everything that has been set in motion will reach its rightful conclusion, and there is little you can do about it.

## 12. The Hanged Man

- This is you in your current state, symbolized by the upside-down nature of the Hanged Man. You feel that your values have been overturned and everything looks the wrong way up. This is a time to find your true centre whilst others only hang around. In suspension, things have a way of settling themselves.
- The challenge of your current issue is to break free of old attachments and values. Your way of looking at life needs to shift, and shift big time! You may want to behave yourself into a new way of belief by doing something totally outside of yourself—something that forces you to break free from your old conditions. Be daring.
- The flow of the next few months is somewhat held in check. You may find yourself waiting on others and not achieving all that you plan. The Hanged Man represents a time to ensure that you are sticking true to your highest ambitions and not selling yourself short. A period of review is ahead, but little change.
- The past in relation to this issue is one of waiting, waiting, waiting. It seems like nothing changed and you were left hanging out to dry. You may have felt that no one understood quite what you were getting at or thought your ideas were plain upside down. This time is passing, so your ideas may now be seen in a different light—stick with them.

- You should set your sights on your highest ambitions and not compromise on the way. Although the end may not justify the means, you must not lower yourself to others expectations. Keep true to your highest ideal, and strive ever towards it.
- The resources you can draw upon include your earliest ambitions. The Hanged Man is sometimes called the "drowned giant," and in this case, the giant is your most powerful hopes, springing from the depths of your past. Go deep inside and reconnect with your original self. Although your hopes may have been sleeping, it is time to awaken them; although the giant may have been drowning, it is time to rescue him! Revive your ambitions, no matter how unlikely they seemed in the past.
- Your own state in this matter is one of suspension. It is possible you are caught in a no-win situation or swinging between two opposite courses of action, like a pendulum. Inside, there is conflict. Perhaps there is a middle way.
- Those around you see you as plainly hanging around! You are not seen as a decision-maker or leader, but a steady influence. However, this has little impact on the decisions of others. You have to come down off your high horse and get involved. It is time to become the difference that makes a difference!
- The concerns you have which are not actual are that things are not changing. You feel worried that change will not come, or the conflict will not resolve itself. This is a temporary matter and your concern is unfounded. Look to the other cards to see the manner in which this change of circumstances will come.
- The overall outcome of this matter is summarised by the awkward Hanged Man. As an outcome card, this image is not an absolute resolution, but a half-way point. The conflict will not be over soon; it will merely turn into another phase. You are advised here to stick to your original goal wherever possible as a guide, and not let yourself be swayed one way or the other or pulled entirely off course.

# 13. Death

- This is you in your current state, symbolized by the Death card, one of deep transformation. In this position, this card is powerful—a statement of inevitable and profound change, happening from your current situation and self, combining together to produce a whole new you. Do not expect this to be easy; remember that from the ashes the phoenix will arise.

- The challenge of your current issue is all about transformation. In the Death card, we see a call to change from one state to another. Those who resist due to holding on to old beliefs, power, or childish hopes are not spared. Do not waste the invitation by playing it safe—you have everything you need to make that change.
- The flow of the next few months is one of gradual change leading to a transformation of the current situation. The Death card is an excellent card to receive in this position, for it means that everything is already present for your ambitions to be realised. You should embrace new experiences as much as possible to get the most out of the next few months—it's easier to accept the inevitable change.
- The past in relation to this issue is one of gradual change. The sort of change that kills the old state of affairs and turns it into something entirely new—perhaps you didn't see this one coming until afterwards. Nonetheless, now that the Death card has made itself known, it is time to move on from the new situation; there can be no going back to old, outworn habits.
- You should set your sights on learning and transforming yourself. You are looking for a big make-over, and with it will come the struggle to release old ways of thinking and behaving. You have to learn that there is always change, and although it feels like a part of you is dying, that may be because it is time for that old part to give way to something new. Think of the caterpillar and the butterfly!
- The resources you can draw upon include your ability to embrace change. The Death card is a powerful card here and shows that you can—when you wish— make a new start from the ashes of the old. It is time to recover and step into that new self, even if it feels like letting go of important things. Those things may now belong to your past, not your future.
- Your own state in this matter is one of change—but are you accepting or resisting the inevitable transformation you're having to make inside? This is a truly challenging card here in this position, and it calls for you to be ready to let go and accept new ways of thinking, new ways of acting. It's your choice—are you ready to grow up into the new you?
- Those around you see you as undergoing a slow change. It may be that they see it clearer than you. Try asking those who know you well if they have noticed

how you're changing just now? They may have a lot more to tell you than you presently know.

- The concerns you have which are not actual are that you are not yet ready for this change. You are.

- The overall outcome of this matter is summarised by the powerful card of Death, signifying transformation and change of circumstances. Rarely if at all an actual physical death, this card does show that a big change is inevitable in this situation, and you must be prepared to work with all it brings. Often, this card in this position indicates that you are already seeing how this change will occur; it will not be sudden, shocking, or surprising but a gradual build-up to a particular tipping point.

# 14. Temperance

- This is you in your current state, symbolized by the angelic figure of Temperance. She shows that your situation is one in which things are coming together, but at great cost to yourself. You are being tested in the fires and tempered like steel— first hot, then cold, then both again. You might recall the adage "what does not kill me makes me stronger"—you will surely come out of this much stronger.

- The challenge of your current issue is to maintain balance at all costs. The figure of Temperance appears to blend the contents of her two chalices with little effort. You have to keep a light touch and bring things together; you have to do a lot of work keeping the peace without stressing yourself too much. It is indeed a challenging time, but you will learn much afterwards.

- The flow of the next few months is one of give and take. Things will come together, but it will take time and not happen in one single event. You may have to go backwards and forwards. As they say, two steps forward, one step back. The card here is a good one: it means that although your patience might be tested, you will stay the course to the best possible outcome.

- The past in relation to this issue is one where you have had to bring a lot together to get where you are now. This may have cost you in terms of stress and personal energy, so perhaps you will pleased to know you can take your hands from the controls just now. You did the best you could, and now it is up to others to take charge and run the show.

- You should set your sights on the process of combination. There are many things you are going to need to blend to attain success, and the measures of each will be most important. Are you sure you have the right ingredients in the proper proportions? This will be an experiment, so be prepared to make many changes along the way without losing sight of the reason by which you started.
- The resources you can draw upon include your ability to combine the best of all worlds. Whether it is the heart and the mind, science and art, or one person's opinion and someone else's, you are able to blend apparent opposites into a satisfactory conclusion. A true diplomat, you should draw on your skill to see the best and measure accordingly.
- Your own state in this matter is one of having to toe the line between holding forth and holding back. This may be creating tension, so ensure that you have your eye firmly on the desired outcome and are not afraid to keep trying different ways of getting closer to what you want.
- Those around you see you as the peacekeeper, the diplomat, the final say. Ensure that you are prepared to weigh everyone's opinions fairly and combine the best ideas into one solution.
- The concerns you have which are not actual are that you are not able to hold everyone's opinions and values in your own life. You may not feel you are living up to others' expectations. However, this card in this position indicates that you are doing a better job than you may think. Continue as you are and ensure that others show more recognition of your talents.
- The overall outcome of this matter is summarised by the angelic Temperance card. She is the messenger between the higher worlds and the lower world, so expect good news and a well-balanced outcome in proportion to the effort you have made so far. All is good and all manner of things will be well.

# 15. The Devil

- This is you in your current state, symbolized by the Devil card. This card shows how you are chained to your current habits, opinions, and behaviour. Things are not as they appear, and it is time to let go of what seems to be most important. There is the possibility of deceit and treachery. Ensure that you have all the facts, and trust no one before taking action.

- The challenge of your current issue is to uncover what is being deliberately hidden from you or face up to your own deception. You may think that something is more important than it actually is. However, this is no excuse for hiding your head in the sand. The Devil is a difficult card in this position, but that does not mean that you cannot overcome the challenge.
- The flow of the next few months is somewhat constrained. There will be difficulties and deceptions lying in wait for you. You should not expect immediate results. The Devil card often signifies deliberate deception or an attachment to wasteful activity. You should ensure that you keep everything open and honest during the next few months; otherwise someone may call your bluff.
- The past in relation to this issue is one of attachment and illusion. Things were never as they appeared to be, and until this was discovered you were chained to wasteful behaviour and thinking. That is all in the past, and you can move on now knowing that everything that needs to be known as been brought out into the light.
- You should set your sights on the material things in life for once. It is time to get real and down-and-dirty with your life. This may seem self-indulgent…but it is time to be selfish for once!
- The resources you can draw upon include your ability to trust your own senses. What feels wrong probably is—you should take this into account. Where you feel constrained you should find the strength to persevere. This is a challenging card in this position, telling that the fight will be worth it.
- Your own state in this matter is one of self-imprisonment. You may feel as if you cannot make any progress at all. But perhaps things are not as they appear to be and there are more opportunities if you can face your fears. The Devil is a terrifying force that is easily dispelled by the light of honesty and truth.
- Those around you see that you have attached yourself to an unworthy goal. They may not support you because they do not understand what you get from your current behaviour. You should examine your own motivations and be honest with yourself if other ways of obtaining your rewards exist.
- The concerns you have which are not actual are to be found in the dark card of the Devil. It is possible that you are reading too much into the situation and scaring yourself unnecessarily. Although it may seem that you are chained within these events, you may have more freedom than you feel. It is up to you to face

the facts and have the courage to call other people's bluff or say that the king has no clothes.

- The overall outcome of this matter is summarised by the Devil. This card shows material ambition being fulfilled; however, it also shows an attachment to bad habits and thought patterns. You must be careful not to be too attached to the goal and view it as a temporary step towards your higher ambitions.

# 16. The Blasted Tower

- This is you in your current state, symbolized by the Blasted Tower. The Blasted Tower is a card of sudden change. It symbolises a clearing out of all that has gone before so that new foundations can be built. Although it may feel as if everything is in ruin, there is now an opportunity to see a new horizon.

- The challenge of your current issue is to recover whatever has been left by the recent changes. There will be some parts of your life that have weathered the storm better than others. Although it has been a testing time, you can rebuild with stronger stones as your foundation.

- The flow of the next few months is one of sudden change. In the next few months, things that have been built up will come to a sudden head. This may be very disruptive; however, you may find that it clears the air and allows a new beginning. Be prepared to spend time picking up the pieces.

- The past in relation to this issue is one of abrupt change. This may have been a shocking revelation or a sudden surprise. It may have toppled you and shattered your beliefs. However, this is now in the past, and it is time to decide what it is you wish to build next.

- You should set your sights on communicating clearly all you have planned. You should not be arrogant and think that you can do things by yourself. Others can help you build something longer-lasting and more stable than you could alone. Keep within your resources, and do not plan too ambitiously.

- The resources you can draw upon include your ability to take action when action is required, no matter the consequences. You can soon topple those whose ideas are not stable or long-lasting. You may have to shatter some illusions that your ability to see what is fixed and right will see you through.

- Your own state in this matter is somewhat unstable. You feel as if you are on rocky ground and may lack the confidence to see your plans through. It may be worth testing the ground and ensuring that everybody agrees on what is planned. You may need to communicate yourself more clearly with others.

- Those around you see that you have encountered a sudden change of heart. You may feel as if you are still on the same path others may disagree with. Often this card symbolises a dramatic shift in your values or beliefs. Your friends and family may have realised this before you. It might be worth checking whether people still understand what it is you are about.

- The concerns you have which are not actual are that you have not communicated clearly your intentions. You may worry that there will be sudden changes ahead. However, you will be pleased to know that this card in this position signifies that these worries are unfounded. Your current work will lead to a long-lasting and stable result.

- The overall outcome of this matter is summarised by the Blasted Tower, sometimes called "the tower struck by lightning." This shows what happens when pride takes a fall. You must not rest on your laurels; keep building no matter what shocks may be in store for you. You may find that when you think you have finished, you are just at the beginning of a new start.

# 17. The Star

- This is you in your current state, symbolized by the delightful Star. This card is one of hope and vision. It shows that you have a clear goal in mind, one which is ahead of you, like a guiding star. You must keep this vision in mind as you progress and ensure that all your effort goes towards moving closer to the star and does not fall on barren soil.

- The challenge of your current issue is whether the reality matches your hopes. Sometimes things don't live up to your expectations and you must learn to compromise what is possibly against your ideal vision. This can be difficult when you have a clear picture of what it is you desire. This card shows that you have to balance what is possible to achieve and what is ideal to achieve.

- The flow of the next few months is one where your hopes will become increasingly more manifest. The things you seek will seem to be in reach. However, you must keep striving towards your vision and not waste time or energy wallowing in your dreams. You must ensure that you pour the waters of reality into the pool of your hopes.

- The past in relation to this issue is one full of hope. It may be that the honeymoon is now over and reality has set in. You should aim to find a new balance and a new vision now that the dreams have passed. The figure on this card in her nakedness symbolises openness and honesty; think of it as a guide for your own actions moving forward.

- You should set your sights on maintaining a clear vision of what it is you are aiming for. In this position, it signifies a leading light to you and that everything should be directed towards accomplishing the goal you have set for yourself. The Star card here is in a strong position and suggests the likely accomplishment of your vision.

- The resources you can draw upon include your ability to measure out your time and effort to accomplish what to other people would remain a mere hope. You have the ability to guide yourself and others towards an ideal solution, and it should not be underestimated. Your ability to provide this guidance is something you should draw upon more to assist others.

- Your own state in this matter is perhaps too hopeful. Whilst the Star card is very positive, it can sometimes signify unrealistic or unrealised hopes. It may be time to take a reality check in order to maintain your own balance and position in the world.

- Those around you see you as an idealistic dreamer with little chance of accomplishing your goals. In this case you should perhaps share with them your vision and allow them to help you realise it.

- The concerns you have which are not actual are in the world of hopes and dreams. You may have set expectations that seem unrealistic and you do not appear to have the resources to deliver. However, this is just a concern; so long as you keep your goal in sight at all times, the results will follow.

- The overall outcome of this matter is summarised by the Star. This card is ambiguous in this position and may signify the realisation of your hopes so long as the preceding cards have been positive. If they had been somewhat negative, then this card symbolises an outcome where your dreams will not be realised.

# 18. The Moon

- This is you in your current state, symbolized by the Moon card. This is the card of the unconscious and of those concerns and fears that prevent us from moving forwards. The crayfish does not want to come out of the water and journey down the forbidding path. In this position the card suggests that we should listen to our own intuition and unconscious through dreams and feelings in order to decide the best path forwards. This may not be the one that makes most sense.

- The challenge of your current issue is that events seem to keep going around without any resolution. This can be a frustrating time, particularly when it feels as if there's nothing you can do about it. Often this situation results in feeling isolated and concerned about opening to others. We should, however, remember that moonlight can guide our path so long as we take careful steps.

- The flow of the next few months is one of cycling changes. These changes may not come to any apparent resolution; however, you will be proceeding down the path of change. Although there will be no direct outcome in the next few months, it will be worth reviewing how far you have travelled at a later time.

- The past in relation to this issue contained some fear of the unknown. You may have stumbled upon a new power or been uncertain of the future. However, you had the courage to continue and braved the journey to get to where you are now. Although the last few months may have seemed somewhat wasted, be assured that they were an essential part of your journey.

- You should set your sights on setting new routines that allow you to concentrate on a few important things in life. You should establish new habits and try to delegate work, freeing you up to consider new horizons. It is possible you have allowed yourself to get into a rut, and it is time to break out of those old shells that have accumulated around you.

- The resources you can draw upon include the deeper and unconscious parts of yourself. It is in these reflective moments and strange visions that you can see the path ahead. You should draw upon your intuitions, which are particularly strong at this time. Although the path ahead may be winding, with a little courage you will find it is better lit than you thought.

- Your own state in this matter is one of quiet reflection. The Moon symbolises the unconscious and the feminine. In her light we go deep inside ourselves, and in those depths find true meaning. At the present time the answer lies within you, not without.

- Those around you see you as somewhat dreamy and reflective. Perhaps they don't believe you are engaging fully in the work at hand. They may be reacting to your expressed concerns, so you should do your best to assure them that your heart is in the right place.

- The concerns you have which are not actual are symbolised here by the Moon. The card signifies fear of the unknown and the depths of the unconscious. In this position it suggests that you have made for yourself many hopes and fears without any evidence to support either. It is time for a reality check to ensure you are not worrying without due reason. In a sense, the Moon is positive here, as it suggests your worries have no basis in your surroundings.

- The overall outcome of this matter is summarised by the changeable Moon card. She is full of cycling change, though never chaotic. There will be no fixed resolution to the matter but rather a new rhythm, as if a new music had come into your life.

# 19. The Sun

- This is you in your current state, symbolized by the wonderful card of the Sun. This card is full of light, and the young child signifies youthful innocence and delight. You are presently open to new experiences, and your awareness is ready to expand to new horizons. Whatever you put your mind to at this time will lead you to wonderful new experiences.

- The challenge of your current issue is to find the joy of life present in all creative acts. You may feel as if the current situation is dull and monotonous—inject some fun into it! It is a time to release your inner child and play with the situation rather than be overly serious.

- The flow of the next few months is one of increasing lightness and joy. Any weight will be lifted off your shoulders, and you will be free to explore new opportunities and avenues. To take advantage of the next few months, you should adopt a childlike attitude and not take anything too seriously.

- The past in relation to this issue is one of innocence and openness. In fact, you may have left yourself too exposed to the influence of others. Although it was a joyful time, it has now passed, and you should find yourself taking on new responsibilities.

- You should set your sights on those things which make you feel wonderful. Although this may seem somewhat selfish, there is a great deal to be said for remembering your inner child. You should look towards those things that give you the most pleasure and joy. There will be another time to be serious and grown up, but that time is not now.

- The resources you can draw upon include your sense of play and a childlike exploration of the world. There was a time when you felt invincible and the world was yours as a playground. It is this attitude that will serve you well if you remember it now.

- Your own state in this matter is one of innocence. You are trying to remain open to all of the possibilities and welcome any suggestions from others. Whilst admirable, this attitude may leave you open to manipulation. You may feel as though you are playing a game whilst others may be playing *you*.

- Those around you see you as having a delightful innocence and being the soul of the party. If you are happy in this role, take delight in it.

- The concerns you have which are not actual are of leaving yourself too vulnerable to others. You may wonder if you can preserve your own innocence and openness in the current situation. This card in this position suggests this is merely a concern, not a reality. You will be able to remain trusting despite any events that may follow.

- The overall outcome of this matter is summarised by one of the most positive cards in the deck, the Sun. This signifies great success in everything you are trying to accomplish. Indeed, it suggests that your rewards will be greater than you expect. Accept everything given to you with open arms and as they say, never look a gift horse in the mouth.

# 20. The Last Judgement

- This is you in your current state, symbolized by the Last Judgement card. This card shows the dead arising to the call of the great trumpet. In everyday terms, it is a call to action. You are being called to respond, and it is insistent. Now is the time to do something rather than close your ears and eyes to the opportunity. Doing anything at this time will be better than doing nothing.

- The challenge of your current issue is to find your calling. Without a sense of purpose and direction it is sometimes hard to motivate ourselves to action. In your present situation you need to reconnect to your highest values and attempt to enact them in your life. Without this connection you will struggle unnecessarily to achieve even minor accomplishments.
- The flow of the next few months is one in which you will see a great deal developing. Others will be called into your life to join with you in a variety of activities. There is going to be a great deal of action and work ahead leading to grand results.
- The past in relation to this issue is one of judgement. This is a card of action and indicates that you have taken action that has led you to your present situation. There was no going back then, and there is no going back now. You can only move forwards from this position. You should take a moment to recall what it was that caused you to make the big decision of the past in order to make the best decision for the future.
- You should set your sights on deliberate action and causing results to occur in accordance with your will. Your aim should be to achieve noticeable goals with clear consequences. The time away thinking is over and the time for action is now. Go do it!
- The resources you can draw upon include your ability to call others to do the best they can and to truly be themselves. You are able to draw people into your project and your life because they feel it is important to them. Don't be afraid of blowing your own trumpet!
- Your own state in this matter is one of judgement. You feel as if you have all the information you need to make your decision. If anything is preventing you from making this decision, it is a projection coming from outside yourself and should not be heeded. In effect, the decision has already been made.
- Those around you see you as being very decisive and able to make good judgement calls. If you feel uncertain in the responsibilities given to you, be sure to make clear that you require assistance. This card in this position also signifies that others believe that you are a good motivator and will respond well to any requests that you make of them.
- The concerns you have which are not actual relate to whether you are able to make a decision at this time. Although it may seem like a one-way street, the fact

is that you are already halfway down it. You must snap out of your own doubt and see the reality of the situation, which is already in motion.

- The overall outcome of this matter is summarised by the Last Judgement card. This card shows an angel blowing the trumpet at the end of time, signifying a final judgement, one in which all actions are considered. The card is extremely powerful in this position and shows that there will be a definite and clear outcome in this case. The nature of this outcome will have already been determined by all the events so far; you should look to the other cards for the overall judgement.

# 21. The World

- This is you in your current state, symbolized by the final card of the major arcana, the World. This is a card of synthesis and completion, showing that you have everything you need at the present time, whether you realise it or not. There is no need to look outside of the present situation to find anything new.
- The challenge of your current issue is to ensure that everything is being held together in a creative way. Loose ends should be tied up and distractions should be set aside. This is a difficult card in this position; it means a significant amount of work to put everything in its place.
- The flow of the next few months is one in which many things will come together. As someone said, " I love it when a plan comes together!" It will be a good time for the realisation and completion of many tasks and an equally good time to discard obsolete ambitions.
- The past in relation to this issue is one in which many things came together. It may have seemed like everything came to an end, yet this was merely the start of a new beginning.
- You should set your sights on bringing all the elements in your life together and establishing a harmonious balance. This is a card of synthesis and completion that suggests when you keep to a simple aim and do not complicate matters, your outcome will be positive. This is not a time to take on new things; rather, tidy those things that are presently in play.
- The resources you can draw upon include your ability to see the big picture and summarise things completely. You should ensure that things have been put away tidily and no loose ends remain. This card is the card of all four elements, so

you should look to resolve any issues using common sense, logic, intuition, *and* practicality together.

- Your own state in this matter is one in which you feel you have everything together and everything is under your control. You feel as if you have an overview of the whole situation and all the resources required to deal with it. In this position, this card is a naturally powerful symbol of your own ability to manage your affairs.

- Those around you see that you are holding everything together and that it is effortless for you. If you feel this is not the case, it is time to bring other people into the situation. Do not be afraid to fit people into your life where they can add to the party.

- The concerns you have which are not actual are that you may be overwhelmed with too many things to do or you may not have the resources to accomplish everything required of you. These concerns are not justified, and with the card in this position, you will find that you have more than enough energy to accomplish everything.

- The overall outcome of this matter is summarised by the card which signifies…completion! The World is a very powerful card—in fact, the most powerful card—in this position. It can be interpreted to mean that the outcome will be completely successful and everything will come together in exactly the way that you intend. If there are negative elements in this reading, you may wish to concentrate on removing them, resolving them, or mitigating against their effect so they will have no place in the final outcome.

# Appendix 3:
## *The Tarosophy Code*

## Standards of Conduct, Performance, and Ethics for Professional Tarot Readers

*It is important as a contemporary tarot card reader to have a solid code of standards. We have provided here a template for your consideration, one used by members of Tarot Professionals. It is based on professional codes from similar fields, geared towards tarot readers. It does not include terms and conditions of trading or local legislative requirements—these must be determined by your local conditions.*

**Tarot reading** is a form of divination originating in fifteenth-century Europe. The tarot is a deck of cards in various forms which gained popularity in northern Italy and spread in usage, as a game, as an inspiration for poetry, and as a means of fortune-telling. Its usage for fortune-telling is documented from the late 1500s, though it was more popular from the late 1700s to the early 1800s.

The word *tarot* is French, and the earliest name for the cards was the Italian *carte da trionfi,* the "cards of the triumphs."

The use of tarot as a means of self-development, fortune-telling, divination, and therapy has grown worldwide. There are now more than a thousand tarot decks available in print, and many more have been published in the last century, particularly in the last fifty years.

**Tarot Professionals** is a global organisation of professional tarot readers based in a UK-registered limited company. Our vision is to restore the spiritual dignity of tarot and offer authentic readings, study, and development of the cards, all with integrity and respect. Our mission statement is "tarot to engage life, not escape it."

This Standards document is our statement of that vision in practice. If you are a **member** of Tarot Professionals, these standards are for your adoption. If you are a **client** of a member of Tarot Professionals and believe the member has not upheld these standards, you may make a complaint to the company's directors. We take all such complaints seriously, and any member found in breach of these standards will be advised, warned, or have membership with Tarot Professionals removed as the situation dictates.

The people for whom we perform divination by tarot must be able to trust you with their well-being. To justify that trust, you must:

- Make the care and informing of your client your first concern, respecting their dignity and the dignity of the process of divination;
- Provide a high standard of practice in accordance with local legislation;
- Be open and honest, act with integrity, and uphold the reputation of your profession.

As a member of Tarot Professionals, you are personally accountable for actions and omissions in your practice and must always be able to justify your statements to the client.

You must always act lawfully, whether those laws relate to your professional practice or personal life. Failure to comply with this code may bring your practice into question and endanger your registration with Tarot Professionals.

This code should be considered with all other advertising, legal, and trading standards and regulations which apply to your personal circumstances, geography, or online presence. Tarot Professionals has appointed a "Legal Eagle" role to collate and provide material in this regard.

Though it was stated earlier, the following bears repeating: **Make the care and informing of your client your first concern, respecting both their dignity and the dignity of the process of divination.**

## Treat People as Individuals

- You must not discriminate in any way against those for whom you read;
- You must treat people kindly and with consideration.

## Respect Client Confidentiality

- You must ensure all information given is treated in confidence;
- If you record any information, the client must be made aware of this;
- You must keep any such information securely.

You must disclose information if you believe that somebody may be at risk of harm (or causing harm to themselves or others) in line with the law of the country/state in which you are practising.

## Inform Your Client as to Your Practice

You must inform your client as to the nature of your practice. They must be well informed as to what to expect from their reading before it commences. This includes but is not limited to such practices as mediumship, aura reading, Guides, Channelling, Reiki, etc. It is recommended you inform the client about any combination of approaches you may use during the session.

You may wish to respond to client concerns (implicit or expressed) about the Death card or receiving "bad" cards, etc.

## Welfare of Children and Young People

You must be aware and make response to local regulations with regard to the welfare of children and young people (aged up to 19 in the UK, 24 if they have disabilities). This is presently covered in the UK through the ECM (Every Child Matters) initiative and the Children Act of 2004. The website for this topic is **http://www.everychildmatters.gov.uk**.

If the client lacks capacity to make informed decisions, such as being under the influence of alcohol or drugs, or suffering severe mental distress, you should stop the reading and possibly refer the client to a mental health professional. You must ensure as best you are able there is informed consent for the divination.

It is recommended you maintain or have access to a contact list of organisations who can offer specialist support in alcohol dependency, gambling, and other issues that go beyond the divination process you are offering.

## Maintain Clear Professional Boundaries

This means that you must:
- Refuse any gifts or favours that might be interpreted or used to imply fraudulent activity outside of the agreed contract;
- Not ask for loans or accept loans from clients;
- Establish and actively maintain clear physical and emotional boundaries at all times.

**Provide a High Standard of Practice and Care**. This means that you must:
- Ensure any advice you give is justifiable and within your professional capacity;
- Keep your skills and knowledge up to date;
- Keep clear and accurate records;
- If you maintain records of your readings, ensure they are clear and accurate reflections of the reading which has taken place.

You must be aware of the requirements of law with regard to information. In the UK and Europe, laws pertain to the recording and provision of information under both the Data Protection Act (1998) and the Freedom of Information Act (2005). You can get more information on these at the Information Commissioner's Office **http://www.ico.gov.uk/**. (There is presently no single act in the US with regard to data protection.)

**Be open and honest, act with integrity, and uphold the reputation of your profession.**

## Act with Integrity

· You must adhere to the laws of the country in which you are practising.

## Deal with Problems

· You must offer a constructive and honest response to any criticism of your service.

· You must act immediately to address any complaint.

## Uphold the Reputation of Your Profession

· You must cooperate with the media only when you can confidently ensure the reputation of divination and tarot is upheld. Tarot Professionals can put you in contact with others to advise on publicity.

## Information about Insurance

Tarot Professionals Ltd. offers a UK-based insurance scheme providing public liability insurance. You should consult with your local business advisors, venue organisers, etc., as to insurance requirements for your services.

## Establishing Terms and Conditions

As part of the performance of your services, you should establish terms and conditions according to local requirements.

These may include but are not limited to:

· Length of session;

· Payment terms;

· Refund policy;

· Cancellation policy;

· Follow-up sessions;

· Contact protocol (i.e., hours of business).

# Endnotes

1. See The Tarot Review site at **http://www.thetarotreview.com**.

2. See *Tarot Flip*, Marcus Katz & Tali Goodwin, (Forge Press, 2010.)

3. You can explore more about Kabbalah at **http://www.kabbalahcourse.com**.

4. Bruce Patison, *Modern Methods of Language Teaching* (Oxford University Press: 1964), p. 3.

5. To discover more about NLP, please visit our site at **http://www.nlpmagick.com**.

6. In NLP terms, this is a strategy composed of a visual, kinesthetic, and auditory sequence.

7. First presented in *Tarot Twist*, Marcus Katz & Tali Goodwin (Forge Press, 2010).

8. First presented in *Tarot Flip*.

9. Louis, p. 247.

10. Bunning, p. 42.

11. Gearhart, p. 56.

12. Zodiastar, p. 71.

13. Pamphlets and teaching material in private collection.

14. Papus, *The Tarot of the Bohemians*, ed. A. E. Waite (North Hollywood: Wilshire,1973), p. 308.

15. http://www.tarotprofessionals.com/tarotarticles.html.

16. Tarot-Town is at: http://www.tarot-town.com.

17. This spread is very powerful when combined with the *Tarot of Ceremonial Magick* by Lon Milo Duquette.

18. For the entire history of the Celtic Cross spread, see *Tarosophist International* vol 1, iss. 2.

# GET MORE AT LLEWELLYN.COM

Visit us online to browse hundreds of our books and decks, plus sign up to receive our e-newsletters and exclusive online offers.

- Free tarot readings • Spell-a-Day • Moon phases
- Recipes, spells, and tips • Blogs • Encyclopedia
- Author interviews, articles, and upcoming events

# GET SOCIAL WITH LLEWELLYN

**Find us on Facebook**

www.Facebook.com/LlewellynBooks

**Follow us on**

www.Twitter.com/Llewellynbooks

# GET BOOKS AT LLEWELLYN

## LLEWELLYN ORDERING INFORMATION

 **Order online:** Visit our website at www.llewellyn.com to select your books and place an order on our secure server.

 **Order by phone:**
- Call toll free within the U.S. at 1-877-NEW-WRLD (1-877-639-9753)
- Call toll free within Canada at 1-866-NEW-WRLD (1-866-639-9753)
- We accept VISA, MasterCard, and American Express

 **Order by mail:**
Send the full price of your order (MN residents add 6.875% sales tax) in U.S. funds, plus postage and handling to: Llewellyn Worldwide, 2143 Wooddale Drive Woodbury, MN 55125-2989

**POSTAGE AND HANDLING:**

STANDARD: (U.S. & Canada)
(Please allow 2 business days)
$25.00 and under, add $4.00.
$25.01 and over, FREE SHIPPING.

INTERNATIONAL ORDERS (airmail only):
$16.00 for one book, plus $3.00 for each additional book.

Visit us online for more shipping options. Prices subject to change.

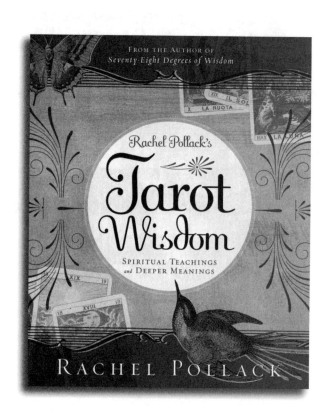

FROM THE AUTHOR OF
*Seventy-Eight Degrees of Wisdom*

Rachel Pollack's

# Tarot
# Wisdom

SPIRITUAL TEACHINGS
*and* DEEPER MEANINGS

RACHEL POLLACK

# Rachel Pollack's Tarot Wisdom
### *Spiritual Teachings and Deeper Meanings*
### Rachel Pollack

Beloved by nearly half a million tarot enthusiasts, Rachel Pollack's *Seventy-Eight Degrees of Wisdom* forever transformed the study of tarot. Finally—after thirty years—the much-anticipated follow-up to this revered classic has arrived! Enhanced by author's personal insights and wisdom gained over the past three decades, *Rachel Pollack's Tarot Wisdom* will inspire fans and attract a new generation of tarot students.

Alive with a rich array of new ideas, yet reverent to the history and tradition of tarot, *Rachel Pollack's Tarot Wisdom* is a comprehensive guide for all levels. All seventy-eight cards are explored from fresh angles: tarot history, art, psychology, and a wide variety of spiritual/occult traditions. Pollack also takes tarot reading in new and exciting directions—spanning predictive, psychological, magical, and spiritual approaches. Featuring a wealth of new spreads, anecdotes from the author, and innovative ways to interpret and use tarot, this all-encompassing guide will reinvigorate your practice.

**978-0-7387-1309-0, 504 pp., 7½ x 9⅛**                **$24.95**

---

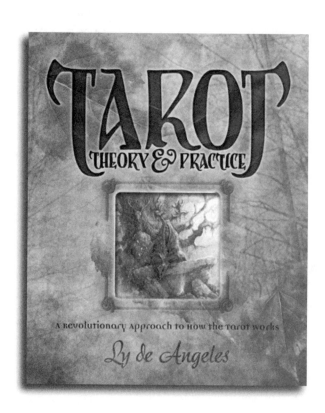

TAROT
THEORY & PRACTICE

A Revolutionary Approach to How the Tarot Works

Ly de Angeles

## Tarot Theory & Practice
### Ly de Angeles

In this groundbreaking book, Ly de Angeles shares her own original ideas on the nature of prophecy and using tarot to predict the future.

Exploring quantum physics, free will, and fate, de Angeles poses a bold new theory, suggesting tarot can impact your reality … and your future. She also introduces Time, the god of tarot, and reveals insightful correlations between tarot and the Kabbalah Tree of Life, astrology, and the four elements. Sprinkled throughout are exercises and personal case histories that illuminate these complex ideas.

Ly de Angeles also offers guidance for putting theory into practice, along with card interpretations and sample spreads. There's advice for handling the deck, timing events, and giving accurate readings. Also included are tips for going professional: setting up a space, maintaining confidentiality, reading objectively and responsibly, communicating bad news, staying safe, avoiding burnout, and much more.

978-0-7387-1138-6, 312 pp., 7½ x 9⅛                    $16.95

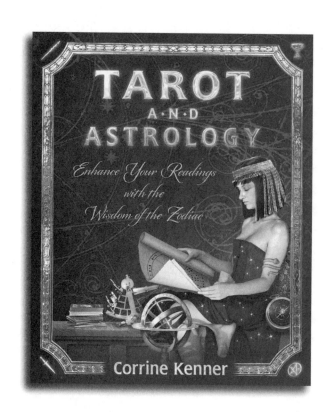

## Tarot and Astrology
### *Enhance Your Readings with the Wisdom of the Zodiac*
#### Corrine Kenner

Enrich and expand your tarot practice with age-old wisdom from the stars.

Entwined for six centuries, the link between tarot and astrology is undeniably significant. This unique and user-friendly guide makes it easy to explore and learn from this fascinating intersection—and you don't even need to know astrology to get started. Discover how each major arcana corresponds to an astrological sign or planet, where each minor arcana sits on the Zodiac wheel, how the court cards and tarot suits are connected to the four elements—and what all this means. Also included are astrological spreads and reading techniques to help you apply these new cosmic insights.

978-0-7387-2964-0, 312 pp., 7½ x 9⅛                    $17.95

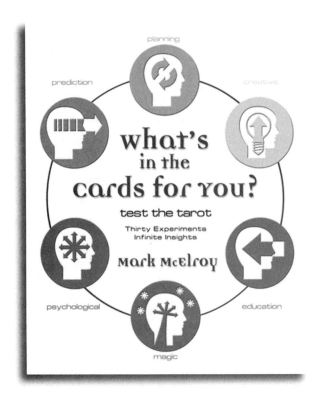

planning

prediction

creative

what's
in the
cards for you?

test the tarot

Thirty Experiments
Infinite Insights

Mark McElroy

psychological

education

magic

# What's in the Cards for You?
## *Test the Tarot*
### Mark McElroy

Modern society still harbors outdated notions about the tarot, associating it with fortune-telling scam artists, slumber party hijinx, or what they've seen in movies. With good-natured humor and charm, Mark McElroy acknowledges these misconceptions and offers skeptics a hands-on approach to learning the true benefits of tarot.

No dry lectures on tarot history and symbolism will be found here. Instead, McElroy engages readers with thirty fun and practical exercises for exploring the power and utility of tarot. These easy activities take only fifteen minutes each and illustrate the many applications of tarot as a tool for self-understanding, relationship insight, dream analysis, brainstorming, writing inspiration, meditation, problem-solving, and making difficult decisions.

**978-0-7387-0702-0, 192 pp., 7½ x 9⅛**                    **$14.95**

---

## Tarot Prediction & Divination
### *Unveiling 3 Layers of Meaning*
### Susyn Blair-Hunt

Bring more depth and power to your tarot readings—it's easy once you learn to understand the three dimensions of the tarot. Popular tarot teacher and author Susyn Blair-Hunt presents an original, step-by-step approach that shows how to use tarot's visual cues as a means to awaken inherent psychic abilities and decipher the predictive, therapeutic, and spiritual messages hidden within the cards. Beginning readers will find everything they need to get started immediately, while experienced readers can use this guide to expand their abilities, refresh their perspective, and take their interpretive skills to the next level.

This unique system offers expanded meanings that give more versatility to your tarot interpretations. With fifteen original layouts, thirty sample readings, and a series of helpful correspondence charts, this book will teach you how to draw more insight from the tarot, making your readings more effective and profound.

978-0-7387-2172-9, 312 pp., 7½ x 9⅛                    $18.95

## Tarot: Get the Whole Story
### *Use, Create & Interpret Tarot Spreads*
### JAMES RICKLEF

Creating original spreads is a rite of passage for many ambitious Tarot students. James Ricklef gives valuable lessons in doing just that—with advice for finding inspiration, defining positional meanings, and structuring a layout.

*Tarot: Get the Whole Story* is also for those who want to peer over the shoulder of a Tarot master as he demonstrates a variety of new spreads. Readers will learn which spreads are best for relationship concerns, personal transformation, New Year's resolutions, life decisions, and more. Each chapter discusses a new spread with detailed explanations of positional meanings and dynamics between the cards. Also included are illustrations and entertaining sample readings featuring Clark Gable, Marie Antoinette, Hera, Don Juan, and other historical, literary, or mythological figures.

**978-0-7387-0345-9, 240 pp., 7½ x 9⅛**                    **$15.95**

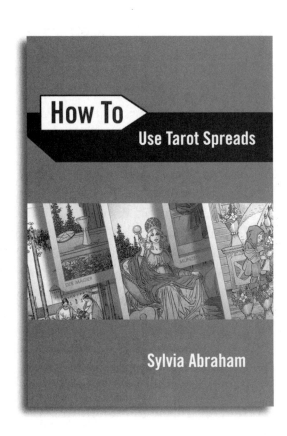

# How To

## Use Tarot Spreads

### Sylvia Abraham

# How To Use Tarot Spreads
## Sylvia Abraham

Being a skilled tarot reader requires the ability to address the querent's specific concerns in a way that is understandable and memorable. Now, for the first time, there is a book of specific tarot spreads that will provide the answers to the most commonly asked questions about love and romance... home and family... business and finance... major life events such as marriage, pregnancy, and divorce... travel and relocating... inner fears and personal development... spiritual growth and past lives.

A common problem for tarot readers is how to put the cards together so they make sense. It helps to be a good story teller, to bring the cards to life in a dramatic way that stays with your querents long after they have gone home. The 37 time-tested spreads in this book help you gain the confidence to do just that. You will also see real-life readings for each spread that were conducted by the author. Plus, *How To Use Tarot Spreads* includes the upright and reversed meanings of each card as well as the steps to conducting a positive tarot reading.

**978-0-7387-0816-4, 308 pp., 5³⁄₁₆ x 8**                              **$9.95**

---

SPECIAL TOPICS IN TAROT

# TAROT
# TIPS

EIGHT OF PENTACLES

RUTH ANN AMBERSTONE
& WALD AMBERSTONE

FOREWORD BY MARY K. GREER

## Tarot Tips
### Ruth Ann Amberstone and Wald Amberstone

Get answers to just about any question you could have about the Tarot.

Since its start in 1998 as a free email newsletter, "Tarot Tips" has grown into one of the major newsletters of its kind, answering queries from readers around the world. Now its correspondence is reprinted in this new book by the same name.

In small pieces, easy to grasp and digest, one technique after another is laid out before you. From low-impact shuffling methods, to how to get yes-no answers from the cards, to using the Tarot to help you cope with hard times, answers are given in the form of reasonable guidelines drawn from the authors' long experience.

**978-0-7387-0216-2, 192 pp., 6 x 9**                    **$15.95**

---